Modern Nicaraguan Poetry

Modern Nicaraguan Poetry

Dialogues with France and the United States

Steven F. White

Lewisburg
Bucknell University Press
London and Toronto: Associated University Presses

Associated University Presses
440 Forsgate Drive
Cranbury, NJ 08512

Associated University Presses
25 Sicilian Avenue
London WC1A 2QH, England

Associated University Presses
P.O. Box 338, Port Credit
Mississauga, Ontario,
Canada L5G 4L8

Some of the acknowledgements (p. 9) constitute an extension of the copyright page.

The paper used in this publication meets the requirements
of the American National Standard for Permanence of Paper
for Printed Library Materials Z39.48-1984.

Library of Congress Cataloging-in-Publication Data

White, Steven F., 1955-
Modern Nicaraguan poetry : dialogues with France and the United States /
Steven F. White.
      p.   cm.
  Includes bibliographical references and index.
  ISBN 0-8387-5232-2 (alk. paper)
  1. Nicaraguan poetry—20th century—History and criticism.
2. Nicaraguan poetry—French influences. 3. Nicaraguan
poetry—American influences. I. Title.
PQ7512.W48   1993
861—dc20   91-58938
                                                                        CIP

PRINTED IN THE UNITED STATES OF AMERICA

For Nancy and for David McKenzie

Contents

Acknowledgments

The author would like to express his gratitude to Juan Armando Epple, Françoise Calin, Roy Caldwell, Daniel Goldrich, Gwen Kirkpatrick, and Barbara May. For their invaluable guidance and friendship, many thanks to Jorge Eduardo Arellano and Alfred Gross. Special appreciation is due Judith E. Deshotels, Laurie Olmstead, Richard Kuhta, and the staff at the O.D.Y. Library, as well as St. Lawrence University's Faculty Development Fund for help during the final stages of the preparation of the manuscript.

The author also wishes to thank the following poets, literary executors and publishers for their permission to cite from previously published and unpublished material: José Antonio Argüello, Ernesto Cardenal, José Coronel Urtecho, María Luisa Cortés, Pablo Antonio Cuadra, Vicente García-Huidobro S. (Fundación Vicente Huidobro), Carlos Martínez Rivas, and Luis Pasos Argüello.

Lines from "Conquistador" from *Collected Poems, 1917-1982* by Archibald MacLeish, reprinted with permission of Houghton Mifflin Company.

Lines from "The Hill" from *Spoon River Anthology* by Edgar Lee Masters, originally published by the Macmillan Company. Permission by Ellen C. Masters.

Portion of a letter to Pablo Antonio Cuadra from Thomas Merton, dated December 4, 1958. Reprinted with permission of the Merton Legacy Trust.

Lines from "Poetry" reprinted with permission of Macmillan Publishing Company from *Collected Poems of Marianne Moore*. Copyright 1935 by Marianne Moore, renewed 1963 by Marianne Moore and T. S. Eliot.

Poems from *Collected Poems* by Siegfried Sassoon. Copyright 1918, 1920 by E. P. Dutton. Copyright 1936, 1946, 1947, 1948 by Siegfried Sassoon. Used by permission of Viking Penguin, a division of Penguin Books USA Inc.

Lines from "Le Retour" and "Le Gaucho" from *Débarcadères*, and lines from "Le matin du monde" from *Gravitations* by Jules Supervielle, (c) Editions GALLIMARD.

Every effort was made to trace the copyright holder of material cited from *Sailing South American Skies* by James Saxon Childers, originally published by Farrar & Rinehart, 1936.

Introduction

Poets in Nicaragua, beginning in the nineteenth century with Rubén
Darío's *modernista* revolution, consistently have engaged in a
transformative dialogue with French and North American authors as a
means of creating a Nicaraguan literary identity. It is difficult to
conceive of Darío undertaking his verbal innovations without having
immersed himself in the verse of Baudelaire, Hugo, and Mallarmé. At
the same time, however, the *modernistas* were not content with merely
imitating the French, but wanted, instead, to create their own work that
was modern and cosmopolitan yet still Hispanic American in terms of
thematics and vitality.[1] They assimilated an internal vision, a way of
perceiving the world, that subverts models of servile European cultural
dependence.[2] The mutable, multifaceted nature of this process has led
Pere Gimferrer to speak of Darío's "protean gift" as a writer.[3] The same
spirit of mimetic independence describes Darío's relationship with the
poetry of Whitman: Darío incorporates Whitman's expansive, euphoric
discovery of the American continent in his verse, yet he rejects the
democratic principles that are inseparable from Whitman's excellence as
a poet. Darío's strategy for the assimilation of foreign literatures
resembles that of his country's future generations of poets, which are the
subject of this book. The work of seven preeminent, modern Nicaraguan
poets (Alfonso Cortés, Salomón de la Selva, José Coronel Urtecho, Pablo
Antonio Cuadra, Joaquín Pasos, Carlos Martínez Rivas, and Ernesto
Cardenal) reveals an important characteristic of twentieth-century poetry
in Nicaragua: that it cannot be understood fully without examining the
French and American literary traditions.

The diverse literary dialogues between writers from Nicaragua,
France, and the United States require a rigorous, but flexible, analytical
methodology that includes socio-political and historical considerations,
comparative literature, common literary themes, the arcane
understanding between authors known as "communicating vessels," and,
also, intertextuality, defined by Gérard Genette as "a relation of
copresence between two or more texts."[4] We agree with Michael
Riffaterre when he proposes in *Text Production* that, as readers, we are
engaged on two levels, simultaneously deciphering the text before our
eyes as well as other texts returning concomitantly in our memory.
Riffaterre believes that "the imitated poem underscores, if only by

11

reduplication, the effects of the poem imitating it."[5] Because all literature is intelligible only in relation to other texts, an understanding of how one text "rewrites" another is a way of entering into the dialogue that literature requires in order to generate meaning and evolve.

By creating a limited international context for Nicaraguan poetry in terms of linking it to France and the United States, I have necessarily excluded in this study other important "conversants" in the dialogical process.   My intent is certainly not to deny the importance of Nicaragua's literary evolution with regard to that of its Central American neighbors, Cuba, or especially its relationship with Mexico, where de la Selva, Cuadra, Ernesto Mejía Sánchez, Martínez Rivas, and Cardenal all lived for extended periods of time. With regard to Mexican verse, Nicaraguan poets have assimilated a great deal: for example, like Enrique González Martínez, they had their own swans' necks to twist; José Juan Tablada, an Hispanic American Imagist, gave them the opportunity to experiment with Japanese verse forms; from Ramón López Velarde they learned innovative ways to incorporate political themes in their poetry, and to achieve a balance between the cosmopolitan and their own potentially asphixiating provincialism; José Gorostiza helped them develop the poetics of the long poem.   José Emilio Pacheco cites Salvador Novo and Salomón de la Selva as part of the "other" Hispanic American vanguard linked to modern poetry in the United States.[6]   In addition, an entire anthology of poetry could be compiled on the theme of Nicaragua's long and ongoing literary dialogue with Spain.[7]

Although the traditional method of classifying Nicaraguan poetry by generations is not entirely unproductive, we have chosen to group the poets in this study in keeping with certain fundamental poetic affinities, rather than the year they happened to be born. Thus, in the book's first section, "A Dialogue with France," one finds Alfonso Cortés (1893-1969), Pablo Antonio Cuadra (b.1912), and Carlos Martínez Rivas (b.1924), each belonging to a different, successive literary generation. Similarly, section three, "A Dialogue with the United States," is composed of Salomón de la Selva (1893-1958), José Coronel Urtecho (b.1906), and Ernesto Cardenal (b.1925). The work of Joaquín Pasos (1914-1947), which is the topic of the second section, "A Dialogue with France and the United States," embraces both literary traditions to a greater degree than perhaps any other Nicaraguan poet, with the exception of Rubén Darío.[8] In this sense, Pasos's poetry proves that the Nicaraguans' dialogues with France and the United States are not mutually exclusive. Furthermore, the tripartite division of the book is of a non-absolute nature: for example, Martínez Rivas assimilates the aesthetics of Baudelaire in order to describe life in the United States;

Pasos uses the Chilean poet Vicente Huidobro as his bridge to avant-garde French literature; de la Selva consciously rejects the United States for political reasons before history opens and closes his dialogue with England. Nevertheless, the poetry of Nicaragua remains a metamorphosed engendering of its predominantly double lineage.

Together, the seven chapters create a septipartite definition of modern Nicaraguan poetry as gnostic, a balance of myth and history, painterly, apocalyptic, testimonial, linguistically innovative, and ethical. The method of analysis, as I stated earlier, varies from chapter to chapter, depending on the kind of poetry being discussed. For example, in chapters 2, 6, and 7, the reader will find full discussions of Nicaragua's national historical context and its complex relation to Nicaraguan poetry. The first chapter, "The Journey Toward God in the Poetry of Cortés, Baudelaire, Rimbaud, and Mallarmé," links the spiritual quest of Alfonso Cortés with that of several nineteenth-century French poets who maintain a heterodox position with regard to traditional Catholicism. The theme of the New World as a space that simultaneously lends itself to the imaginary projection of utopian ideals and to the conflict of history's transformative powers forms the basis of the second chapter, "Pablo Antonio Cuadra and Jules Supervielle: Utopia, National Identity, and History." The third chapter, "Carlos Martínez Rivas and Charles Baudelaire: Two Painters of Modern Life," expands the definition of intertextuality to include the pictorial and the metapictorial qualities of texts portraying urban existence in accordance with the ideas Baudelaire expresses in his essay "Le Peintre de la Vie Moderne" (The painter of modern life).

Chapter 4, as we have said, links the intertextual dialogues between Nicaragua, France, and the United States: "The Eschatological Voyage in the Poetry of Joaquín Pasos, Vicente Huidobro, and T. S. Eliot," is a study of three long metaphysical poems with vast spatial and temporal scopes, in which there is a metaphorical union of the theme of the voyage with the treatment of "last things" such as death and the possibility of redemption.

The fifth chapter, "Salomón de la Selva: Testimonial Poetry and World War I," examines the curious case of a Nicaraguan poet militantly engaged in a conflictive, interlingual/intertextual dialogue *with himself.* Between the publication of *Tropical Town and Other Poems* (1918) and *El soldado desconocido* (The unknown soldier) (1922), there is a remarkable movement in de la Selva's verse toward a colloquial poetic diction of verisimilitude and, more importantly, a conscious, permanent abandoning of a language (English) that the poet had used to express himself with relative success in the literary circles of the United States.

The last two chapters of this book really should be read together, given the similarities of the poetic projects of Coronel and Cardenal. Chapter 6, "Translation and Intertextuality: José Coronel Urtecho's Dialogue with North American Literature," explores Coronel's dual use of U. S. poetry in translation to renovate Nicaraguan verse and to oppose the negative aspects of North American culture imposed on Nicaragua. The final chapter, "Ernesto Cardenal and North American Literature: the Formulation of an Ethical Identity," describes the process by which Cardenal finds in texts by Pound, Williams, MacLeish, and certain anonymous Amerindian poets a means to create his own definition of moral and social responsibility.

In many ways, the synthesis of these two major foreign literatures and their subsequent transformation into poetry that is an undeniably Nicaraguan element of national identity is complete. New poets are assimilating verse from France and the United States in a secondary fashion from older Nicaraguan writers whose longevity and, of course, the quality of their verse, have enabled them to continue to dominate Nicaraguan literature. It remains to be seen if the younger writers will be able to maintain an *active*, rather than passive, openness to literatures of other countries and epochs as an effective way to extend the borders of their country.

Modern Nicaraguan Poetry

Part I

A Dialogue with France

1

The Journey toward God in the Poetry of Cortés, Baudelaire, Rimbaud, and Mallarmé

Nicaragua's truly outstanding, though relatively unknown, poet Alfonso Cortés (1893-1969) belongs to the line of visionary poets that seek to penetrate another world beyond tangible, visible appearances. The spiritual quest for an Absolute in Cortés's poetry makes Cortés a descendent of certain nineteenth-century French poets who, despite evident differences, do share some fundamental preoccupations and obsessions. As Alice Coléno points out in her book *Les Portes d'ivoire* (The ivory doors), these poets describe a world of essence rather than appearance which, for Baudelaire, is unity, for Rimbaud, purity, for Mallarmé, the Absolute, and for all three poets, beauty. Their mission consists of revealing these qualities to the reader.[1] We have chosen these three particular French poets for comparative purposes in this chapter because their work contains the drama, the ecstasy and the crisis of the individual engaged in spiritual combat—qualities that also characterize the poetry of Cortés. It is important to establish from the onset that Cortés was deeply involved in the study of French poetry. He wrote at least one poem in French, "Chanson sans paroles," (Song without words)[2] and also translated poetry by Verlaine, Hugo, Moréas, and Guérin.[3] So immersed was Cortés in nineteenth-century French Symbolist poetry that his intellectual friends nicknamed him "Mallarmé."[4]

Cortés is a peculiar case: the poet was afflicted by clinically-diagnosed schizophrenia, spent long periods of time chained to the wall of his home in León (the former house of Rubén Darío), and later endured decades as a virtual prisoner of an asylum in Managua. It is virtually impossible not to succumb to the Nicaraguan tendency to substitute personal anecdotes and speculations regarding Cortés's brooding anger, explosive and dangerous violence, and humorous, profound lunacy for the supposedly more scientific and objective approach of literary criticism. Cortés not only lived (quite literally) in the shadow of Darío, he also is buried in the cathedral of León near the drunken stone lion sprawled over Darío's tomb. Unlike Darío, the great cosmopolitan, Cortés lived the triple isolation of Nicaragua, provincial León in the first decades of the twentieth century, and the asylum. Cortés's early attempts to establish himself as a journalist were frustrated by an illness that rendered him apolitical and almost completely oblivious to world events. His family, especially his sister María Luisa, preserved his works (presumably against the wishes of the doctor, who had forbidden him to write) and published them in small editions locally. Despite the fact that the majority of Cortés's most accomplished poems were published from 1931-1935, he was discovered by his compatriots José Coronel Urtecho and Ernesto Cardenal in the early 1950s. At that time, Cardenal edited and published a very selective anthology of poetry by Cortés, and, later in the decade, encouraged Thomas Merton to translate some of Cortés's visionary work into English. Although Cortés has an established reputation in Nicaragua as a key figure in his country's literary history, as well as a modicum of recognition and praise outside Nicaragua, it is difficult to find his work in general anthologies of *modernista* or twentieth-century Latin American poetry. For now, according to John Beverley and Marc Zimmerman, the "very powerful sense of cosmic utopian subjectivism"[5] in the poetry of Alfonso Cortés has been limited to a great impact on successive generations of Nicaraguan poets. This is especially true in the case of Ernesto Cardenal, whose book-length poem *Cántico cósmico* contains at least a dozen references to Cortés's poetry.

While most Nicaraguan critics choose to emphasize the radical singularity of Cortés, others have attempted to link his work in a very tentative way with *modernista* poets such as the Mexican Enrique González Martínez. It may also be fruitful to compare Cortés with other late *modernistas* such as Leopoldo Lugones and Julio Herrera y Reissig in light of Gwen Kirkpatrick's remarkable study *The Dissonant Legacy of Modernismo*, especially considering the sort of eroticism and metaphoric renewal that one finds in Cortés's poetry. Generally, however, the Nicaraguans cite the similarities between Cortés's poetry and certain nineteenth-century French poets, though these same critics, in my opinion, fail to establish the precise manner in which Cortés engages in a literary dialogue with these authors that are so important in the development of his work.[6] For this reason, I will examine what may be the principal theme that links Cortés with Baudelaire, Rimbaud, and Mallarmé: the poet's open or covert opposition to the tenets of orthodox Catholicism. This conflictive heterodoxy manifests itself in his poetry as an anguished search for knowledge of God (*gnosis*) that determines the conditions under which the poet can aspire to transcendence, understood as the eternal conflict between gravity and grace, or, in a stricter Gnostic sense as defined by Hans Jonas, the manner in which "the spirit stripped of all foreign accretions reaches the God beyond the world and becomes reunited with the divine substance."[7]

The first of three sections in this chapter will compare four poems by Baudelaire and Cortés so as to establish the primacy of spatiality as a factor in the poets' ability to embark on their respective transcendent journeys. Baudelaire describes infinity in the Christian framework of Hell and Heaven, whereas Cortés encounters the infinite in the extreme existential dualism of expansive and reductive modes of being. In the second section, I will analyze two poems by Cortés with titles and themes that closely resemble two texts by Rimbaud and Mallarmé as a means of explaining, through the metaphorical objects of the boat and the window, the positive and negative aspects of the transcendent voyage. In this case, Cortés adopts a more measured and less self-destructive approach to the visionary experience than Rimbaud; Cortés and Mallarmé experience a similar grave psychological threat when they discover the Ideal that they desire intensely lies beyond their reach. The final section will demonstrate how a current of Gnosticism in the poetry of Cortés defies conventional Christian transcendence and thus enables Cortés to realize his identity as a Nicaraguan poet.

Spatiality and Modes of Being

The sense of spatiality predicates the poet's relationship with the world. Cortés's "Irrevocablemente" (Irrevocably) and "La canción del espacio" (The song of space) and Baudelaire's "L'Irrémédiable" (The irremediable) and "La Mort des Pauvres" (The death of the poor) provide an interesting point of departure for a discussion of the importance of reductive and expansive spatiality in determining the propitiousness of transcendence.

"Irrevocablemente" is perhaps the most pessimistic poem in Cortés's oeuvre, with the possible exception of "Sin nombre" (Nameless). It recounts what might be considered a third Fall of humanity, outside the parameters of a traditional theological framework. The symbolic language that characterizes Catholicism is curiously absent in this poem describing an encounter not with the damnation of Hell, but with "la Nada" (Nothingness):

> Por donde quiera que escudriña la mirada,
> sólo encuentra los pálidos pantanos de la Nada;
> flores marchitas, aves sin rumbo, nubes muertas . . .
> Ya no abrió nunca el cielo ni la tierra sus puertas!
> Días de lasitud, desesperanza y tedio;
> no hay más para la vida que el fúnebre remedio
> de la muerte, no hay más!, no hay más!, no hay más

que caer como un punto negro y vago
en la onda lívida del lago,
para siempre jamás . . .

(Poesías 23)

(Wherever the gaze finally comes to rest, / it finds only pale swamps of
Nothingness, / dead clouds, birds without bearing, withered flowers . . . /
Both earth and sky have closed their doors! / Days of lassitude, hopelessness,
tedium— / nothing more for life but the funereal remedy / of death, nothing
more, nothing more, nothing more / except to fall like a point, black and
vague, / on the livid wave of the lake / forever and ever . . .)

The expulsion from Paradise signified a loss of the universal Adamic
tongue of Eden, a language that was mimetic of the divine syntax, which
caused objects to leap into being as they were named. The destruction of
the tower of Babel and the resulting scattering of languages further
alienated humanity from the original unity of speech. The Fall in
Cortés's poem "Irrevocablemente" seems to signal the possibility of an
even greater incapacitation—a reduction of human limits so great that the
individual will no longer be able to formulate language and express
reality.

The poem is a fatalistic enumeration of images of non-being. The
poet relies on the empirical information that the human eye is capable of
registering and characterizes the void that surrounds him as "pálidos
pantanos," as if the swamps had taken on a bloodless, human quality—or
as if the poet-phenomenologist himself were the sum total of the non-
living things he perceived. Perhaps these are "les marais occidentaux"
(the Occidental swamps) that Rimbaud refers to in *Une Saison en Enfer*
(*A Season in Hell*) in "L'Impossible" ("The Impossible"; *Oeuvres* 235):
the impossibility of attaining spiritual wisdom in the Occident. Cortés
sees, then names, the individual elements that, together, form the exterior
world: withered flowers, birds that have lost their bearing, dead clouds.
The natural space defined by the poem is a moribund landscape with no
regenerative purpose. The vastness of the swamps that stretch as far as
the eye can see are inversely proportional to the narrator's diminishing
mode of being.

Because the narrator's voice is curiously disembodied (the first
person is submerged in a state of despair so profound that it can no
longer function on the surface of the poem), the "fúnebre remedio de la
muerte" exerts a powerful attraction that draws all living things toward it.
The centripetal forces at work in the poem are heightened by the
conspiracy of both sky and land not to open their doors to the poet's
mind. Hopelessness and boredom give way to a longing for death that the
poet imagines as an extreme diminishing or collapse of his body's limits

(as if the poet, in celestial terms, were a supernova abruptly becoming a black hole). This point, incidentally, differs completely from T. S. Eliot's "still point of the turning world" in "Burnt Norton." In Cortés's poem, consciousness has been so severely restricted that it no longer possesses a vantage point from which to view the spinning planet. The poet, representing each individual manifestation of human awareness, is helpless in his eternal fall toward the water below. This losing of one's human dimension and being reduced to a dimensionless geometric object ("un punto negro y vago") that has no property except a specific location in space resembles another of Cortés's poems "El poema cotidiano," (The quotidian poem) in which the poet asks: "¿es que yo he de ser siempre un punto alucinado/donde resuena el múltiple eco del universo?" (*Tardes de oro* [Afternoons of gold], 3) (Will I always be an hallucinating point / where the multiple echo of the universe resounds?)

Neurologist Oliver Sacks, author of *Awakenings*, a difficult to classify work that W. H. Auden has called "a masterpiece," discovers a correlation between the kind of reductive spatiality embodied in "Irrevocablemente" and the phenomenon of illness:

> Common to all worlds of disease is the sense of pressure, coercion and force; the loss of real spaciousness and freedom and ease; the loss of poise, of infinite readiness, and the contractions, contortions and postures of illness: the development of pathological rigidity and insistence.[8]

This general, though profound, definition of sickness is an apt description of the overall tone of "Irrevocablemente," a poem with an intense claustrophobic quality in which life ceases to be a flexible series of alternatives. Under these circumstances, transcendence becomes impossible. There is a sense of irremediable closure and entrapment on this journey, despite the fact that, paradoxically, the poem is an approach to infinity since the plummeting of the diminished poet will continue "para siempre jamás."

Baudelaire's "L'Irrémediable" possesses a remarkably similar ambience (beginning, of course, with the poem's title and the consequent hopelessness of ever undoing what has already been done). As does "Irrevocablemente," the poem by Baudelaire lacks the first person narrator that characterizes so many of the poems of *Les Fleurs du Mal* (*Flowers of Evil*). The speaker of the poem may be found in the catalogue of "emblèmes nets" (clear emblems) that form the poem's "tableau parfait / D'une fortune irrémédiable" (perfect picture / of an irremediable destiny). The emblems range from the abstract ("Une idée, une Forme" [An idea, a Form]) to the concrete ("Un navire pris dans le pôle" [A ship trapped at the pole]), and inhabit a landscape that is mythological ("tombé / Dans un Styx bourbeux et plombé" [fallen / into a Styx of mud and lead]) and biblical ("Un Ange, imprudent voyageur"

[An Angel, imprudent traveler]). As in "Irrevocablemente," the poet is surrounded by a vastness that overwhelms him. He is a minuscule, lost figure immersed in a "cauchemar énorme" (enormous nightmare) and battles "un gigantesque remous" (a gigantic whirlpool). The black point plummeting toward the water in "Irrevocablemente" struggles hopelessly in the whirlpool in "L'Irrémédiable" like a swimmer.

In Cortés's poem, the poet is forever suspended above the surface of the earth ("Ya no abrió nunca el cielo ni la tierra sus puertas!"), falling toward it without reaching it. Neither ascent/transcendence nor descent below the earth's surface are possibilities. Baudelaire's poem, though permeated with images of falling such as "un Etre / Parti de l'azur et tombé / Dans un Styx" (A Being / having left the azure realm and fallen / into a Styx) and "Un damné descendant sans lampe" (A damned, lampless soul descending), is a poem that eschews suspension for a limitless capacity for descent into a different sort of transcendence. Baudelaire aspires to the transcendence of damnation, which, ironically, is as beautiful in its perfection as the poem that describes (and is a consequence of) "La conscience dans le mal"(the conscience submerged in evil).

One might summarize what certain French critics have written regarding Baudelaire's ambiguous Catholicism by means of the following questions: Are personal transgressions confessed by the poet himself as sin at the end of his life? Is his a highly marginal relationship with the Church in which the poet rejects the Christ of Calvary in order to appropriate certain aspects of a symbolic language that he manipulates with his own objectives? Is it an ability to believe not in the Word made flesh, but in the flesh made Word by means of the imaginary conversion of human experience into verse, a phenomenon parallel to religion and priesthood?[9]

Baudelaire's poem, unlike Cortés's (which seems stripped of Christian terminology), achieves access to an underworld "oú nul oeil du Ciel ne pénètre" (Where no eye from heaven can penetrate) precisely because of Baudelaire's lucidity and ability to penetrate human consciousness within the framework of morality as defined by Catholicism. It is a world in which the "Diable" (Devil), irremediably linked phonetically to the title of the poem, "fait toujours bien tout ce qu'il fait" (always does well whatever he does). The limits of the self in Baudelaire's poem, though not reduced to the degree of "un punto negro y vago," are nevertheless constrained and entrapped ("un navire pris dans le pôle"). But the poet is able to achieve a heightened sense of awareness by means of "le mal": Evil gives birth to the poem's symbolic language appropriated by the poet from the language of Christianity. Cortés, on the other hand, incapacitated by his reductive mode of being, has already lost his human dimension and seems on the verge of forfeiting his ability to communicate reality as perceived by human consciousness.

That this sense of "le mal" is absent in "Irrevocablemente" raises a serious question. Is there an existential impossibility of salvation in Cortés's poem? Cortés may ultimately fare far worse than Baudelaire, the damned, in that the conditions set forth in "Irrevocablemente" are perhaps more irrevocable than those presented in "L'Irrémédiable."

At the opposite end of the ontological spectrum is the expansiveness that the self can absorb and use, not only as a source of well-being, but as a means to achieve transcendence. For Baudelaire, in "La Mort des Pauvres," it is not "le Mal," but death that beneficently enables the individual to approach certain mystical aspirations. Death serves a double paradoxical function: it is simultaneously one's only respite as well as the force (because of one's fear of it) that makes one continue to live. The poem, in which death is portrayed as the very goal or purpose of life, is a series of equations, all of which begin with "C'est" (It is), that attempt to name or to approximate the ultimate unknowable quantity that is death. The freedom and consolation of death in "La Mort des Pauvres" are not, of course, an available alternative in "L'Irrémédiable" since the damned individual must remain alive within certain parameters so that he can continue the ritual process of purification through suffering. The "fúnebre remedio" that Cortés mentions in "Irrevocablemente" becomes a pleasing, intoxicating "elixir" in "La Mort des Pauvres." The attraction of death in the form of the Angel with magnetic fingers does not result in a loss or a reduction of consciousness (as it does in "Irrevocablemente"), but in a source of heightened awareness that resembles the "gloires uniques" (sole glories) in "L'Irrémédiable": death offers "le sommeil et le don des rêves extatiques" (sleep and the gift of dreams of ecstasy).

Most important, however, is Baudelaire's conception of death in the final stanza of the sonnet. The end of life is, first of all, a means to know the glory of the Gods. Baudelaire, by referring to "Dieux," avoids a monotheistic approach to religion in order to embrace a fuller spirituality that is both Christian and pagan. The second and third phrases metaphorically link death to an accumulation of spiritual sustenance ("le grenier mystique" [the mystical granary]) and wealth ("C'est la bourse du pauvre" [It is the purse of the poor]) from which the poor can draw: these possibilities of transcendence through death do not exist in "Irrevocablemente." The last, expansive image of "La Mort des Pauvres" addresses spatiality and modes of being most directly: the final equation is an open-ended approximation of infinity. The doors of the sky that would be closed in "Irrevocablemente" are thrown open onto the unknown in the last line of Baudelaire's poem.

This sense of spatiality is an appropriate place to begin an analysis of Cortés's "La canción del espacio":

La distancia que hay de aquí a
una estrella que nunca ha existido
porque Dios no ha alcanzado a
pellizcar tan lejos la piel de la
noche! Y pensar que todavía creamos
que es más grande o más
útil la paz mundial que la paz
de un solo salvaje . . .

Este afán de relatividad de
nuestra vida contemporánea—es—
lo que da al espacio una importancia
que sólo está en nosotros,—
y quién sabe hasta cuándo aprenderemos
a vivir como los astros—
libres en medio de lo que es sin fin
y sin que nadie nos alimente.

La tierra no conoce los caminos
por donde a diario anda—y
más bien esos caminos son la
conciencia de la tierra . . . —Pero si
no es así, permítaseme hacer una
pregunta:—Tiempo, dónde estamos
tú y yo, yo que vivo en ti y
tú que no existes?

(*Poesías* 47)

(The distance from here to / a star that never existed / because God has not succeeded in / stretching the night's skin / that far! And to think we still believe / that world peace is more / useful, greater, and comes before / the peace of a single savage . . . / This fascination with relativity / in our contemporary life: that's / what gives space an importance / found only in ourselves. / And who knows when we'll learn / to live like the stars— / free amidst all that has no end / and needing no one to feed us. / The earth does not know the roads / where it journeys every day. / Yet those roads are the / earth's awareness . . . But allow me / a question if this is not so: / Time, where are we, / you and I, since I live in you / and you do not exist?)

Even formally, this poem reflects a euphoric vision of life that is far more hopeful than in its psychological counterpart, "Irrevocablemente." The rhyme scheme, metrics, punctuation, and line breaks of "La canción del espacio" are quirky, open, and irregular—Cortés even rhymes an article with a preposition ("la" and "a"). All that cements the disparate elements in the poem is the symmetry of its three eight-line stanzas. "Irrevocablemente," on the other hand, is a poem hermetically-sealed (as is the poet's fate) by three couplets with consonant rhymes followed by a quatrain with an *a b b a* rhyme scheme (reminiscent of the pattern sustained throughout the ten quatrains in "L'Irrémédiable").

The distance experienced by the poet in "La canción del espacio" (the first five lines of the poem form a breathless exclamation that is an incomplete sentence) is so vast that not even God can cover it with the night's skin. But to what God does Cortés refer? If this God is the omnipotent God of Catholicism, why is there an act (the stretching of the night's skin) beyond realization?[10] Why would God be subject to the power of a night characterized in human terms as possessing skin? As we shall see, Cortés's transcendent encounter with infinity is spatial, not religious in the traditional sense. It begins in egocentric terms and ends with an expansion of the self's boundaries so great that the individual ceases to exist.

"La canción del espacio" is filled with fragmentary thoughts and abrupt tonal shifts that give the poem a varied structure. The poem's individual, seemingly-unrelated components achieve a unity precisely because of the predominance of space over time in the poem. The reader, as Joseph Frank states in *The Widening Gyre*, must possess the ability "to undermine the inherent consecutiveness of language, frustrating the reader's normal expectation of a sequence and forcing him to perceive elements of the poem as juxtaposed in space rather that unrolling in time."[11] The space in Cortés's poem is also, of course, internal. The poet's encounter with a non-threatening vastness (quite different from the spatial aspects of "Irrevocablemente") has taken him deep within himself. Gaston Bachelard in *The Poetics of Space* describes this kind of immensity as existing within ourselves.

> It is attached to a sort of expansion of being that life curbs and caution arrests, but which starts again when we are alone. As soon as we become motionless, we are elsewhere; we are dreaming in a world that is immense.[12]

Such is the spirit of independence in Cortés's poem that the speaker wonders when humanity will learn to live like the stars, transcending even the need to be fed ("sin que nadie nos alimente"). Baudelaire, on the other hand, envisions death as "l'auberge . . . Ou l'on pourra manger" (the inn . . . Where one can eat). Indeed, Baudelaire's conception of death (until the sonnet's final stanza) seems ordered and terrestrial: the poet even gives the disenfranchised their own "patrie antique" (ancient motherland). In "La canción del espacio," Cortés seems more celestial and freer of temporal considerations than Baudelaire. Bachelard might say that Cortés inhabits an ambiguous space in which "the mind has lost its geometrical homeland and the spirit is drifting."[13]

Cortés mentions "relativity" in "La canción del espacio," a poem written in 1927, as the key to recognizing "lo que da al espacio una importancia que sólo está en nosotros." In an infrequently cited prose piece by Cortés entitled "La Belleza Perfecta" (Perfect beauty), the poet describes his understanding of Einstein's theory of general relativity (1916):

> I think that Einstein's theory of relativity, which intuitively serves me as a norm to appreciate things in this way, is a rational and scientific truth possessed by that which is concrete in Nature and in the absolute unity possessed by the abstract in God. This concept, or way of seeing things, obliges me to think that God is the Point of Reference of the absolute and that Humanity is the point of reference of the relative. This I also see clearly and precisely.[14]

Cortés's flawed, intuitive interpretation of Einstein's theory is limited to a perception of the divine as absolute and of the human as "relative." For Cortés, God is an absolute means by which the "relativity" of humanity is measured. This, certainly, is not what Einstein had in mind when he formulated his revolutionary concept of the physical universe. Too, Cortés's geometry seems stranded in Euclidean perceptions; his is a universe (especially in "La canción del espacio") in which space is infinite, parallel lines never meet, and a straight line is the shortest distance between two points. Einstein's discovery changed this perception of reality, according to scientists Lawrence LeShan and Henry Margenau:

> Its consequences included the acceptance of a new mode of explanation in which space was no longer infinite but had a finite radius; the shortest distance between two points in the neighborhood of a star was no longer a straight line; two bodies moving along parallel lines would meet after a long but finite time. . . . The finite radius of space was continually expanding . . . [and] time became the fourth dimension of space.[15]

While Cortés does incorporate some of these complexities in other poems, his use of the word "relatividad" in "La canción del espacio" is, at best, misleading.

Because the movement of the human toward the divine in Cortés's poetry has to do primarily with self-knowledge, one wonders if the poet's absolutism can be defined within the parameters of traditional Catholicism. This is especially true in the beginning of the final stanza of "La canción del espacio." Cortés, as a result of his expansiveness, perceives an entire planet as a sentient being. The poet seems to be creating a paradigm of human awareness: even if one were able to walk all the innumerable paths of consciousness (the frequency—"a diario"—having to do with how often one examines one's life), one would not be able to "know" its mysteries. Perhaps these lines also allude to the manner in which the individual may delude himself into thinking that he knows the paths of consciousness he travels habitually, when, in fact, one cannot know the unknowable.

The final lines of the poem are directed apostrophically to time itself. The poet wonders where he and time are located in space. Individual consciousness at this point, is still intact. This is because the poet recognizes that he is subject to and encompassed by the laws of temporality ("yo que vivo en tí"). But then, in the remarkable final line of the poem, the poet establishes the definite primacy of space over time by negating the existence of both time and himself as an individual ("y tú que no existes?").

It would seem that the reductive and expansive modes of being (with their respective desperate and euphoric emotional states) lead Cortés to the same Void. In "Irrevocablemente," the self is infinitely reduced and experiences "la Nada." The infinitely expanded limits of the individual in "La canción del espacio" result in an erasing of the self and a subsequent merging of the self with pure space. In both cases, the poet's existential anguish and ecstasy do not depend on faith in a traditionally-defined God. Cortés's poetic world is one in which the human "conciencia" recognizes the primary importance of spatiality and rejects the Christian terminology of "le conscience dans le Mal." Perhaps this distinction hinges on the two alternative meanings of the Spanish "conciencia" and the French "conscience." The reader must weigh the significance of the difference between consciousness and conscience. In Baudelaire's poetry, the poet maintains a certain ambivalent faith in the conscience of the individual oppressed by temporal and material considerations: transcendence becomes possible through the act of writing and death. Cortés discovers that, within the realm of human consciousness, transcendence means an understanding, however temporary or partial, of how the infinitely vast equals the infinitely small.

Boats and Windows: the Transcendent Journey

A similar spatial axis in terms of the preoccupation with a "here" and a "there" exists in Cortés's "El barco pensativo" (The pensive ship) and "Ventana" (Window) as well as in Rimbaud's "Le Bateau ivre" (The drunken boat) and in Mallarmé's "Les Fenêtres" (The windows). All four texts are visionary poems that treat the theme of the transcendent voyage either by means of the metaphor of navigation by ship or the perception of the sky through a window.

Rimbaud's "Le Bateau ivre," written in 1871, may be read as the poetics of the *je* (I) becoming *autre* (other), a process of open revolt against traditional Christianity whose meaning depends on the very framework of thought that the poet negates. According to Pierre

Messiaen, during this period, "if [Rimbaud] speaks of Christianity in his poems, he tends to caricature it, denigrate it, insult it."[16] As the object of the poem, the divided self can study its own capacities for visionary creation and self-destruction, principles that are directly proportional in "Le Bateau ivre": the greater the destruction, the fuller the awakening. The poem addresses the critical issue of the extent to which an individual can aspire to transcendence without seeking refuge in a greater power that lies beyond the self.

Of "Le Bateau ivre"'s twenty-five quatrains, seven are dedicated at the beginning to describing the process of the poet-boat's liberation. This process depends on the violent *depopulation* of all humanity borne by the vessel, specifically "les haleurs" (the bargemen) and then the rest of the crew, without which the rudder and anchor lose control over the boat. Consequently, the poet feels the onset of transcendence as his limits expand in the presence of the "Poéme / De la Mer" (Poem / of the Sea). The next ten quatrains, beginning with the line "je sais les cieux crevant en éclairs . . ." (I know the skies rent by lightning . . .), form the central part of the poem and enumerate the images of the *je* as *voyant* (seer), a state facilitated by the subject's expansive mode of being. The final eight quatrains express the ultimate failure of the truncated project embarked upon by the poet at the beginning of the poem with such high, almost desperate, expectations. The poet discovers that his *je* has not been permanently divided and that there is no escape from the reality of Europe with its "anciens parapets" (ancient parapets). The vast expanses of water that the poet-*bateau* experiences during his journey are reduced, finally, to a toy boat and a single "flache / Noire et froide" (puddle / black and cold).

"El barco pensativo" begins on an ocean beach (not on the banks of a river as in Rimbaud's poem) in a boat with masts and sails. Cortés's ship seems potentially seaworthy from the start and is reminiscent of images from the opening lines of Dante's *Purgatorio* in which the human spirit leaves the cruel sea of the *Inferno* and hoists its sails on its journey upward to Paradise. The main difference between the tone of the two poems may be found in the adjectives that are the third words of the titles: "ivre" and "pensativo." For Rimbaud, drunkenness (associated in the poem with the motion of the river) is one means to achieve the "dérèglement de *tous les sens*" (the disordering of *all the senses*) that would lead to an altered consciousness. A pensive state of meditation (related, perhaps to the calm sea that forms the poem's setting), for Cortés, produces a more tranquil but no less intense sense of heightened awareness:

EL BARCO PENSATIVO
En la sonante playa, con ímpetu afanoso
y movimiento vivo,

tiende sus velas tristes al viento poderoso
    el barco pensativo.
Es el hombre. Sus sueños, como marinos graves
    van en callada tropa;
mujeres siempre bellas y trémulas como aves
    se sientan en la popa.

La incógnita esperanza, petrel de largo vuelo,
    en los mástiles ronda
y un coro de recuerdos, coronados de cielo,
    se aleja sobre la onda.

Vienen del puente voces, se ordena y se trabaja
    bajo las ciudadelas
estáticas de éter; mientras el viento ultraja
    el telón de las velas.
El sol imprime exámetros de plata en las espumas,
    en el azul se lanza
una ciudad de luces y de brumas;
    el horizonte danza.

Y el Capitán, en tanto que la visión celeste
    de la hora se disipa,
se acerca a una alta verga y ve alejarse al Este
    el humo de su pipa.

(Poesías 9)

(The Pensive Ship
    On the roaring beach, with a painful impulse / and lively movement / the
pensive ship / spreads its sad sails to the powerful wind. / It is man. His
dreams, like solemn sailors / journey in silent ranks; / Trembling, ever-
beautiful women like birds / sit in the stern. / The unknown hope, petrel of
long flights, / circles the masts / and a chorus of memories, crowned by the
sky, / recedes over the waves. / Voices come from the bridge. Orders are
given and work is done / Beneath the static / citadels of ether; meanwhile,
the wind buffets / the canvas of the sails. / The sun engraves silver
hexameters in the surf, / a city of lights and mist is hurled / into the blue; /
the horizon dances. / And the Captain, as soon as the celestial vision / of the
hour dissipates, / approaches a high spar and sees smoke from his pipe /
recede in the East.)

In "El barco pensativo," the poet gradually *populates* the vessel that
he is. The poet gives his own dreams (likened to sailors) the task of
guiding the ship as he sets sail. Fellow passengers include beautiful,
passive women, perhaps embodiments of certain feminine aspects of his
unconscious. Suddenly, in the third stanza, there is an effacing of the self
in preparation for the coming instant of transcendence. The poet's

unknown hope, metaphorically portrayed as a sea-bird capable of long flights, circles the masts, physically separated from the psyche that produces it. Individual memories, which together form the foundations of the poet's personal past and identity, become a chorus that recedes over the waves, leaving the poet emptied, open and prepared to incorporate the vastness of the sea and sky that surround him. This parallels the process of self-purgation in "Le Bateau ivre": the sea on which the poet navigates into the vision (the poem of the sea, the sea of the poem) even increases its limitlessness by reflecting the stars in the sky. Nevertheless, Rimbaud's self is not only intact but insistently present ("Je sais . . ."; "J'ai vu . . ."; "J'ai rêvé . . ."; J'ai suivi . . ."; J'ai heurté . . ." [I know . . . I've seen . . . I've dreamed . . . I've followed . . . I've touched]). The poet, having rebelled against all superior authority (including God), is determined to achieve his visionary state on his own.

It is immaterial whether or not Rimbaud's epiphany is of greater duration than Cortés's. In the recreation of the transcendent moment by means of the written word, Rimbaud would have the reader believe that the poet was somehow able to maintain himself in the presence of the vision for an extended, although unspecified, period of time. Nevertheless, "Le Bateau ivre" is a poem of immense bitterness and sadness. Rimbaud recounts the visions nostalgically in an ecstatic past tense. Cortés, on the other hand, observes the "ciudadelas estáticas de éter," "exámetros de plata en las espumas" and "ciudad de luces y brumas" in an exalted present, *en route*. Perhaps this is the particular formula of the alchemy of the word that Rimbaud has been seeking all along: the ability to describe visions in the present tense without being overwhelmed by the falseness of what he was seeing (or not seeing) and writing.

Rimbaud's retrospective mourning of the loss of transcendence is so great toward the final stanzas of the "Le Bateau ivre" that he longs for death, for a final immersion in the infinite: "O que ma quille éclate! O que j'aille à la mer!" (O let my keel burst! O let me go to the sea!). Cortés, on the other hand, sustains the moment of grace by ending the poem in the here and now at a calm peak which, oddly enough, depends not on the vision itself (which dissipates) but on the presence of the God-like Captain who peacefully watches smoke from his pipe recede in the East. The beauty of this final image lies in the transience and substancelessness of smoke—like life itself:[17]

It is the poets' relationship to a superior being that denotes the greatest difference between these two voyage-poems by Cortés and Rimbaud. The intensity of Cortés's "visión celeste" gives way to a prolonged tranquillity. Cortés implies that the soul's journey toward God, toward the "port" from which it originally departed, can be undertaken only in the guiding presence of God (a phenomenon that does not enter the configurations of "Irrevocablemente" and "La canción del espacio"). Rimbaud, in "Le Bateau ivre," ultimately rejects all authority and finds, in his inability to replace God with himself, that he may not be able to navigate "les cieux délirants" (the delirious skies) at will and on his own. He is left with only the "nuits sans fond" (bottomless nights) that may or may not house his "future Vigeur" (future Strength). The poet has believed all along that he would have to rely on his own reserves of visionary imagination without the benefit of divine guidance of the kind that the "Capitán" provides in "El barco pensativo."

In the case of "Les Fenêtres" by Stéphane Mallarmé, the transcendent voyage depends not on a superior being or a series of stunning self-induced visions but on the individual's capacity to perceive the mystical qualities of Nothingness that lie beyond an object as simple as a window. Much has been written by French authors such as Flaubert, Proust, Valéry, as well as the poems in French by the German Rilke, about the seemingly safe act of looking through a window. But "Les Fenêtres" and Cortés's poem "Ventana" specifically deal with the psychological dangers that Gaston Bachelard, in *The Poetics of Space*, calls "the dialectics of outside and inside."[18] Bachelard believes that the two intimate spaces, because of their mutual hostility, are always ready to be reversed. This is very similar to the "inherently antithetical" worlds of illness and well-being that "confront one another in perpetual hostility"[19] as described by Oliver Sacks in *Awakenings*. In light of these spatial considerations, then, a window might be regarded as the transparent, reflective border, or surface, of this perpetual conflict.

The two speakers in "Ventana" and "Les Fenêtres" are divided from the exterior world under similar circumstances: from a single perspective within a closed area, the speakers regard the exterior world through a window. The comments of critic José Varela-Ibarra regarding the window in Cortés's poem also apply to "Les Fenêtres":

> In the window, the interior space (physical and spiritual) and the exterior space (everyday and universal) are juxtaposed. . . . For this reason, the sensation of perspective that it creates is simultaneously that of a space that is both more vast and more reduced than the natural space. The window is the bridge between "here" and "there," "now" and "then," "inside" and "outside," "madness" and "saintliness."[20]

Both poets utilize the window as an aperture through which they project themselves and their own interior space out of the phenomenal world toward an Ideal. As Cortés writes in the introduction to *El poema cotidiano* (The quotidian poem), the sky forms the natural setting for this projection: "In the sky of thought, the ideal stands out as the perennial symbol of its real and certain substantial nature. . . . Art stands out as the effective incarnation of all mental longing."[21] This longing ("anhelo") in

line 4 of "Ventana" is a key word, and is linked to "cielo" (sky) in line 2
by rhyme:

> Un trozo azul tiene mayor
> intensidad que todo el cielo.
> yo siento que allí vive, a flor
> del éxtasis feliz, mi anhelo.
>
> Un viento de espíritus, pasa
> muy lejos, desde mi ventana,
> dando un aire en que despedaza
> su carne una angélica diana.
>
> Y en la alegría de los Gestos,
> ebrios de azur, que se derraman . . .
> siento bullir locos pretextos,
> que estando aquí, ¡de allá me llaman!

(30 poemas 17)

(A bit of blue has greater / intensity than the whole sky. / I feel that my
longing lives there / on the level of happy ecstasy. / A wind of spirits passes /
far away from my window, / creating an air in which an angelic diana / tears
her flesh apart. / And in the happiness of the Gestures, / inebriated with
azure, that overflow . . . / I feel the crazy pretexts boil, / which, being here,
call me from the distance!)

The window itself frames the portion of external space that is
available to the speakers in both poems. While Mallarmé discovers a
panoramic view, for Cortés, the fragment of blue sky defined by the
window is more intense than the entire sky. Cortés's desperate longing
for the "éxtasis" embodied in the blue sky's open space corresponds to
Mallarmé's intense desire to experience the *azur* which, for him,
represents purity in poetry.

The moribund figure in "Les Fenêtres," "las du triste hôpital" (weary
of the sad hospital) and in an advanced state of decrepitude, crawls to the
window "pour voir du soleil sur les pierres" (to see the sunlight on the
stones). Through synecdoche, Mallarmé singles out a part of the body,
the mouth, to signify an entire physical and mental state. In a complex
synesthetic series of stimuli, the mouth is feverish as well as voracious in
its longing for the "azur bleu" (blue azure). And it is by means of the
mouth that the poet may use the lips and their "long baiser amer" (long
bitter kiss) to make loving contact with the surface of the warm, golden
windowpanes. This act produces a potent, therapeutic state of inebriation
in which the subject of the poem, now rejuvenated, removes himself
from the horrors of the hospital-world around him. He is able to

transform his view of the sunset bleeding over the rooftops of the city into "galeries d'or . . . sur un fleuve de pourpre et de parfums" (galleries of gold . . . over a fragrant purple river).[22]

The visionary moment in "Ventana" occurs in the poem's second stanza, a remarkably complex juxtaposition of biblical and mythological imagery that masks what is essentially a violent sexual fantasy. Eduardo Zepeda-Henríquez detects the tone of vehemence in this poem, as well as a kind of transcendence that "belongs to the order of what is vital. . . . Here, there is nothing metaphysical, only life: the life of the man, Alfonso Cortés."[23] The vision in which the violence is directed against a female figure occurs in a space far from the speaker. The words "despedaza" and "diana" are strangely resonant of the myth of Acteon and Diana: Acteon interrupts Diana while she is bathing and, as a punishment, Diana transforms him into a deer then hunts him down with dogs; Diana, the chaste huntress-goddess associated with the moon, allows no one to view her nakedness. In other words, Acteon pays for his curiosity (and, most likely, his sexual desire) with his life. The correspondence of the myth with Cortés's poem is not direct at least, of course, in terms of the results: it is not the poet as Acteon who is hunted down by the divine "diana." The goddess, of flesh and blood, even though she is floating through the sky, rips her flesh to pieces—almost as if the invisible dogs had rebelled and killed her instead of attacking Acteon. Is this a violent, repressed vision of revenge (a projection of the poet's own desires) on a woman who would not permit sexual intimacy? Perhaps, as Beryl Rowland suggests, it is an example of modern psychology's approach to the Acteon myth as "a youth, confronted with sex for the first time, shocked into impotence."[24] If one continues this line of thought, it is difficult to read lines 9 and 10 as anything but a kind of strange, euphemistic language describing an ejaculation, a masturbatory sense of euphoria after having destroyed the unattainable purity. How should one interpret the justifications that follow this ebullience? Are they the voice of the conscience as defined by Catholicism, in other words, "la conscience dans le Mal" and the guilty person's self-inflicted psychological punishment?

"Ventana" is an intensely personal poem related by a first person voice in the present tense. "Les Fenêtres" maintains a certain objectivity until, halfway through the poem, immediately following the transitional sixth stanza, the "je" surfaces abruptly. In a cinematographic replaying of what has come before, the subject in Mallarmé's poem confronts himself in the window that, like the two halves of the poem itself, has become a mirror. Whereas "Ventana" recounts the destruction of purity embodied in the "angélica diana," "Les Fenêtres" is a nostalgic attempt to reinforce purity: "le matin chaste," "Une peau virginale" (the chaste morning, a virginal skin). In the window, the subject of Mallarmé's poem also sees his own reflection transformed into that of an "ange" (angel) and foresees his death embodied in the image of the old man from the beginning of the poem. But he also senses the possibility of a cycle that mystically goes beyond death to rebirth.

Nevertheless, the impurity of his surroundings with its stench (the sense of smell functioning here as a counterpart to the perfumed river) overwhelms him. He must hold his nose—even as he marvels in the presence of "l'azur." His final question, on the ontological order of Hamlet's "To be or not to be," remains unanswered. To leave behind the phenomenal world, to leave *himself* behind, he must break the glass and pass through the shattered window, the consequences of which might mean not the controlled flight through eternity, but the plummeting through the void of deep space with his two plucked wings of little use—like a doomed Icarus with no more power over his movement than the dropping point in Cortés's "Irrevocablemente." There are, of course, mystical aspirations in "Ventana" and "Les Fenêtres," but there is no reference to God. Is this because both poems are highly existential? Is it because, at least in the case of Mallarmé, we are dealing with mystical poetry that is essentially atheistic?[25]

The Sacred Pores and the Circle with No Center

Until now, the object of this transcendent voyage has remained somewhat ill-defined. In the first two sections of this chapter, we have examined the differing, unorthodox interpretations of Catholicism in the poetry of Baudelaire, Rimbaud, and Mallarmé as well as the ways powerful collages of symbolic languages, all approximating the same infinity, operate in the work of these writers. John Porter Houston's following observation on Rimbaud's "mystical" poetry also applies to certain poems by Baudelaire and Mallarmé:

> The essential problem is that Rimbaud's "mystical" poems are syncretic after the manner of much nineteenth-century religious literature. They have an artistic coherence and pattern but no clear theological grounding.[26]

At this point, it is important to clarify our definition of mysticism, because, strictly speaking, Baudelaire, Rimbaud, Mallarmé, and Cortés are not mystical poets, but poets with mystical *inclinations*. There are, of course, important differences between the poets: for Baudelaire and Rimbaud, mysticism is achieved through carnality, a debauched urban life, and self-immolation; Mallarmé's enormous intelligence impedes him as a mystic and the kind of total surrender that this implies; Cortés, a provincial poet isolated from the world, might be considered more mystical than the others in terms of the purity of Being that characterizes his ontological and spiritual search. Nevertheless, traditionally, the mystical experience (such as that of San Juan de la Cruz) describes the union of the soul with God. The individual passes through three different stages: 1) *vía purgativa* 2) *vía iluminativa* and 3) *vía unitiva*. The purgative stage describes the escape from the dark night of the senses and the subsequent loss or erasure of the self. In the illuminative stage, one sees and feels the presence of God. This stage is followed by one in which the transformed "individual" becomes one with God. None of the poems by Cortés or the three French poets transcends the second stage. The journey of these poets, therefore, must be described as a movement *toward* God that falls short of achieving unity with God.

However, in the case of Cortés, what sort of God does the poet hope to reach? Francisco Fuster cites a creed-like passage from Cortés's "La Belleza Perfecta":

> To summarize: I believe in God, I believe in Religion and I believe that its future is rationalist and not dogmatic, not because I do not believe in the dogmas, but precisely because I think that all nature is a dogma that is subject to being penetrated by Reason—when Man is truly Humanity, and because of this understands that Truth, which is God, is nothing but Perfect Beauty.[27]

Fuster then makes the following comment:

> He certainly has original and luminous ideas, but they do not coincide with the truth of religion and even less with the message of authentic Catholicism.[28]

Cortés's poetry is Christian but not in keeping with traditional Catholicism due to a strong current of Gnosticism that permeates his work.

If this is true, it would simply place Cortés and his religious thought in a long line of other "rebel" poets, whose works, according to Octavio Paz, manifest a fundamental conflict:

> The opposition between poetic and sacred writings is of such a nature that every alliance made by modern poetry with an established religion always ends in scandal. Nothing less orthodox than the Christianity of a Blake or a Novalis; nothing more suspect than that of a Baudelaire; nothing more alienated from the official religion than the visions of a Shelley, a Rimbaud, or a Mallarmé . . ."[29]

Paz goes on to say that the influence of Gnosticism on these poets is undeniable. As we have said before, given the syncretist tendency of the poetry that we are investigating in this chapter, one cannot say that the authors are writing purely and solely in a Gnostic tradition. However,

Gnosticism does form an important foundation for the pursuit of spiritual knowledge in the poetry of Baudelaire, Rimbaud, Mallarmé, and Cortés.

In her book *The Gnostic Gospels*, Elaine Pagels states that, in its desire to be universal, the orthodox Catholic church opened itself to anyone who did not challenge the three basic components of the system: doctrine, ritual, and clerical hierarchy. The Gnostics questioned all three. As Pagels says, "only by supressing gnosticism did orthodox leaders establish that system of organization which united all believers into a single institutional structure."[30]

One of the Gnostic beliefs that the orthodox leaders were particularly interested in supressing was the idea that self-knowledge is the equivalent of knowledge of God. Pagels elaborates on this aspect of Gnosticism:

> Whoever comes to experience his own nature—human nature—as itself the "source of all things," the primary reality, will receive enlightenment. Realizing the essential Self, the divine within, the gnostic laughed in joy at being released from external constraints to celebrate his identification with the divine being.[31]

According to Pagels, the Gnostics believed (against orthodox Christianity) that "the psyche bears *within itself* the potential for liberation or destruction."[32] An example of this inner, human power (which bears a remarkable resemblance to modern psychotherapeutic interpretations) are the following words attributed to Christ in the Gnostic *Gospel of Thomas*:

> Jesus said, "That which you have will save you if you bring it forth from yourselves. That which you do not have within you will kill you if you do not have it within you."[33]

If one considers Dante a paradigm of Christian orthodoxy (even though the perspicacious critic Kenneth Rexroth believes that there are "traces of Gnostic cosmology" throughout Dante),[34] Cortés's poem "La Pregunta del Dante" (Dante's question; *Treinta poemas* 113) illustrates the hetorodox Christian viewpoint that Cortés assimilated from French poetry. In *The Divine Comedy*, Dante frequently addresses, warns, and admonishes his readers. The opening question of "La Pregunta del Dante" makes it seem as if Dante discerned Cortés among the more valiant of his readers and asked him, perhaps annoyed that someone might have had the audacity to have followed him so far, "What are you doing there?" Cortés gives the orthodox Dante a quite unorthodox, Gnostic interpretation of the meaning of life: "no hay más saber que el ser, ni otra manera / de ser que ejercitar el inconsciente / individual" (There is no greater knowing than being, nor any other way / of being than exercising individual unconscious). A curious counterpart to "La Pregunta del Dante" is Cortés's poem "El Policírculo" (The polycircle) (*Las siete antorchas del sol* 127) in which God constructs the Immense Circle that is Paradise then says to the poet who lives there, "Qué hace allí" (What are you doing there). The answer to Dante's question lies in the psyche of the individual, according to Cortés, and can be elucidated only on the basis of an inward journey into the unconscious.

Cortés seems eager to confront Dante on his own territory: he even writes his poem in Dante's *terza rima* and hendacasyllables. The poem, despite its heretical view ("cada cosa es como la interpreta / uno mismo" [each thing is as one / interprets it]), is deferential to the great Italian poet: "la razón completa de mi existencia para tí en tí vive" [the complete reason for my existence lives for you and in you]). The fifth tercet of Cortés's poem is a homage to the supreme moment of transcendence in *Paradiso* when Dante ascends with Beatrice from the Primum Mobile to the realm of the Empyrean. The Point of Light that is God overcomes Dante, a Point that paradoxically seems enclosed by that which It encloses. Dante then perceives the endless flowing of God's grace: "e vidi lume in forma di rivera / fulvido di fulgore, intra due rive / dipinte di mirabil primavera" ("and I saw light that took a river's form— / light flashing, reddish-gold, between two banks / painted with wonderful spring flowerings.")[35] In Cortés's poem, the poet himself is the divine being who circumscribes himself and his own actions. It is the poet who sees, flowing from his own distant center ("aquel foco en silencio que recibe/toda la luz" [that center in silence that receives/all light]), a stream of poetry that reflects the poet's "conciencia humana" (human consciousness). The stream of poetry exists simultaneously within all human consciousness and within the poet himself individually:

> . . . Y como el que circunscribe
> a sí propio su acción ví que fluía
> de aquel foco en silencio que recibe
>
> toda la luz un chorro de poesía
> que reflejaba mi conciencia humana
> y que era en ella pero en mí existía.—
> Y comprendí la Trinidad cristiana.

(And like he who circumscribes / his actions himself, I saw flowing / from that center in silence that receives / all light, a stream of poetry / that reflected my human consciousness / and that I was in it but that it existed in me. / And I understood the Christian Trinity)

Cortés's final line ("Y comprendí la Trinidad cristiana") is an expression of revelation on the same level as Dante's encounter with the supreme geometry of the Trinity, which Dante describes as three equal circles, the second reflecting the first, and the third (the Holy Spirit) being the fire of Love that is breathed from the first two. For Dante, the second circle (the Son, the Logos, the Word, the Idea) contains within itself our human form as a manifestation of Christ's human form. Before he loses consciousness, Dante comes to know how the total incompatibility of the human and the divine (the square and the circle) is made compatible.

Cortés's understanding of the Trinity is altogether different from Dante's. Cortés only perceives the second circle, the Logos. But the Logos as an aspect of the divine contains its own tripartite unity: for Cortés, the Christian Trinity consists of potentially divine human consciousness, the individual consciousness that pursues *gnosis,* and poetry. Max Pulver, in an article entitled "Jesus' Round Dance and Crucifixion According to the Acts of St. John," says that, at the beginning of the third century, Christianity was most permeated with Gnosticism. He continues with an explanation of the original significance of the Logos:

> At that time the Logos meant not only the creative word, but also the inwardness, the Spirit. Thus the Logos, interpreted as inwardness, can also encompass . . . silence.[36]

The journey toward God, for Cortés, is one that is undertaken within the self either in silence or by means of the creative word. It is in this way that self-knowledge leads to knowledge of and equality with God. As Cortés says in his poem "La Verdad" (Truth): "Y Dios es en el hombre / lo que él en Dios" (And God is in man / what he [is] in God; *Las rimas universales* 97). This echoes John 10:38 when Jesus says, "the Father is in me, and I in him."

Cortés's great poem of the *vía iluminativa,* in which he senses the proximity of God is "Pasos" (Steps), a text in which the solitude and silence of the first stanza produce the ecstasy of the second:

> Cuando, en el tumulto de la Tierra,
> sientan los seres su soledad,
> dará una tregua eterna la guerra
> del Ruido; hundirá en la antigüedad
>
> sus pasos el Hombre y la Mujer,
> surcarán la arruga de la frente
> de Dios, donde del éxtasis de Ayer
> se alza vapor incesantemente . . .

(*Poesías* 58)

(When, in the tumult of the Earth, / the beings feel their solitude, / the war of Noise will make / an eternal truce; / Man and Woman will sink / their steps in antiquity, / they will plow the wrinkle of God's / forehead, where, from Yesterday's ecstasy, / vapor rises incessantly . . .)

According to Gnostic beliefs, in order to become like God, or even approach God, one must leave one's body either temporarily in ecstasy ("se alza vapor incesantemente") or permanently in death. Cortés uses the third person singular form in the future tense of the verb "hundir" (to sink), even though the subject of the verb, "el Hombre y la Mujer" (Man and Woman), is plural. Apparently, the poet is seeking some kind of unity and equality (Gnosticism is strongly matriarchal and antipatriarchal) of humankind, a oneness in the presence of God that precedes a oneness with God. By having humanity plow the wrinkled brow of God in the poem's second stanza, the poet creates a metaphorical link between the terrestrial and the celestial.

The lovers, grouped in pairs, (as a point of comparison, Beatrice leaves Dante on his own in the final transcendent cantos of *Paradiso*) in the third stanza are in a trance-like state of wakefulness, perhaps enlightenment:

> Y quedarán los enamorados
> —como despiertos—y dos a dos,
> la mirada fija en los Sagrados
> Poros, de eterno sudor bañados,
> de la frente arrugada de Dios!

(And the lovers will remain / —as if awake—and two by two, / their gazes fixed on the Sacred / Pores, bathed in eternal sweat / from the wrinkled forehead of God!)

Is this an example of what Thomas Merton calls "the strange, infallible certainty of Zen"[37] in Cortés's poetry? The lovers seem to have reached a level of awareness filled with every possibility in which the self knows all things, questions nothing, and rejects nothing.

Cortés uses synecdoche, the same technique one finds in Mallarmé's "Les Fenêtres," to create a staggering sense of enormity in "Pasos." The single gaze of each couple is fixed on the Sacred Pores of God's forehead. It is difficult to imagine a more stunning example of the humanization of the divine. Dante is very adept at this, too, in *Paradiso*. But, ultimately, his God is an abstract, geometric shape. In this particular poem by Cortés, God sweats like the rest of us!

Nevertheless, in other poems, Cortés's approximation of God involves a high degree of abstraction. "Yo" (I) (*Treinta poemas* 105), for example, is a poem that moves from the concrete, natural world of "El viento, el mar, la lluvia, el grito / de los pastores" (the wind, the sea, the rain, the call / of the shepherds) to an abstract "divina feria" (divine fair) that defines a space in which "el infinito es círculo sin centro" (the infinite is a circle with no center). Given the title of the poem and its subject matter, "Yo" is an ontological piece on reaching conclusions about the meaning of life by experiencing the different possibilities life offers. Although these alternatives are far more restrained than Rimbaud's radically unconventional approaches to the attainment of vision and wisdom, Cortés enumerates certain options suggested to him by others in the first stanza and rejects them:

> Muchos me han dicho:—El viento, el mar, la lluvia, el grito
> de los pastores . . . Otros:—La hembra humana y el cielo;
> otros:—La errante sombra y el invisible velo
> de la Verdad, y aquellos:—La fantasía, el mito.
>
> Yo no . . .

(Tardes de oro 101)

(Many have told me: the wind, the sea, the rain, the call / of the shepherds . . . Others:—the human female and the sky; / others:—the wandering shadow and the invisible veil / of Truth, and still others:—fantasy, myth. / Not for me . . .)

The answers, according to the poet, lie in the ineffable ritual presided over by a flying chorus of archangels. "Yo" is a poem of many paradoxes. Sometimes Cortés links two words (whose meanings seem to cancel each other) in the single syntactical unit of an oxymoron. For example, although Cortés appears to reject "la hembra humana"—one recalls Rimbaud's "Mais l'orgie et la camaraderie des femmes m'etaient interdites" (But the orgy and the camaraderie of women were forbidden me) in "Mauvais Sang" (Bad blood) (Oeuvres 216)—he characterizes eternity as if it were an animal searching for its mate: "la eternidad vive en sagrado celo, / en el que engendra el Hombre y pare lo infinito" (Eternity lives in sacred heat, / in which it engenders Man and gives birth to the infinite). Within eternity's endless mating season, humanity, because it procreates, is mimetic of infinity, which also gives birth.

This paradoxical image of reproduction that is simultaneously sacred and profane is a key approximation of God and infinity in Cortés's poetry. The epiphany in "Yo," a poem probably written in the early 1920s, closely resembles new theories concerning the nature of the universe. One of the most controversial of these more recent theories is explained in physicist David Bohm's book Wholeness and the Implicate Order. In an interview, Bohm summarizes his view of the universe in the following way:

Everything enfolded in one whole, and unfolding from an infinite ground
into finite moments. All moments enfolded within each other, and unfolding
from a totality which is beyond time.[38]

Cortés's creative words—the poem that expresses humanity's mystical
inclinations, the Logos interpreted as both word and silence—produce
the paradox of "mis palabras son silencio hablado" (My words are
spoken silence). The text of the poem defines a silent rather than a
spoken space. Silence becomes a prerequisite for spiritual knowledge
(*gnosis*)[39]; all that one thinks one knows becomes difficult, while one's
encounter with the unknown becomes easy. The poet likens himself to
the Merchant (someone engaged in sacred numerical transactions) at a
divine fair:

> Yo soy el Mercader de una divina feria
> en la que el infinito es círculo sin centro
> y el número la forma de lo que es materia.

> (*Tardes de oro* 101)

(I am the Merchant of a divine fair / in which infinity is a circle with no
center / and the number [is] the form of that which is matter.)

These final lines of "Yo" are extremely complex definitions of the
nature of the universe. Cortés may be offering an explanation of God (or
human enlightenment) as a circle with no center. Perhaps he is
attempting to describe the nature of a universe with a finite radius that is
infinitely expanding. Perhaps the last line is a description of the creation
of matter by a subaltern God, a number held by one of the fundamental
books of the Kabbala (the "Sefer Yezirah" which means "Book of
Creation") to be an emanation from God, the Ein-Sof.[40] Varela-Ibarra
believes that Cortés is drawing on the language and philosophy of
Pythagoras to express the essence, mystery, and beauty of life in "Yo."[41]

In other poems by Cortés, there are different degrees of abstraction in
terms of the perceiver and the perceived God. For example, in "En
silencio" (In silence) (*Las siete antorchas del sol* 74), the poet who lifts
his eyes toward God in a moment of despair is given the curiously
abstract denomination "el pobre supernumerario" (the poor
supernumerary). The palpability of God, as described by the poet in
God's presence, can be simultaneously abstract (in a non-geometric,
human way) and concrete as in "La chimenea" (The fireplace) (*Las siete
antorchas del sol* 115): "¿Sientes? En este sitio en que estamos los dos /
huele a gas, huele a infancia, huele a mujer y a Dios . . ." (Do you smell
it? In this place where both of us are, / it smells like gas, it smells like
childhood, it smells like a woman and God). Any combination in his

poetry of the abstract and the concrete, the divine and the human, is, as far as Cortés is concerned, an appropriate use of symbolic language to approach the oneness of being.

What Cortés, Baudelaire, Rimbaud, and Mallarmé have in common is their faith in the power of human consciousness to engender the analogies necessary to link seemingly unrelated objects and ideas. As poets, they share an obsession with metaphor, metamorphosis, and synthesis as ways of naming the unnameable source of all spiritual knowledge. Although these poets retain in their verse certain sacred and profane linguistic structures derived from Catholicism, they seem dissatisfied with the limitations of Christianity's symbolic language and seek other systems of thought (Gnosticism, for example, but also the Platonic manifestations in the theories of Emmanuel Swedenbourg, as well as the occultism and magic of Eliphas Lévi), that enable them to approximate the original oneness of being.[42] The syncretic convergence of the diverse systems in the verse of these four poets moves toward the creation of a single, all-encompassing text.

Pablo Antonio Cuadra believes that Cortés learned from Baudelaire's "Correspondances" (Correspondences) "to see in the existing reality a hidden side, an immense store of analogies, an entirety of figures to be deciphered."[43] If Cortés, in his poetry, is engrossed in the interpretation of the "forêts de symboles" (forests of symbols), a system by which symbols and humanity engage in familiar, mutual observation, it is because he seeks the "ténébreuse et profonde unité / Vaste comme la nuit et comme la clarté" (tenebrous and deep unity / vast as night and light) that Baudelaire describes in "Correspondances." Gaston Bachelard would add that "it is the principle of 'Correspondances' to receive the immensity of the world, which they transform into intensity of our intimate being."[44]

What, finally, is the significance of the powerful Gnostic current in the poetry by Cortés? First of all, Gnosticism forms the basis of Cortés's unique identity as a Nicaraguan poet, linking him to a tradition of rebellion. Furthermore, as Harold Bloom points out, Gnosticism is a paradigm not only for religious self-knowledge, but also for a theory of reading poetry. A deep, comparative reading of the poems by Cortés as well as the other poets cited in this chapter, for example, contains the potential for an understanding of what Bloom calls "the multi-layered text of the *psyche*."[45]

2

Pablo Antonio Cuadra and Jules Supervielle: Utopia, National Identity, and History

In a fascinating essay on the New World, More's *Utopia*, and Cuba, Ezequiel Martínez Estrada describes the first European encounters with the unique and confusing beauty of the landscape of the American continent. According to Martínez Estrada, the strange flora and fauna as well as the inhabitants with their exotic customs and beliefs disturbed the humanist and the naturalist to such a degree that the Europeans transformed their discovery into "a mythology and a legend that covered the entire, as yet unexplored territory, turning it into a region of fabulous beings and occurrences."[1] For Nicaraguan poet Pablo Antonio Cuadra and French poet Jules Supervielle, the landscape of the New World is a space that lends itself to the imaginary projection of certain utopian ideals, a theme that has a solid tradition in literature from Latin America since the time of Christopher Columbus and his descriptions of the earthly paradise in America, to Ernesto Cardenal's desire to establish the kingdom of God on earth by combining Christian, indigenous, and Marxist precepts.[2] Despite Cuadra's acknowledged literary "apprenticeship" with the Uruguayan-born French writer Supervielle, there is a critical difference between the early works of the two poets: the history of the American continent that is entirely absent from Supervielle's landscapes in *Débarcadères* (Wharfs) (1922) and *Gravitations* (Gravitations) (1925) plays a crucial role in Cuadra's *Poemas nicaragüenses* (Nicaraguan poems) (1934) in that Cuadra's paradisaical world enters into a conflict with the transformative power of historical events. Cuadra, unlike Supervielle, consciously incorporates the indigenous culture and mythology of the so-called New World in his poetry.

The first section of this chapter describes how both poets create a narrator-traveler in their work as a means of entering and depicting the landscape. In the second part, we will discuss the Edenic impulse itself in the early works of both poets and the ways that Cuadra undercuts and refutes the myth of the peaceable kingdom. The third section will focus on several poems by Cuadra in which a particular moment of history (the

45

occupation of Nicaragua by the U.S. Marines in the 1930s) jeopardizes
the existence of the idealized landscape. It is this balance of the historical
and the mythical, unaddressed by Supervielle, that enables Cuadra to
establish a national identity of his country successfully. At the same
time, however, in a process that involves the assimilation of mythical
models and actions associated primarily with Central America, Cuadra
manages to achieve an archetypal universality in his poetry.

The Traveler in a New World

In a short prose piece eulogizing Supervielle, Cuadra expresses what
it was that was miraculously revealed to him in 1930 (when he began to
compose the poems in *Poemas nicaragüenses*) as a result of reading
Supervielle's verse-journeys into the South American landscape:

> When I was searching for the expression of my land in my first Nicaraguan
> poems, an angel of the sort that assists poets, brought to my awareness
> *Débarcadères* and *Gravitations*, two books of poetry by Supervielle prior to
> 1925. This must have been in 1930. The discovery of the Uruguayan pampa
> by Supervielle, or, what might be better characterized as the magical light
> with which his eyes illuminated the landscape as he contemplated it by
> means of poetry, was like the instantaneous opening of a window to the
> morning light. I saw there a horizon open for my own discovery of the
> Nicaraguan land.[3]

According to Cuadra, it was not only the theme of Supervielle's poetry
that attracted Cuadra's passionate attention, but the French poet's manner
of presenting his subject in a way that combined a subjective lyricism
with an epic narrative power:

> That rhythm on horseback that I managed to transfer to my Nicaraguan
> mount; that moderate approach to the epic, stripped of all eloquence; that
> eluding of the old rhetoric of beauty (foreign lace hung in the window
> through which the poet looked at his land) so that one could see clearly and
> serenely; . . . an entirely new scale of poetic virtues prompted by Supervielle
> enabled me to create the first rebellion of my poetry.[4]

It is clear in Cuadra's eulogy of Supervielle that Supervielle's poetry
holds a double value for Cuadra: it is, first of all, the impetus for a
journey into a national landscape; and secondly, Supervielle gives
Cuadra a modern technique with which he can express his new
perception of this landscape. Supervielle converts Cuadra into a traveler
in a new world that is both Nicaragua and the innovative literary world
of the 1920s and '30s. Supervielle's brand of realism and quasi-
surrealism enables Cuadra to express a personal geographical reality

which the Nicaraguan poet came to know through his travels by boat, on horseback and on foot.

According to Jorge Eduardo Arellano, the theme of the journey, inspired in part by Cuadra's reading of French verse, played a critical role in the development of Cuadra's early poetry:

> In *Poemas nicaragüenses* as well as in *Cuaderno del sur* (Southern notebook)[5] he engages in an itinerant discovery of the interior of the country in the first book and the exterior . . . in the second. Over both works, a traveler's eye presides, a characteristic that the poet acquired in literary terms through his reading of the French poets of the Vanguard such as Blaise Cendrars, Valery Larbaud, Paul Morand, and especially Jules Supervielle.[6]

The fascination with the journey motif in French poetry was a characteristic not only of poems by Cuadra but also by Cuadra's generational literary compatriots known collectively as the *movimiento de vanguardia* (Vanguard Movement). In an issue of the Nicaraguan literary journal *El Pez y la Serpiente* (The Fish and the Serpent), there is a gathering of the poems that the *vanguardistas* (primarily José Coronel Urtecho, Cuadra, and Joaquín Pasos) translated in a group effort from the French and published in the supplement *Vanguardia* between 1931 and 1932.[7] Of these poems, Supervielle's "Le Retour" (The return) may have had the more profound impact on Cuadra as a poet.

"Le Retour" is a poem in which the poet has embarked on a journey that is simultaneously a return to the poet's native land (Uruguay) after an extended absence and an attempt to recover the lost, more perfect, world of his childhood. In this poem, Supervielle, who characterizes himself in a book published in 1919 as the "Ulysse Montévidèen" (Ulysses from Montevideo) (*Poèmes* 96), appears to be seeing the landscape and himself, in the light of a sort of primitive Ideal, for the first time. Perhaps in this way Supervielle's narrator-traveler resembles his counterpart (as defined by William Nelson) in Thomas More's classic *Utopia* (1516):

> When the Utopian traveler Raphael Hythloday is described at the beginning of the book he is compared with Plato and Ulysses, a comparison that serves neatly to define the principal roots of More's work: the imagination of a "best state of a commonwealth" and the report of a wise traveler to strange lands.[8]

It is the traveler's wisdom and his ontological preoccupations that distinguish "Le Retour" from the enumeration of people and places that often characterizes panoramic travel poems. Christian Sénéchal says the following about the difference between Supervielle's voyage poems and those of many of his contemporaries:

An evasion outside of society or oneself—this is what travelling meant for
many of our contemporaries, or perhaps a way of knowing the picturesque
and diverse world. For Supervielle, it was a necessity, an act as natural as
tides.[9]

Sénéchal goes on to say that Supervielle's non-escapist descriptions of
his travels take their sustenance from the stuff of the world, enriching the
poet, turning him inward to an exploration of the self, without which the
world would not exist.

"Le Retour" opens with the poet's endeavor to establish the poem's
and his own spatial coordinates. In his French text, Supervielle leaves the
Spanish word *gauchos*. Despite the fact that this particular word is
charged with the literary, historical, and cultural character of a particular
space (the pampa in Uruguay and Patagonia), the poet explores none of
these traditional associations with any depth. He relies on an exotic,
stereotypical "aura" that the word evokes in his reader. The rhythmicality
of these men on horseback initiates the process of physical location:

> Le petit trot des gauchos me façonne,
> Les oreilles fixes de mon cheval m'aident à me situer.

> (*Choix de poèmes* 13)

(The quick trot of the gauchos shapes me, / the fixed ears of my horse help
me situate myself)

The second line of the poem expresses a certain geometry: the two fixed
points of the horse's ears together with the third point that is the poet
himself form a plane whose dimensions are as infinite as the pampa
appears to the human eye. But where is the poet exactly? As he says in
the poem, he becomes one with the landscape that possesses neither
mythology nor history:

> Je fais corps avec la Pampa qui ne connaît pas la
>   mythologie. . . .
> Je m'enfonce dans la plaine qui n'a pas d'histoire . . .

> (*Choix* 13)

(I merge with the Pampa that does not know mythology. . . . / I sink into the
plain that has no history . . .)

Somehow outside of all mythical and historical considerations, the poet
is located in the "nowhere" that underlies the word "utopia"
etymologically.

When the traveler-narrator in the opening poem of Cuadra's *Poemas nicaragüenses*, "Introducción a la tierra prometida" (Introduction to the promised land), incorporates the landscape into his own body, he is, at the same time, bringing himself into contact with an immemorial tradition—the history of his forebears:

> ¡Oh tierra! ¡Oh entraña verde prisionera en mis entrañas: tu Norte acaba en
>   mi frente,
> tus mares bañan de rumor oceánico mis oídos
> y forman a golpes de sal la ascensión de mi estatura.
> Tu violento Sur de selvas alimenta mis lejanías
> y llevo tu viento en el nido de mi pecho,
> tus caminos, en el tatuaje de mis venas,
> tu desazón, tus pies históricos,
> tu caminante sed.
> He nacido en el cáliz de tus grandes aguas
> y giro alrededor de los parajes donde nace el amor y se
>   remonta.

(OPC vol. 1, 116)

(Oh earth! Oh green entrails imprisoned in my / entrails: your North ends in my forehead, / your seas bathe my ears with oceanic sounds / and form the ascension of my height with blows of salt. / Your violent South of jungles feeds my distances / and I carry your wind in the nest of my chest, / your roads in the tattoos of my veins, / your uneasiness, your historical feet, / your walking thirst. / I was born in the chalice of your great waters / and I spin over the places where love is born and soars.)

In both "Le Retour" and "Introducción a la tierra prometida," there is an expression of oneness of the poet with his landscape that one finds in much of the poetry of Pablo Neruda. A significant, fundamental difference, however, distinguishes the two poems: Supervielle, from a European perspective, seems to divorce the New World from a sense of tradition. The pampa, according to Supervielle, is unencumbered by the mythology and history of the Old World:

> Je me mêle à une terre qui ne rend de comptes à
>   personne et se défend de ressembler à ces
>   paysages manufacturés d'Europe, saignés par
>   les souvenirs.

(Choix 14)

(I mix myself with a land that yields to no one and refuses to resemble those manufactured landscapes of Europe, bled by memories)

The traveler in the fourth line of "Le Retour," for example, in saying "Toute la Pampa étendue à mes pieds" (The entire Pampa stretched out at my feet) expresses a single individual's limited awareness. Cuadra, on the other hand, converts the landscape itself into a wayfarer ("tus pies históricos") (your historical feet) that resembles the poet, though on a larger, collective scale.

Like Cuadra, Supervielle gives the names of the flora and the fauna native to the landscape he describes during the course of his travels. But Supervielle fails to mention the native tongues that originally named the objects that the poet perceives. This is not to say that the Uruguayan lifestyle is absent from Supervielle's poetry. On the contrary, it is a contribution to Uruguayan culture that is treasured by the Uruguayans themselves.[10] But Supervielle, in what may be described as an overzealous Adamic instinct, diminishes the indigenous traditions in his portrait of the New World. The "hirondelles" (swallows) in "Le Retour," unlike the "urraca vagabunda de las fábulas campesinas" (wandering magpie of peasant fables) in Cuadra's poem, are disconnected from the matrices of popular mythology and are, therefore, less rich in meaning. Both Cuadra and Supervielle share a cosmic, sacred link with their respective American landscapes. But, while sacredness for the latter poet signifies an escape from the European into a recognizable, transhistorical childhood world, the former is fully aware that by moving through the mythical landscape of his ancestors he thereby reintegrates himself into a sacred past.

Cuadra, unlike Supervielle, describes travels other than his own, and travelers other than himself. One such figure (both mythical and historical) is the subject of the sole poem in *Poemas nicaragüenses* that refers to Nicaragua's Atlantic coast. "El Negro" (The black man) is a narrative poem about a shipwrecked black slave named Sarabasca who finds freedom in what is now known as Nicaragua when he is accepted into the Indian tribe of King Miskut. The poet, presumably staring out over the Caribbean in the Nicaraguan coastal city of Bluefields, is reminded by the landscape (the place where Sarabasca won his freedom) of an historical incident that, over the centuries, has acquired an archetypal significance, thereby winning a place in the collective memory of the Nicaraguan people:

> Alto de mí, el sol de sal
> se cierne sobre el mar con su ojo incandescente.
> Yo renuevo una memoria abandonada y canto
> este lugar donde puso su pie blanco
> el negro, el fugitivo de las islas encadenadas

cuando la muerte levanta su viento crepitante
para agitar las terribles arenas infinitas.

(OPC, vol. 1, 154)

(High above me, the sun of salt / blossoms over the sea with its incandescent
eye. / I renew an abandoned memory and sing / this place where the black
man put / his white foot as a fugitive of the islands in chains / when death
raises its crackling wind / to stir the terrible, infinite sands.)

As much as the sea represents for Sarabasca a road to freedom in a
particular epoch (one that condones slavery), it is also "sin tiempo"
(timeless) and as dangerous in its infinity as death. Sarabasca, reaching
the country whose only flag is the greenness of the jungle, is himself one
of history's smoking pages:

Navegaba en un ataúd de remos sin manos
bajo la estrella oscura de Aphar o de Magreb
con una lágrima de sal hiriente
en sus ojos sin patria. Sarabasca
hijo del fuego, herrado a fuego, cuerpo
de carbón aquí quemó su último exilio
y miró las selvas con sus banderas verdes
levantando gritos de papagayos y gavilanes marinos.
Sarabasca: humeante página del siglo . . .

(OPC, vol. 1, 154-55)

(He navigated in a coffin with oars but no hands / under the dark star of
Aphar or Magreb / with a wounding tear of salt / in his eyes with no
homeland. Here, Sarabasca, / son of fire, branded by fire, body / of coal,
burned his last exile / and watched the jungles with its green flags / lifting
cries of giant parrots and sparrow hawks. / Sarabasca: smoking page of the
century . . .)

Sarabasca shows the Indian King Miskut his scarred back, which the
King reads with pity, as if the scars were taken from the unpublished
books by all the anonymous historians who carry with them the emblems
of history, linear time indelibly engraved in their flesh:

Tienes escritos en tu carne
nuestras peregrinaciones y destierros.
Tienes grabados en tu piel
los caminos errantes de los hijos de los ríos.
te has posesionado de la piel de nuestra tierra.

(OPC, vol. 1, 156)

(Written in your flesh are / all our wanderings and exiles. / Engraved on your skin / the errant roads of the children of rivers. / You have taken possession of the skin of our land.)

Sarabasca escapes the sea navigated by the buccaneers and adventurers who enslaved him, so that he can live in freedom and work the land. The poem also functions as a sort of creation myth in that it describes the foundation of the Atlantic coast's cultural diversity—the "other" Nicaragua with its black and indigenous heritage.

The sea, as it relates to the traveler's journey, is quite different in the early work of Cuadra and Supervielle. Cuadra, unlike Supervielle, is essentially a landlocked poet. Though Nicaragua is a small country with the Pacific to the west, the Caribbean to the east, and a vast body of fresh water in its center, Cuadra's eyes are turned toward an isolated interior of jungles and plains. The few references to the sea in *Poemas nicaragüenses* are indicative of what is perhaps the only significant gap in his early poetry: the failure to fully develop a *complete* national identity that reflects Nicaragua's diverse cultures and geography. The poet rectifies this in a truly magnificent way in *Cantos de Cifar y del mar dulce (Songs of Cifar and the Sweet Sea)* (composed from 1969-1979), a series of poems that describe the culture of the Great Lake, Nicaragua's inner sea. Even when one considers *Cuaderno del sur*, a dozen poems written during Cuadra's travels by sea to South America in 1934-35 (contemporary with the composition and publication of *Poemas nicaragüenses*), it is clear that Cuadra continues to view his journey in terms of the land he knows. In "Mástiles" (Masts), for example, the ship's masts remind the poet of high trees:

> Yo amo
> estos altos
> y solitarios
> árboles
> y corto
> aún verdes
> sus rutas
> olorosas a delfín y a gaviota.

(*Cuaderno del sur* 13)

(I love / these high / and solitary / trees / and still green / I cut their routes / that smell of dolphin and gull.)

According to Christian Sénéchal, a similar confusion of land and sea and longing exists in the poetry of Supervielle, though without the historical resonance of Cuadra's poetry:

For Supervielle, the sea was nothing more than a second pampa, more monotonous than the one in Uruguay.[11]

As James A. Hiddleston points out in his analysis of the sea in Supervielle's poetry, the marine landscape produces a distinct persona which Hiddleston calls "un moi-mer" (a self-sea). Hiddleston believes that the poet benefits from a state of therapeutic forgetfulness.[12] This therapy provided by the sea seems to follow death by drowning, the ultimate risk and the secret desire of the marine traveler in the Romantic tradition à la Shelley. A complex spatial matrix in which the poet's infancy is joined to the paradisaical world exists at the bottom of the sea in Supervielle's "Le Survivant" (The survivor), a poem in which the drowned man lives peacefully with all the creatures of his childhood and Creation.

In *Poemas nicaragüenses*, the reader searches in vain for this "moi-mer" that Cuadra develops with such "freshwater" distinction in *Cantos de Cifar* nearly forty years later. The sea in Cuadra's early poems usually remains in some unattainable distance that the traveler is unwilling to negotiate. In "Oda fluvial" (Fluvial ode), for example, the poet has indirect access to the sea by means of other bodies of water. The Río Frío flows into the Río San Juan which flows from Nicaragua's Gran Lago into the Caribbean. This river that finally reaches the sea contributes simultaneously to a sense of universality and to the construction of a national identity: Cuadra's river resembles Supervielle's sea in that it bears the eternal temporal emblem of "la constante hoja desprendida" (the constant fallen leaf); it differs, however, from the often unreal worlds contained in the bodies of water in Supervielle's seascapes because the river also reveals "la secreta historia del contrabandista" (the secret history of the smuggler), an important reference to the economic history of Nicaragua. When Supervielle travels beneath the waves of high seas he invents mythical/biblical paradises populated with the human and animal life that the poet once knew when he inhabited the land. The parameters of utopia in Cuadra's *Poemas nicaragüenses* define a land situated in this world, subject to the history and to the myths of a particular country—Nicaragua.

The Edenic Impulse

According to the authors of *Utopian Thought in the Western World*, Columbus, the paradigmatic traveler, on his third voyage in 1498, withdrew from the mouth of the Orinoco River as a result of his enormous fear of entering Paradise:

Columbus was manifestly in a state of disarray. He was close by the terrestrial paradise, but he knew, as he wrote to the Spanish sovereigns, that no one might enter it except with the will of God. Frightened by the forbidden paradise and the ultimate secret it held, he fled back to Hispaniola.[13]

One can imagine Columbus' immense difficulties, psychologically speaking, when it came time to take possession of Paradise itself in God's name. How was Columbus going to imitate the act of Creation in a zone that was supposedly already sacred? In *The Myth of the Eternal Return*, Mircea Eliade discusses mythic implications of the discovery of the New World:

> Better still, a territorial conquest does not become real until after—more precisely, through—the ritual of taking possession, which is only a copy of the primordial act of the Creation of the World. . . . It was in the name of Jesus Christ that the Spanish and Portuguese conquistadores took possession of the islands and continents that they had discovered and conquered. The setting up of the Cross was equivalent to a justification and to the consecration of the new country, to a "new birth," thus repeating baptism (act of Creation).[14]

Eliade summarizes the Edenic impulse as the attempt to create a sacred center of the cosmos, a zone that defines an absolute reality.

In *Poemas nicaragüenses*, a book whose original title was *Campo* (Countryside), Cuadra seems to have conquered Columbus's fear perhaps as a result of something as unremarkable as the Nicaraguan poet's birthright. The landscape in Cuadra's "Introducción a la tierra prometida" takes on a biblical, utopian quality that is reminiscent (at least in terms of the poem's title) of the "land flowing with milk and honey" promised by God to Moses in Exodus 3:8. But the poem begins with an invocation and characterization of the sun as a timeless, ancestral peasant that is rooted in the mythology of Central America:

> Portero de la estación de las mieses,
> el viejo sol humeante de verdes barbas vegetales
> sale a la mañana bajo una lluvia de prolongados
>   tamboriles
> y vemos su hermoso cuerpo luminoso como en un
>   vitral,
> labrador de la tierra,
> abuelo campesino de gran sombrero de palma,
> cruzando con sus pesados pies la blanda arcilla
>   gimiente.

(*OPC*, vol. 1, 115)

(Keeper of the season of the fields of grain / the old, smoking sun with its green beard of plants / rises in the morning under a prolonged drumming rain / and we see his lovely, luminous body as if in a window, / worker of the earth, / grandfather peasant with a great palm hat, / crossing the soft moaning clay with heavy feet.)

This image of the sun as keeper of the seasons with a brilliant, almost divine, body is reminiscent of Náhuatl and Quechua literatures from the Aztec and Incan empires, especially from the early colonial period when indigenous and Christian symbolic, religious languages became inextricably intertwined.[15] The poem continues with several images derived from this mixture of paganism and Christianity, most notably in the following lines:

> Ahora estamos ya en el mes de las mariposas
> y, alrededor del grano cuya resurrección ellas
>   anuncian disfrazadas de ángeles,
> brotan también las palabras antiguas caídas en los
>   surcos . . .

(*OPC*, vol. 1, 115)

(Now we are already in the month of butterflies / and, around the grain whose resurrection they announce disguised as angels, / the ancient words that fell into the furrows sprout, too . . .)

Often, the Christian themes predominate as in the use of "resurrección" and "ángeles" in the fragment cited above, or, later, in the line "He nacido en el cáliz de tus grandes aguas" (I was born in the chalice of your great waters). There are many other instances, however, of the non-Christian merging with the Christian, for example in Cuadra's description of the migratory patterns (that echo the biblical Exodus) of the two high cultures that existed in Nicaragua before the arrival of the Spaniards: the Nahuas, who immigrated from the north, and the Chorotegas, from the south:

> Voy a enseñarte a ti, hijo mío, los cantos que mi
>   pueblo recibió de sus mayores
> cuando atravesamos las tierras y el mar
> para morar junto a los campos donde crecen el
>   alimento y la libertad.

(*OPC*, vol. 1, 115)

(I am going to teach you, my son, the songs that my people received from their elders / when we crossed the lands and the sea / to dwell next to the fields where food and freedom grow.)

Supervielle's self-centered Adamic impulse may be precisely what erases all traces of history (as well as myths of a clear regional origin) other than the poet's own personal sense of nostalgia for a lost "Eden." French critic Yves-Alain Favres believes that it is significant that poems by Supervielle such as "Le matin du monde" (The morning of the world) and "Montevideo" are permeated by the light at daybreak, a world of innocence, recovered beauty, and purity, in which each morning is a rebirth, the first day of Creation.[16]

"Le matin du monde," like the paradisaical world Cuadra portrays in "Introducción a la tierra prometida," begins at sunrise. The poem combines a series of images of birth and purity to create an Edenic world that reveals itself empirically to the poet. Perception is, at first, self-reflexive, the way the world would necessarily appear to its first inhabitant:

> Alentour naissaient mille bruits
> Mais si pleins encor de silence
> Que l'oreille croyait ouir
> Le chant de sa propre innocence.

(*Choix* 43)

(In the surroundings, a thousand sounds were born / but again so full of silence / that the ear thought it heard / the song of its own innocence)

The village, or city, between sea and countryside is a microcosm that emerges into being as if it were a great insect acting as a protagonist for "l'éclosion de son âge" (the eclosion of its age). At first, the poet relegates human beings to a plane of secondary importance. "Les palmiers" (the palm trees), "les oiseaux" (the birds), and "un cheval blanc" (a white horse) precede the discovery of "l'homme" (the man), who then takes precedence as he moves in an anthropocentric fashion "avec la Terre autour de lui" (with the Earth around him). Suddenly the world comes to life and the streets are filled with women and children engaged, according to the poet, in some spiritual quest ("S'assemblaient pour chercher leur âme") (they gathered to search for their souls). What Supervielle has done is transform the quotidian into a moment of epiphany. The poem is a kind of genesis stripped, as Jaques Robichez says, "of all religious reference," leaving only a "paganised myth."[17] This revelation at dawn in an urban environment appears to depend on the natural world that surrounds it—"les frontières de la campagne" (the borders of the countryside) on one side, and "les vagues de l'océan" (the ocean waves) on the other.

It would seem, then, that the poet is attempting to recreate not only the innocence and purity of paradise, but Adam's capacity, according to

George Steiner, to name "all that comes before him in a closed garden of perfect synonymy."[18] In *After Babel*, Steiner discusses the original language in terms of its being an intermediary between God and humanity:

> According to the medieval Kabbalah, God created Adam with the word *emeth*, meaning "truth," writ on his forehead. In that identification lay the vital uniqueness of the human species, its capacity to have speech with the Creator and itself.[19]

It is this possibility of mimesis of divine dialogue or creation that both Supervielle and Cuadra seem to be seeking in certain Adamic poems. In an article about Cuadra's *Poemas nicaragüenses*, Jorge Eduardo Arellano points out, "like a native Adam, the poet names what is his: an innumerable quantity of natural and human elements."[20] Not surprisingly, it is Cuadra's encounter with Supervielle's pampa during Cuadra's travels in 1935 to Uruguay that produces the most overt example of this phenomenon, in the poem "Creación de la mujer en la pampa" (Creation of woman on the pampa):

> Atravesando la pampa
> tú puedes decir:
> soy el primer hombre sobre la tierra
> y mirar inútilmente la infinita distancia
> sometida al silencio de la luna.

> (*Cuaderno del sur* 22)

(Crossing the pampa / you can say: / I am the first man on earth / and (you can) look uselessly at the infinite distance / subjected to the silence of the moon.)

In Supervielle's poetry, the poet's contact with the natural world enables him to touch and to move with all of its objects—much like Rimbaud's sensual poem "Aube" (Dawn), in which the poet personifies Nature as a woman, tears away all her veils, and experiences her immense body. By repeating the cosmogonic gesture, Supervielle creates his own life, in the sense of giving it a hitherto unknown meaning:

> It is in the Uruguayan countryside that, for the first time, I had the impression of touching the things of the world and pursuing them.[21]

The process is a circular one in which each stage depends on the other: the poet, imitating the primordial act of Creation, names all the things into being; these things inspire the poet and grant him the gift of "song" in the form of words; these words serve to celebrate the poet's country, which gives him the power to name. Cuadra, as a national poet, is the voice of a land where words seem *anxious* to be expressed. Supervielle, a French-Uruguayan hybrid, is lost in a kind of no man's land, a region devoid of myth and history because the poet fails to perceive these traditions.

The problem of converting the landscape into words depends not only on the naming of the objects in the landscape, but on the possessing of them with all one's senses (a phenomenon that manifests itself in Rimbaud's "Aube" as an almost sexual embrace). As in "Aube," a youthful pantheistic urge dominates the paradisaical poems of Supervielle and Cuadra. Cuadra addresses some of the landscape's objects directly in "Introducción a la tierra prometida":

> Y vosotros, árboles de las riberas,
> nidos de los pequeños hijos del bosque,
> alas al sol de los buitres,
> reses en los pastos, víboras sagaces:
> dadme ese canto,
> esa palabra inmensa que no se alcanza en el grito
>   de la noche
> ni en el alarido vertical de la palmera,
> ni en el gemido estridente de la estrella.

(OPC, vol. 1, 116-17)

(And you, trees of the shoreline, / nests of the small children of the forest, / vultures with wings extended to the sun / cattle in the pastures, wise snakes: / give me that song, / that immense word that cannot be reached in the scream of the night / or in the vertical howling of the palm tree / or in the strident moaning of the star.)

The speaker in Cuadra's poem asks elements of the landscape to grant him poetry's song, even though the poet senses that it lies beyond his reach—perhaps drowned out in the different noises produced by the things that are normally incapable of generating such sounds associated with humans and animals. In the *mythic* landscape, all things animate and inanimate, tangible and intangible, possess a voice. When the word loses its capacity for communicative speech (however inadequate it may have been), the results are devastating—Cuadra uses the word "holocausto" (holocaust) to describe the magnitude of the disaster of "esa palabra sin voz" (that voiceless word). By speaking, Cuadra recreates a primordial past. The poem is a sacred text passed on through the generations:

> y aquí escuché las estrofas de este himno campal
> que entonaban nuestros padres en la juventud de los
>   árboles

y que nosotros sus hijos repetimos, año tras año,
como hombres que vuelven a encontrar su principio.

(OPC, vol. 1, 116)

(And hear I heard the stanzas of this hymn from the countryside / that our
fathers intoned in the youth of the trees / and that we, their children, repeat,
year after year, / like men who find their beginning again.)

By the end of the poem, the poet, confident of his power, engages in an
intimate fury of naming:

> Eres tú, colibrí,
> pájaro zenzontle, lechuza nocturna,
> chocoyo parlanchín verde y nervioso,
> urraca vagabunda de las fábulas campesinas.
> Eres tú, conejo vivaz,
> tigre de la montaña, comadreja escondida,
> tú, viejo coyote de las manadas,
> zorro ladrón,
> venado montaraz,
> anciano buey de los corrales.
> Eres tú, ¡oh selva!
> ¡Oh llano sin lindes!
> ¡Oh montaña sin sol,
> laguna sin olas!
> Eres tú, capitana de crepúsculos.
> Noble historia de pólvora y laureles.
> Porvenir de trigales y de niños:
> ¡Amor nicaragüense!

(OPC, vol. 1, 117)

(It is you, hummingbird, / zenzontle bird, nocturnal owl, / chocoyo,
chattering, green and nervous, / wandering magpie of the peasants' fables. /
It is you, vivacious rabbit, / mountain tiger, hidden weasel, / you, old coyote
from the packs, / thieving fox, / wild deer, / old ox of the corrals, / It is you,
oh jungle! / Oh limitless plain! / Oh mountain without sun, / lake without
waves! / It is you, captain of twilight. / Noble history of gunpowder and
laurels. / Future of fields of wheat and of children: / Nicaraguan love!)

In considering the poem's final three lines, it is clear that human beings,
both as makers of history and abolishers of historical time, form an
integral part of Cuadra's world. Nicaragua's noble history is composed
of gunpowder and the laurel of victory in battle; its future depends on
fields of wheat and children. All is motivated by a profound nationalistic
love.

The two poets' depiction of paradise differs especially in the role that animals fulfill in the landscapes that they inhabit: Supervielle's is generally a peaceable kingdom, whereas a tragic savagery (that mirrors human reality) dominates the natural world as Cuadra describes it. With regard to the animal-inhabitants of Supervielle's world, Robert Vivier discusses their purity of intention, courteous love toward one another, and essential goodness.[22] In his analysis of Supervielle's poetry, Yves-Alain Favres also affirms the utopian presence of the animals in that one has the impression of having returned "to Eden, to the primitive Garden where the beasts, devoid of all ferocity, lived in close sympathy with man.[23]

This is not to say, however, that the hard reality of life on the pampa never enters the poetry of Supervielle, especially in the case of the narrative, descriptive poems of *Débarcadères*. The livestock forming the economic mainstay of the landscape Supervielle describes will eventually be slaughtered. In "Le Gaucho" (The gaucho), for example, the hierarchy among the humans and animals and their different purposes for existence are clearly evident in a simple, everyday scene from life and death on the pampa. The cow with its skinned head haunted by ten different shades of red in Supervielle's "La vache de la forêt" (The cow in the forest) is another example of the rough-edged, closely-observed reality in *Débarcadères*. Certainly, the system of order in the Earthly Paradise was not predicated on the systematic violent exploitation of some of its living members over others.

Compared to the objectively-described, routine slaughter in these two poems from *Débarcadères*, the death of the cow in Cuadra's "La vaca muerta" (The dead cow) is a positively cosmic event that outweighs the death of any human being in *Poemas nicaragüenses* in importance and emotional intensity:

> Era ella, muerta.
> Aislada en las serranías ásperas y desvalidas,
> bajo el eterno paréntesis de sus cuernos sin
> amparo,
> entre las cuatro sombras de sus pupilas vacías.

(*OPC*, vol. 1, 165)

(It was her, dead. / Isolated in the harsh and forsaken mountains, / under the eternal parentheses of her horns with no shelter, / between the four shadows of her empty pupils.)

The dead cow is a loss for the entire world, though it is perceived by few ("las ciudades del Sur, / ignorando, / dormían") (the cities in the South, / ignoring [what happened] / were sleeping). It is especially devastating for the "niño inocente" (innocent child) who receives the sad news perhaps as life's first great blow. In the last stanza, the image of the cow becomes a kind of religious icon or sacred, archetypal Mother to be mourned, worshipped, and adorned with flowers in a regenerative rite:

> ¡Oh, quién buscara la rosa
> para adornarle su testa!

(OPC, vol. 1, 166)

(Oh, that someone should look for the rose / to adorn her head!)

Both poets use animals as links with a primordial world: Supervielle's animals peacefully coexist with each other and humanity in a replica of Eden; and the dead cow in Cuadra's poem is a source of ritual through which, in the words of Mircea Eliade, "every consecrated space coincides with the center of the world, just as the time of any ritual coincides with the mythical time of the 'beginning.'"[24]

Occasionally, however, the "timeless" world associated with the animals in the poetry of Supervielle and Cuadra is quite different. In Supervielle's "Mouvement" (Movement), for example, the horse's senses, far more acute than those of a human being, function in a world (like the one into which the horse gallops in "Le matin du monde") in which linear, historical time vanishes: one horse perceives something invisible that another horse sensed two million years before. The only point of contact between "Mouvement" and Cuadra's "Horqueteado" (see definition below) may be the presence of the double horses in both poems that represent parallel worlds. The normal temporal boundaries that divide past from present cease to exist in "Mouvement." Similarly, there is a convergence of the living and the dead in "Horqueteado," a poem in which a rhythmic equivalence is established between the two galloping horses and the heartbeat of the terrified poet, who senses himself on the verge of entering the timeless world of death:

> Un hombre muerto cabalgaba. Unos ojos solitariamente
>> fijos
> Como si todos los caminos y las sendas se unieran
>> para siempre en un último camino.
>
> . . . Las espuelas que rompieron los ijares de mi
>> potro
> Hasta emparejar mi corazón con el galope,
> Repercutieron en el caballo compañero.

(OPC, vol. 1, 142)

(A dead man was riding on horseback. / Some eyes staring in a lonely way / as if all the roads and paths were joined / forever in a last road . . . / The spurs that dug into the flanks of my colt / until my heart was beating with the rhythm of the gallop, / sounded the same on the other horse.)

Yet there is another richer, more symbolic dimension in "Horqueteado" that has to do with the poem's expression of a Nicaraguan tradition which Cuadra explains in a note in the original 1934 edition of *Poemas nicaragüenses*:

Horquetear.—A system used in Chontales to bury those who die far from their homes. The dead person is mounted on a horse familiar with the route and maintained in a seated position by means of forked sticks, one of which supported the chin, the other, behind, the neck. The poem is a poetic definition of the word, a custom that today is disappearing.[25]

Cuadra uses these traditions and their variations throughout *Poemas nicaragüenses* with brilliant results. For example, when the horse of silence gallops above the trees in "Adormidera" (Poppy), carrying a rider who was hacked to death by a machete, the poet transforms the moon into the white eye of a dead ox:

> Es la hora del miedo
> cuando la noche tiene un ojo blanco de buey muerto

> (*OPC*, vol. 1, 133)

(It is the hour of fear / when the night has a dead ox's white eye)

Too, tradition includes a culture's shared mythology. In "Tigre muerto" (Dead tiger), death on earth is mirrored in the sky itself, as if, in keeping with the mythic story of the jaguar that eats the moon, the terrestrial were able to prey on the celestial:

> Sueña el cadáver del jaguar su última rapiña
> y en el pequeño cielo frío y azul
>   que guarda su pupila
> zopilotes insomnes cierran círculos negros
> sobre el esqueleto de vaca de la luna.

> (*OPC*, vol. 1, 157)

(The jaguar's dead body dreams of its last prey / and in the small, cold, and blue sky that remains in his pupil / sleepless vultures close black circles / above the moon's cow-skeleton)

Throughout his early poetry, Supervielle lacks Cuadra's profound assimilation of tradition as well as Cuadra's movement through the "local" to reach the "universal."

As we have seen, neither poet views America strictly as an idyllic paradise in the biblical sense of perfect harmony and the absence of death. Supervielle, for example, wrote in *Boire à la Source* (Drinking from the source), "The American landscape makes you present for all the agonies."[26] The reader senses this pain most fully in *Débarcadères*, only to feel it dissolve in the warm light of the series of epiphanies in *Gravitations*. For Tatiana W. Greene, the American continent in the poetry of *Débarcadères* is devoid of scruples and possesses a primitive magic.[27] Supervielle moves from his harsh idealized in *Débarcadères* to the serene, often extraterrestrial, utopia of *Gravitations*. Cuadra finds the reality of the landscape he observes incompatible with the unequivocal sustaining of the Edenic myth. Cuadra's attitude is no doubt due, at least in part, to the evolution of scientific thought of his time, which, according to the authors of *Utopian Thought in the Western World*, made the notion of earthly paradise extremely problematic:

> The biological and anthropological discoveries of the nineteenth and twentieth centuries helped to subvert the Edenic myth. The further back one went the more bestial man appeared, and the idea of a heavenly paradise could no longer have a prototype on earth in the beginning of things.[28]

Compared to *Débarcadères*, *Poemas nicaragüenses* depicts a natural world that exists in a more primitive, tragic, and undomesticated state. Three poems in particular, "Monos" (Monkeys), "Escrito sobre el 'congo'" (Written piece on the 'congo' ape), and "Quema" (Fire) are especially relevant in this context.

Cuadra, in what might be termed an attempt at literary demystification, begins "Monos" with the traditional setting of so many idyllic poems—on the banks of a river.[29] But a violent event quickly and abruptly destroys what the reader initially imagines as a typical pastoral scene:

> En las márgenes del Tepeneguasapa
> donde una mañana vi esconderse los garrobos
>   súbitamente
> y perderse un novillo en las fauces de un lagarto
>   lleno de lodo y de lama
> se levantan unos árboles altos y desnudos
> cuyas flacas ramas tiemblan al viento como azotadas
>   de epidemia.

(OPC, vol. 1, 128)

(On the banks of the Tepeneguasapa / where one morning I saw the lizards quickly hide and a calf disappear in the jaws of an alligator covered with mud and slime / there are a few tall, naked trees / whose skinny branches tremble in the wind as if they were being whipped / by an epidemic.)

Without sentimentality, Cuadra transforms the trees of "paradise" into trembling bearers of disease and chooses the image of an alligator devouring a farm animal in order to demystify the Ideal. As a means of revitalizing certain literary situations that had become cliches, the poet continues in "Monos" by recognizing another traditional association—the forest as a meeting place for lovers. But instead of humans, the poet encounters a group of lascivious monkeys, which he describes with a certain embarrassed modesty.

Both "Monos" and "Escrito sobre 'el congo'" are examples of a parodic derogation of several types of traditional discourse. In "Monos," Cuadra uses a documentary, realistic language associated with the positivist tradition in order to express his lack of faith in this kind of scientific diction as a sole means of approaching reality. The poet observes the monkeys (in the present tense, as if he were making an entry in a scientific diary) with a zoologist's precision. In describing the way that the monkeys collectively swing across the river, the poet uses certain words that generally have no place in lyric poetry: "pericia" (expertness), "cálculo" (calculation), "paralelo" (parallel), and "matemáticamente" (mathematically). But Cuadra inserts a surprising metaphor in the last stanza of "Monos" that lifts the poem from the plane of realism and expands the poem's context to include the act of writing. Precise calculations and careful, mathematical planning in literature, too, sometimes fail, ending in total disaster:

> Sin embargo,
> esta delicada operación resulta a veces fallida
>   como este poema
> porque un cálculo mal apreciado
> deja entre las aguas el último mono
> —que es siempre el que se ahoga—.

(OPC, vol. 1, 129)

(Nevertheless, / this delicate operation sometimes results in failure like this poem / because one calculation poorly estimated / leaves the last monkey in the waters / and this is the one who always drowns.)

In "Escrito sobre el 'congo'," Cuadra compares natural images derived from his personal experience in the Nicaraguan jungle with the fabulists' portraits of animals so that he can reject the discourse of the fable, which forms part of the official pedagogical language used to reinforce moral ideas in schoolchildren. The poem begins with the recounting of some of the animals from the fables the poet learned as a boy and an observation on the way we, as human beings, attempt to project a false moralism on the animal world. Cuadra goes on to create his own fable and morals concerning humanity based on a description of the "congo," an ape that inhabits the Nicaraguan jungles. The "congo" is by turns lazy, fierce, territorial, dictatorial, sexually voracious, motivated by hatred and the desire to kill all rivals. In replacing warring Roman gladiators with this savage struggle between an old ape and his young challenger, Cuadra is parodying the epic heroism of the Greco-Roman tradition as well:

> Recordé la estúpida gloria del golpe en el vértigo
>   muscular de la lucha romana
> Ojos implacables y vidriosos de la cólera animal.
> El jadeo de los anchos pulmones bombeando la sangre
>   ennegrecida por la rabia
> Y los angulosos colmillos descubiertos para una
>   risa funeraria
> Para un hambre de odio
> Para ese férreo mordisco que el viejo indomable
> clava en el borbotón yugular de su enemigo.

(OPC, vol. 1, 132)

(I remembered the stupid glory of the blow in the muscular vertigo of the Roman struggle / the implacable and glassy eyes of the angry animal. / The panting of the wide lungs pumping the blood blackened by rage / And the angular eyeteeth disclosing a funereal smile / for a hunger of hatred / for that ironclad bite that the indomitable old ape nailed into the bubbling jugular of his enemy.)

In certain poems, as we have seen, Cuadra accepts the innovative literary language of Supervielle and, at the same time, parodies several kinds of official discourse (positivist, pedagogical, and Greco-Roman) that limit the poet's ability to describe his poetic world.

Cuadra's earthly paradise, more fragile than Supervielle's, seems constantly threatened by tragedy. The poem "Quema," for example, records the horrifying destruction of flora and fauna in a runaway fire during a time of drought. The poem may be read as an apocalyptic counterpart to the genesis described in "Introducción a la tierra prometida." Many of the same animals listed in the description of the Edenic landscape are enumerated again in "Quema" as the world they inhabit and they themselves are consumed by flames. "Quema" retains a sense of timelessness despite a strong journalistic current that runs through the poem: there is a specific place ("Llanerías de Boaco") (the plains of Boaco) and a specific time that lacks only a year ("A las doce del día miércoles 18 de abril") (at twelve o'clock on Wednesday, 18 April):

> Con furia las llamas y el humo
> Cerraron sus mandíbulas candentes
> Al tiempo que un grito indefinible y humano
> Hería la tranquilidad de los lejanos animales a
>   salvo.

(OPC, vol. 1, 139)

(With fury, the flames and smoke / closed their burning jaws / and at the same time an indefinable and human cry / wounded the tranquility of the distant animals who were safe.)

Cuadra, in contrast to Supervielle, mixes linear and cyclical time in his dual capacity as contemporary reporter and omniscient chronicler of great, quasi-biblical disasters.

A Balance of Myth and History

The violence set in the natural landscape of Nicaragua in *Poemas nicaragüenses* tends to blur the distinction between mythical and historical time. Cuadra derives this temporal perspective not from Supervielle, but from the principal source of ancient Central American indigenous tradition—the *Popol Vuh*. In the introduction to his remarkable translation of this work, Dennis Tedlock describes the *Popol Vuh*, a work with an almost unimaginable temporal range:

> We tend to think of myth and history as being in conflict with one another, but the authors of the inscriptions at Palenque and the alphabetic text of the Popol Vuh treated the mythic and the historical parts of their narratives as belonging to a single, balanced whole.[30]

The landscape in *Poemas nicaragüenses* admits historical qualities that are noticeably absent from or rejected by Supervielle's landscape. As we stated previously, for Supervielle, in "Le Retour," the pampa is "la plaine qui n'a pas d'histoire" (the plain that has no history). When he says in the same poem that the pampa "ne connaît pas la mythologie" (does not know mythology), he means not only the classical mythology ("les Dieux de l'Olympe") (the Gods of Olympus) of the Old World, but the indigenous mythologies of the New World as well. Supervielle possesses what may be termed a colonizer's mentality: the myths and the history of the world he describes begin with his own description of them. Supervielle would have the reader believe that despite its brutal history (the extermination, for example, of an indigenous population by the landowners who established the immense livestock ranches), the pampa is somehow ahistorical, existing in a vacuum unaffected by native traditions.

At least three of the twenty-six poems that now form the definitive text of *Poemas nicaragüenses*[31] contain overt historical references that establish the poems' temporal coordinates with great precision. About this particular moment in Nicaraguan history and its relation to Cuadra's first published book, Carlos Tunnermann Bernheim has written:

> The book is Nicaragua itself, seen by a young man who, during a period of foreign intervention, discovers the charm of his land with a sense of marvel. During the years of North American occupation, Nicaragua produced two great testimonies of nationalism: Sandino in the mountains and Pablo Antonio Cuadra in his *Poemas nicaragüenses*.[32]

It is neither possible nor desirable to divorce Cuadra's *Poemas nicaragüenses* from the historical period in which it was written: Calvin Coolidge sent the U.S. Marines to occupy Nicaragua in 1926; when the troops were withdrawn in 1933, owing mainly to the tenacity of Augusto César Sandino and his poorly-armed, barefoot guerrilla army, the United States installed the Nicaraguan National Guard under the command of Anastasio Somoza García. In order to consolidate his power under the weak presidency of Sacasa, Somoza assassinated Sandino on 21 February 1934. According to Edelberto Torres, there was another telling element that determined the murder of Sandino:

> But the most decisive factor in destroying Sandino consisted of the agreement with the government in Washington. [Sandino's] life was the testimony of its shameful intrusion in Nicaragua, and his presence was an affront to the U. S. government . . . that decided to avenge itself by carrying out an act during peace that it could not achieve during the war. The war lifted Sandino to glory and peace took him to his death.[33]

The conflict of these vertiginous years corresponds exactly to the time Cuadra composed, published, and revised the poems in *Poemas nicaragüenses*.[34] The landscape of Nicaragua shaped the nature of Sandino's struggle in the same way that it defined Cuadra's nationalistic poetry. To write *Poemas nicaragüenses*, Cuadra had to begin to become one with the landscape he was describing—an obligatory factor we mentioned previously in our discussion of the relationship between "Introducción a la tierra prometida" and "Le Retour." To wage his successful guerrilla war, Sandino had to depend on certain expert guides that were members of his army such as Colonel Conrado Maradiaga, who were more than simply well-acquainted with the terrain:

The principal quality of Colonel Maradiaga is that he is the best *chan* [guide] in all these mountains. He has an incredible knowledge, down to the most minute detail, of this labyrinth of rivers, jungles and mountains in the Segovias, in the disputed territory, and the Atlantic Coast to Bluefields. Piece by tiny piece, as if he had taken an X-ray and carried it in his mind. He was the one who always guided me. He knows more than all the excellent guides that the army has. Maradiaga orients himself by instinct, like some animals. He was my perennial guide through these protective jungles. For seven years he guided us as if by some cosmic impulse, with an infallible exactitude.[35]

Whereas Supervielle's poetry often seems tenuously related to the American landscape it describes, almost all the poems in *Poemas nicaragüenses* are from clearly identified places in the Nicaraguan interior and bear the names of specific villages and regions (either at the end of each text or within the text itself as in "Introducción a la tierra prometida" and "Monos"). One particular geographical location, "Nueva Segovia," in the poem "El viejo motor de aeroplano" (The airplane's old engine), will inevitably be associated (for the Nicaraguan reader and for the reader familiar with Nicaraguan history) with Sandino and his remarkably successful war against the superior forces of the United States. In *Poemas nicaragünses*, Sandino, even though his actual name appears nowhere in Cuadra's book, is a mythic, secret guerrilla-presence forever linked to the spatial coordinates defined by the topography of Nueva Segovia in northern Nicaragua.

In contrast to Supervielle's poetry in which no historical figure appears even implicitly, the history of Sandino and his war on the foreign invaders manifests itself in Cuadra's poems most explicitly in "El viejo motor de aeroplano," "Iglesita de Chontales" (Little church of Chontales) and in the powerful, dramatic "Poema del momento extranjero en la selva" (Poem of the foreigners' moment in our jungle). "El viejo motor de aeroplano" is the sole poem in *Poemas nicaragüenses* that makes reference to a specific year ("Era una noche de mil novecientos veinticinco") (It was a night in 1925) in its description of a particular incident in history—the guerrillas shooting down a plane "equipada con ametralladoras y raros telescopios" (equipped with machine guns and strange telescopic sights) piloted by an experienced man from California. The narrator of "El viejo motor de aeroplano" resembles a sympathetic war correspondent (à la Hemingway) who vividly recreates the circumstances of the plane crash, the discovery of the pilot's body, and how nobody in town even realized that the plane had been shot down, except the campesinos who found the plane and sold its engine. The poem's first line is reminiscent of the way newspaper articles are preceded by the name of the city. The next three lines are composed in a prosaic directness that contrasts with the lyrical romanticism of the last line of the second stanza:

> En el Valle de "Ciudad Antigua"
> a doce leguas cansadas de la ciudad de Nueva
>   Segovia
> los campesinos vendieron un viejo motor de
> aeroplano.
>
> Era una noche de mil novecientos veinticinco
> ceñida de jazmines como las doncellas que mueren
>   sin amante.

(OPC, vol. 1, 143)

(In the valley of "Ciudad Antigua," / which is twelve tiring leagues from the city of Nueva Segovia, / the peasants sold an airplane's old engine. / It was a night in 1925 / covered with jasmine blossoms like young girls who die without knowing love.)

Cuadra's landscape is harsh and agressive in a way that differs from Supervielle's precisely because it is permeated with history. In "Le Retour" Supervielle speaks of the "Vent affamé du pôle" (hungry polar wind) and in "Le Gaucho" the natural world is both voracious and tenacious in the perpetual struggle to survive:

> La pampa se descellait, lâchant ses plaines de
>   cuivre,
> Ses réserves de désert qui s'entre-choquaient,
>   cymbales!
> Ses lieues carrées de mais, brûlant de flammes
>   internes,
> Et ses aigles voyageurs qui dévoraient les étoiles,
> Ses hauts moulins de métal, aux tournantes
>   marguerites,
> Ames-fleurs en quarantine mal délivrées de leurs
>   corps
> Qui luttaient pour s'exhaler entre la terre et le
>   ciel.

(Choix 16)

(The pampa uprooted itself, unleashing its copper plains, / its desert reserves that crashed like cymbals! / its square places of corn, burning with internal flames, / and its travelling eagles that devoured the stars, / its high metal mills, to the spinning daisies, / soul-flowers in quarantine, poorly delivered from their bodies that fought to be blown between earth and sky.)

But the reader will find few, if any, instances of Supervielle's landscape characterized in terms of weapons of war. Cuadra's "El viejo motor de aeroplano," due to the circumstances of history, contains the presence of such weapons in both a literal and figurative sense. It is as if Supervielle's "organic" struggle has been transformed by Cuadra into warfare between men:

> La avioneta equipada con ametralladoras y raros
> telescopios
> cubrió de sangre las húmedas espadas del trigal
> y el más viejo aviador de la armada
> abandanó sus cruces de plata por una muerte trágica
> y violenta.

(OPC, vol. 1, 143)

(The airplane, equipped with machine-guns and strange telescopic sights, / covered the swords of the wheatfield with blood / and the squadron's oldest pilot / gave up his silver medals for a tragic and violent death.)

The poet's metamorphosis of spikes of wheat into swords is one example of the bellicose qualities of the landscape that Cuadra develops more completely in "Poema del momento extranjero en la selva": one might even discover this combativeness in the meter of this poem's extraordinary "(Rojas lapas hablan lenguas locas)" (Red macaws chatter in crazy tongues), a line of five consecutive reversed iambic feet (trochees) that contribute to a sense of abruptness and violence in the speech of macaws. Yet even these weapons of war are subject to the transformational powers of the natural world and the poet's imagination. Despite the general indifference to the pilot's death among the adult population of the town, the children make paper airplanes in order to practice "asesinando las aves forasteras" (killing the foreign birds). In a similar superimposition of the natural on something made by human beings, the poet describes the actual wreckage of the plane as "el gran esqueleto del pájaro" (the great skeleton of the bird).

The last stanza of "El viejo motor de aeroplano" is extremely important because it is the only poem in *Poemas nicaragüenses* that specifically mentions the guerrilla army engaged in battle:

> Sólo tú—guerrillero—con tu inquieta lealtad a los
> aires nativos
> centinela desde el alba en las altas vigilias del ocote
> guardarás para el canto esta historia perdida.

(OPC, vol. 1, 144)

(Only you, guerrilla, with your restless loyalty to native skies, / standing guard since dawn in the high branches of the *ocote* tree, / will preserve this lost history in song.)

The sentinel is loyal not to a particular ideology, necessarily, but to "los aires nativos." The earth has elevated him into this sky where he keeps watch in the high branches of the *ocote* tree.

This patriotic stance depends, of course, on the identification of the individual with a pure and inspiring national identity. These more "historical" poems by Cuadra about the defense of national sovereignty provide just such an ideal model and are not incompatible with traditional utopian thought. In More's prototypical *Utopia*, for example, according to Martínez Estrada, "the danger for the people of Utopia is outside their country: it surrounds them and constitutes a permanent threat that obliges them to organize armies of defense."[36] In an article entitled "*Utopia* and Power Politics," Gerhard Ritter points out that given the insular nature of the island's political system, "More's ideal Utopians detested war despite their military prowess and their readiness to defend, come what may, their own country."[37]

In contrast to the absence of the first person narrator in "El viejo motor de aeroplano" (due, perhaps to a certain reportorial "objectivity"), the poet speaks in the first person plural in "Iglesita de Chontales," making his identification more complete with the campesinos who live in Pueblo Viejo:

> Y hay una misa de madrugada allá cada tres meses
> Y un sermón de las cosas buenas
> Que todos lo oímos sentados
> A la orilla de las vacas echadas en la penumbra.

> (*OPC*, vol. 1, 120)

(And there is a Mass at dawn there every three months / and a sermon about the good things / that we all heard sitting / near the cows that were lying in the shade.)

In "Iglesita de Chontales," it is by means of a brief moment of humor (uncharacteristic of the tragic tone that predominates in Cuadra's poetry) that the poet locates his poem in a specific moment in Nicaraguan history. The occupying army of the United States has prohibited the peasants from carrying the weapons with which they are accustomed to hunt and protect themselves from the jungle animals. As a result of the imposition of this law, the inhabitants of Pueblo Viejo can do nothing about the creatures sleeping in the dilapidated church:

Ahora que los yanquis nos prohibieron andar con
    rifles y pistolas
Nadie puede matar las guatuzas y los venados
Que duermen tras los confesionarios y en la
    sacristía.

(*OPC*, vol. 1, 120)

(Now that the yankees have forbidden us to carry rifles and pistols / no one can kill the monkeys and deer that sleep behind the confessionals and in the sachristy.)

A mythical "I"/eye chronicles and even seems to choreograph the movements of history contained in "Poema del momento extranjero en la selva" from a perspective outside linear time. The poem is subtitled "A varias voces" (For several voices). Perhaps these different, though sometimes closely-related, dramatic voices are both human and non-human expressions of the balance between mythic and historical temporality. After a disembodied, omnipresent speaker opens the poem by evoking a timeless Nicaraguan landscape, another voice sounds the alarm when the foreigners invade the country in an historical present:

En el corazón de nuestras montañas donde la vieja
    selva
devora los caminos como el guás las serpientes
donde Nicaragua levanta su bandera de ríos flameando
    entre tambores torrenciales
allí, anterior a mi canto
anterior a mí mismo invento el pedernal
y alumbro el verde sórdido de las heliconias,
el hirviente silencio de los manglares
y enciendo la orquídea en la noche de la toboba.
Llamo. Grito. ¡Estrella! ¿Quién ha abierto las
    puertas de la noche?
Tengo que hacer algo con el lodo de la historia,
cavar en el pantano y desenterrar la luna
de mis padres. . . .

En la médula del bosque
500 norteamericanos!

(*OPC*, vol. 1, 145)

(In the heart of our mountains, where the old jungle / devours roads the way the *guás* eats snakes, / where Nicaragua raises its flag of blazing rivers among torrential drums . . . / There, long before my song, / even before I existed, I invent the stone called flint / and I ignite the sordid green of *heliconias*, / the mangroves' boiling silence, / and I set fire to the orchid in the boa constrictor's night. / I cry out. Scream. Star! Who just opened the night's doors? / I must make something from the mud of history, / dig down in the swamp and unearth the moons / of my forefathers. Oh, unleash / your dark rage, magnetic snake, / sharpen your obsidian claws, black tiger, stare / with your phosporescent eyes, there! / In the heart of the jungle, / 500 North Americans!)

From the onset, it is clear that a destructive natural process is at work, devouring human works (such as roads) in the same way that the bird (Micrastur Zemitorquatus) devours snakes. Although the poet names Nicaragua, the symbol of nationalism, the flag, is composed not of colorful pieces of cloth but of the country's "ríos flameando entre tambores torrenciales." At the end of the poem, "las arañas azules" (the blue spiders) are in the process of weaving "una nueva bandera virgen" (a new virgin flag). Cuadra's predominantly mythic landscape does not preclude the naming of individuals who, as Mískito Indian peasants, not famous historical figures, emerge from anonymity as victims of the agressors:

> Andrés Regules—"tu escopeta era prohibida"—
> Ahora cuelgas del manglar.
> Orlando Temolián
> Fermín Maguel (túngula, túngula).
> Acripena, su esposa (todos mískitos)
> más altas que las palmeras las llamas del caserío.

(OPC, vol. 1, 146)

(Andrés Regules, "Your shotgun is against the law." / Now you hang from the branch of a mangrove tree. / Orlando Temolián / Fermín Maguel (túngula, túngula) [onomatopoetic suggestion of the sound of the bullfrog] / Acripena, his wife (all Mískito Indians). / The flames of the burning village leap higher than palm trees.)

In order to simultaneously create a national identity and a sense of universality, the poet places the reader in the heart of a landscape that both accepts and rejects the constraints of being what is now called the Republic of Nicaragua.

As the Promethean inventor of flint, the poet has become the tribal storyteller, combining limited figures (snake, tiger, ancestors, etc.) capable of limited actions clearly-defined by an oral tradition in order to create his narrative. He must unearth his forefathers' moon, source of his potential wisdom, and understand it as they did—one sign among a series of signs with many meanings which together form a rite. Then, the storyteller must be able to give shape to the mud of history in the form of his narrative—a process that resembles the Creator's shaping of the first human beings according to both Mayan and Christian traditions.[38]

The poet is also a shaman, and his poem a curing ceremony designed to rid the landscape of a "disease" (the "quinientos norteamericanos") by drawing spirits from the animal and natural world. The variation of the incantation that begins the poem also ends it, giving the poem a spiralling quality that is mimetic of the repetitive (though never exactly the same) cycle of: foreign agression/national resistance/triumph over the invaders. Despite the implicit military presence of the Sandinistas, whose principal strategy consists of making themselves as indistinguishable from the jungle as possible,[39] nothing human defeats the enemy. Nowhere in the poem does Cuadra mention Sandino or guerrilla forces of the human sort. The jungle itself is a kind of sentient being with its own vast, labyrinthine "médula" (marrow) and "corazón" (heart). Cuadra's poem attempts to achieve an equilibrium between myth and history, between the man of archaic culture who abolishes history through ritual and the contemporary man who consciously creates history. According to Alvaro Urtecho, however, in Cuadra's poetry what predominates is a view of history that is profoundly cyclical:

> Like those who celebrate the liturgy in the rituals of an ancient and prestigious religion that has disappeared, Pablo Antonio intones his song, invoking the specters of heroes and other mythical figures . . . that have become keys to our inner history . . . not the linear, chronological history of dates, speeches and anniversaries of official calendars, but the cyclical, circular history configured by myth.[40]

In *The Myth of the Eternal Return*, Eliade points out that individual events in history are not embedded in the popular memory unless "the particular historical event closely approaches a mythical model."[41]

It is the mythic landscape of Nicaragua that naturally expels what is foreign to it—in this case the "quinientos norteamericanos" who "entran con ametralladoras" (enter with machine-guns) and "hacen la guerra" (make war). Indeed, to a certain extent, the poem may be read as history's doomed assault (in the form of the invading North American soldiers) on mythic time (in its manifestation as the Nicaraguan jungle). Obviously, if Cuadra's poem were to fall completely into historical time, it would mean, in Eliade's words, "the final abandonment of the paradise of archetypes and repetition."[42]

All the flora and fauna of Nicaragua conspire against the enemy. José Román, in a reconstructed 1933 interview with General A. C. Sandino, quotes Sandino as saying:

> According to the Marines themselves, the ticks, lice, fleas, bedbugs, snakes and all the other jungle critters were ferocious Sandinistas.[43]

The mosquitos in Cuadra's poem, "zumbando y saliendo de las cuencas de su calavera" (buzzing and entering any openings in their skulls), wield "finas espadas de la fiebre" (slender swords of fever). In the tree of night "el silencio empolla gavilanes furiosos" (silence hatches furious hawks). Each bullfrog and bird "atestigua la iniquidad" (bears witness to the iniquity). The landscape abounds with the onomatopoetic sounds ("Túngula," "Top") of its warriors, and wins an ultimate victory:

> 500 norteamericanos van huyendo,
> maláricos
> rastros perdidos de pantano en pantano
> delirantes.

> (*OPC*, vol. 1, 147)

(500 North Americans fleeing / with malaria / their footprints lost from swamp to swamp / delirious.)

Those who survive their incursion into Nicaraguan territory flee. The white bones of those who die are "delicadamente pulidos por las hormigas" (delicately polished by the ants). The repetition of the phrase "500 norteamericanos" in "Poema del momento extranjero en la selva" leaves little doubt regarding the poem's temporal coordinates and the nationalistic sentiments experienced by Cuadra as a young poet in the 1930s. However, removed from the context of being part of a book published in 1934, "Poema del momento extranjero en la selva" seems remarkably well-equipped to describe recent and future invasions of Nicaragua by the government of the United States and its mercenary surrogates.

Finally, it is clear that both Cuadra and Supervielle take the universal myth of the primordial paradise as a point of departure, projecting certain utopian qualities on the landscape of the New World. Supervielle, fleeing from the encumbrance of Old World mythology and history, creates a hermetic poetic world that attempts to exclude *all* myth and history, even the indigenous myths and historical context of Uruguay. Consequently, Supervielle's poetry is limited to self-reflexive description (as in *Débarcadères*) or transcends historical time without having assimilated mythical models or actions (as in *Gravitations*). Cuadra, however, is more conscious than Supervielle of the mythological and historical cultural roots of the American continent. It is as if Cuadra first has shaped his verse from the mud of history and then given it life with the breath of myth.[44] According to José Emilio Balladares, the deeply-embedded awareness of mestizo culture, with its indigenous and Spanish/European traditions (precisely the elements Supervielle rejects), is what enables Cuadra to transcend regional limitations in *Poemas nicaragüenses.*[45] As Gloria Guardia de Alfaro has suggested, Nicaragua becomes an historically-conditioned spiritual center that is, at the same time, the source of Cuadra's individuality within the society in which he evolves.[46]

Cuadra praises and appreciates Supervielle for having given him a theme for his poetry as well as a literary technique with which he can endow the Nicaraguan landscape and its people with a rich symbolic vitality: the nationalistic microcosm reflects the universality of the macrocosm. What allows Cuadra to surpass Supervielle as a poet (something that does not negate the French writer's initial importance to Cuadra as an impetus) is a balance of myth and history illuminating Cuadra's *¡amor nicaragüense!* (Nicaraguan love!)

3

Carlos Martínez Rivas and Charles Baudelaire: Two Painters of Modern Life

There are fundamental similarities between the writer and the painter according to Octavio Paz in the essay "Baudelaire as Art Critic: Presence and Present."[1] From a finite sequence of sounds or from a limited range of lines and colors, certain verbal or visual forms are created. Words and colors exist relatively, defining an approximate meaning in conjunction with the other elements of the printed page or the painted surface. Paz goes on to state that with the exception of most art that is modern or simply decorative, all the pictorial works of humanity present two levels. The first is a representation, a relation of lines and colors. The second, which is beyond the pictorial, is what Paz calls "a real or imaginary object."[2] Both Carlos Martínez Rivas, the Nicaraguan poet born in 1924, and Charles Baudelaire are writers whose literary texts possess "pictorial" and "metapictorial" qualities that depict modern life as defined by Baudelaire in his important essay published in 1863 "Le Peintre de la Vie Moderne" (The painter of modern life): "Modernity is the transitory, the fleeting, the contingent, one half of art, the other half of which is the eternal and the immutable."[3] How does this combination of the ephemeral and the immutable function in the poem? How does the poet extract what Baudelaire calls "la beauté mystérieuse" (the mysterious beauty) from the exterior world then transform it by means of the analogical function of the imagination? We will address these questions in this chapter by examining the relationship between Martínez Rivas's neglected masterpiece "Dos Murales U.S.A." (Two murals: U.S.A.)[4] and "Tableaux Parisiens" (Parisian scenes) from Baudelaire's *Les Fleurs du Mal*.

The Metapictorial Poem

The very titles of these two works suggest a painterly approach to the United States and Paris. Martínez Rivas's long poem is composed of two sections of equal length, each of which is divided into six parts. The

poem is a double mural that presents first the diurnal and then the
nocturnal aspects of an urban landscape. The "Tableaux Parisiens,"
which follow "Spleen et Idéal" (Bile and ideal) and form what might be
called the heart of Baudelaire's *Les Fleurs du Mal*, are a series of
eighteen scenes of Parisian life, which are also informed by the realities
of day and night. Both poets open their respective works with an
invocation of an aerial spirit. The trapped narrator of "Dos Murales
U.S.A." begins to speak "mientras que prisionero de las escalerillas / de
escape" (while a prisoner of the fire / escapes). In Baudelaire's
"Paysage" (Landscape), the poem's speaker considers himself a "voisin
des clochers" (neighbor of the bell towers) and views the world "du haut
de ma mansarde" (from the height of [his] garret). Their elevated
perspectives give the two speakers an omniscient quality that produces a
portrait of a world from which they are curiously detached despite the
terrestrial focus of other sections in the poem by Martínez Rivas or other
poems in the series by Baudelaire. In other words, the poet-painter of
modern life observes the city at ground level among *la foule* (the crowd)
as well as from above—a perspective reminiscent of Pissarro's lofty
visions of Paris.

The merging of creative languages is, for the author of
"Correspondances" (Correspondences), a way of articulating the
wholeness of being. Baudelaire believes that Eugène Delacroix has
interpreted "the invisible, the impalpable, the dream, the nerves, the *soul*"
better than anyone else, and that he has done so not only with the
"perfection of a consummate painter," but "with the exactitude of a
subtle writer, with the eloquence of an impassioned musician."
Baudelaire continues with a commentary on the ontological difficulties
of his times that necessitate a more synthesized approach to the attaining
of spiritual knowledge: "It is, moreover, one of the symptoms of the
spiritual condition of our age that the arts aspire if not to take one
another's place, at least reciprocally to lend one another new powers."[5]
Baudelaire's essays on the visual arts (The Salons of 1845 and 1846 as
well as "Le Peintre de la Vie Moderne") are a clear indication of the
poet's search for an esthetic equivalent of a Unified Field Theory. One
recalls, too, Baudelaire's well-known poem "Les Phares" (Beacons) in
which artists such as Rubens, da Vinci, Rembrandt, Michelangelo,
Watteau, Goya, and Delacroix are a source of guidance and bear witness
to the perpetuity of human passion: "cet ardent sanglot qui roule d'âge en
âge" (that burning cry rolling from age to age).

It is very unfortunate that, due to Carlos Martínez Rivas's intractable
character, the Nicaraguan poet's extensive chronicles of painting exhibits
and visits to numerous museums in Madrid, Paris, New York, and Los
Angeles remain unpublished.[6] In certain poems by Martínez, such as
"Vernissage" (Varnishing), one encounters references to Picasso's

"Guernica" and Botticelli's "Nascita di Venere." But the true and abundant evidence of Martínez's abiding interest in the visual arts is contained in his sole published book of poems *La insurreción solitaria* (The solitary insurrection) (1955). In addition to overt references to da Vinci in "Canto fúnebre a la muerte de Joaquín Pasos" (Funeral song on the death of Joaquín Pasos), Van Gogh in "Retrato de dama con joven donante" (Portrait of a woman with a young donor), Goya in "Cuerpo Cielo" (Body Sky), and Klee in "Arete" (Earring), Martínez Rivas's poetry, according to the poet himself in an interview, contains many buried allusions to specific works of art:

> Painting has always had an enormous influence on my poetry. As an example, let me tell you about two paintings in Paris that I saw in the Louvre. A painting by Lucas de Leiden called "Lot and His Daughters" appears in my poem "Kiss for Lot's Wife." The destroyed city in the painting, Sodom, "rhymes" with some sinking boats in the foreground: "Fireworks over Sodom. / Gold and crimson falling / over the keel of the sinking city." I copied it directly—even the woman. I picture her left behind on the little bridge. . . . Also, a painting by Pieter Bruegel, "The Lepers," has to do with the last part of my poem "Two Murals: U.S.A."[7]

Ultimately, however, the most important shared belief on the part of both poets is the recognition that literature may have serious limitations and that at some point it may be necessary to seek recourse in a different creative language that is not subject to the intangibility of words. Martínez Rivas addresses this issue in "Canto fúnebre a la muerte de Joaquín Pasos," a beautiful elegy to the Nicaraguan poet who died at the age of 32 in 1947:

> Y para todo esto sólo te dieron palabras,
> verbos y algunas vagas reglas. Nada tangible.
> Ni un solo utensilio de esos que el refriegue
> ha vuelto tan lustrosos. Por eso pienso que
> quizás—como a mí a veces—te hubiese gustado más pintar.
> Los pintores al menos tienen *cosas*. Pinceles
> que limpian todos los días y que guardan en jarros
> de loza y barro que ellos compran.
> Cacharros muy pintados y de todas las formas
> que ideó para su propio consuelo el hombre simple.

> (*La insurreción solitaria* 56)

(And for all this, they only gave you words, / verbs, and some vague rules. Nothing tangible. / Not even a single utensil of those that rubbing / has turned so lustrous. That is why I think that / perhaps—like me at times—you would have preferred to paint. / Painters at least have *things*. Brushes / that they clean every day and that they keep in jars / of porcelain and clay that

they buy. / Clay pots covered with paint and of all shapes / that the simple
man devised for his own consolation.

For Martínez Rivas, painting is ostensibly a process that is more
reliable and consoling in its concreteness than the act of writing.
According to Julio Valle-Castillo, the visual arts represent for Martínez
"possession of the material, the fascinating domination of the word's
rhythmic value, meanings, and origins" as well as the possibility of
formal perfection and an emphasis on technique itself.[8] In poems such as
"Dos Murales U.S.A." and "Tableaux Parisiens," the poets imitate the act
of painting. They write with the lines and colors that the artist produces
with brushes and paint in order to create the dynamics by which the
pictorial brings the metapictorial into being.

Octavio Paz believes that a contradictory tension characterizes
Baudelaire's writing as an art critic:

> The opposition between the pictorial and the metapictorial, in the end
> resolved to the advantage of the former, is reproduced too in the
> contradictory relationship between "the eternal and the ephemeral": the ideal
> model and the unique beauty.[9]

The subject of "Le Peintre de la Vie Moderne," Constantin Guys,
embodies these contradictions precisely because, although he fails to
achieve the eternal in his sketches of Parisian life, he succeeds very well
in documenting the fleeting moment and the rapid impressions that form
the basis of Baudelaire's definition of modernity. It is not simply the
evanescent testimony of the present that essentially attracts Baudelaire to
the work of Guys, but the artist's thoroughness. Indeed, the scope of
Guys's work, according to Lois Boe Hyslop, is remarkably complete:

> . . . A study of the hundreds of sketches Guys made during his years in Paris
> furnishes us with an authentic picture of the customs, the clothes, the
> preoccupations and the amusements of the high and low echelons of Parisian
> society of that day.[10]

André Ferran in *L'Esthétique de Baudelaire* (The aesthetics of
Baudelaire) agrees that Guys's merit "is in providing the archives of the
life of his times with clumsiness and nonchalance."[11] But the issue, of
course, is how the "tableau de la vie extérieure" (scene of exterior life),
which Baudelaire finds so admirable in the work of Guys (even though
he is careful to classify it with that of the *poetae minores*), manifests
itself in the poetic text given the poet's awareness that the ephemeral
coexists with the eternal in equal proportions.

Two poems provide examples of how both poets attempt to resolve this esthetic difficulty. No text, perhaps, poses the problem as directly as Baudelaire's "A Une Passante" (To a woman passerby):

> Un éclair . . . Puis la nuit!—Fugitive beauté
> Dont le regard m'a fait soudainement renaître,
> Ne te verrai-je plus que dans l'eternité?

(A flash of lightning . . . Then the night!—Fugitive beauty / I am suddenly reborn in your glance, / Will I never see you again until eternity?)

The fleeting beauty of a woman is swallowed by darkness as she, the passerby, disappears in the crowd on a busy street. The transitory nature of the imagined encounter, powerful enough for the poet to believe that it has brought him to life again, depends on the impossibility of its repetition and on its uncertain conjugation with eternity.[12]

A similar moment occurs in the enigmatic opening section of "Dos Murales U.S.A." by Martínez Rivas. The quotidian event of a woman passing through the automatic glass doors of a department store is transformed by the poet into a meditation on modern life:

> Bajo la alta pública mecida cuna de luz
>   en va y ven;
> por la batiente lámina de reflejo y ráfaga
>
>   entras:
> en sandalia la planta pie celeste.
> A mano grande como pie abierto como risa.
>   Suelta
> la crin de púrpura y herrumbre,
>   greñas
> amparando la negligencia del siglo.[13]

(Under the high public swinging cradle of light / endlessly rocking / through the flapping lamina of reflection and wind / you step in: / on sandaled sole of celestial foot. / Big-handed as foot open like laughter. / Loose / rust-colored purple mane, / mophead / concealing the century's negligence.)

As in the poem by Baudelaire, the female figure moves in a busy, public setting. She is addressed directly by the poet as he reconstructs the observed scene in his imagination even though no personal contact was made. This phantasmal dialogue contributes to a heightened sense of futility and pathos. As the figure equated with the subtitle of the first section of "Dos Murales U.S.A." ("La Muerte Entrante") (Death entering), the woman in sandals with dyed hair is simultaneously representative of her times and linked to eternity.

Both of these women are emblems of beauty as perceived by the respective poets. They have a great deal to do with what Baudelaire calls "the heroism of modern life," an idea he introduces in the "Salon of 1845" ("No one is cocking his ear to tomorrow's wind, and yet the heroism of *modern life* surrounds us and presses upon us.")[14] and develops more fully in his writings on the Salon of the following year:

> Before trying to distinguish the epic side of modern life, and before bringing examples to prove that our age is no less fertile in sublime themes than past ages, we may assert that since all centuries and all peoples have had their own form of beauty, so inevitably we have ours. That is in the order of things.
>
> All forms of beauty, like a possible phenomena, contain an element of the eternal and an element of the transitory—of the absolute and the particular. Absolute and eternal beauty does not exist, or rather it is only an abstraction creamed from the general surface of different beauties. The particular element in each manifestation comes from the emotions: and just as we have our own particular emotions, so we have our own beauty.[15]

Baudelaire goes on to say that private subjects such as the population of the underworld of a great city are more heroic than public and official ones.

Painting the Modern City Full of Dreams

For Baudelaire and Martínez Rivas, modernity is composed of opposites. The intensely subjective, individualistic world of the poet coexists with the reality of the streets, crowds, and popular culture. The "particular emotions" of the two poets that are the subject of this essay define modern beauty as an embodiment of the lives of the miserable. According to Octavio Paz, these characters, which include the old and infirm, beggars, street musicians, criminals, and prostitutes, form an elect whose faces marked by misfortune summarize "the bizarre, the irregular and the deformed, all those attributes of modern beauty. . . . The sign of the modern is a stigma: presence wounded by time, tattooed by death."[16] The poet is a *flâneur*, a solitary observer in the streets, a wandering phenomenologist, a walking compendium of life in the city. There is an anonymous quality to these people as they are portrayed in the poems of Baudelaire and Martínez Rivas despite the detailed description of their physical appearance. One thinks of the "sabots lourds" (heavy wooden clogs) of Baudelaire's "mendiante rousse" (red-haired beggar girl) and the sandals with the wooden soles and stinking straps worn by the unnamed woman at the beginning of "Dos Murales U.S.A."

Both poets depend on an impersonal intimacy with the subject in order to link the particular with an absolute that often expresses universal social shortcomings. In Baudelaire's "Les Sept Vieillards" (The seven old men), for example, the poet is astonished by "ce sinistre vieillard que se multipliait!" (this sinister self-multiplying old man!). The poet seems conscious of the way that the industrializing society of mid-nineteenth century Europe is beginning to mass-produce misery. Life in the twentieth-century urban center in the United States of "Dos Murales U.S.A." has defects of a different nature. Against the emptiness and alienation of modern life as he perceives it, Martínez Rivas opposes the "heroic" lives and beauty of some of the same marginal characters that populate Baudelaire's poems:

> ¿Acaso
> aquí, el grito
> del vendedor; el silbido
> de la ramera; el *toc*
>   *toc*
>   del cojo;
>   los arrastriscos
> contrahechos en sus muñones, como
> candelabros arrumbados;
>   ¿acaso
> el pobrecito hablador;
> la miseria y su tonadilla—digo,
> su desdentado hueco músico—halló
> pérdida
> pozo
> eco en la colmenar oreja vacía de la piedra?

(Perhaps / here, the cry / of the vendor; / the whistle / of the harlot; the *toc* / *toc* / of the lame; / the dragging / deformed on their stumps, like / candelabra cast aside; / perhaps / the little babbler about town; / misery and its strain—I say, / its toothless musician hollow—found / loss / pit / echo in the empty beehive-ear of stone?)

The narrator in the poem by Martínez Rivas is bereft of stone and the human history associated with a certain architecture that exists in Baudelaire's Europe, but not in the United States, a country in which the present is deafening and the past is silent. It would seem that as far as the speaker of "Dos Murales U.S.A." is concerned, the present of Baudelaire's "Tableaux Parisiens" is preferable to a contemporary world characterized by Martínez Rivas in another poem as "plástico, supermodelado y vacío" (plastic, supermodeled, and empty).

The living victims of modernity possess for both poets a kind of heroism that is, in a sense, transferable to the process of creating literary beauty from a painful and alienating reality. Critic Jean Starobinski elaborates on these heroic possibilities that the present offers the poet:

> Against the vulgarity or apathy of the modern age, Baudelaire opposes not an art of the past, but rather an art of *modernity*. Against a disastrous present he opposes an heroic present. It is clear that for Baudelaire the *present* is, at the same time, the point of the most painful disillusion, of the most profound discouragement, and the place where the new and disruptive beauty should emerge.[17]

Nevertheless, the question of realism and how elements from the exterior world are transformed into poetry is extremely problematic. What does the poet add to the strictly documentary (if such a rational, empirical category were possible) in order to create a poem such as "Les Aveugles" (The blind) or the devastating third part of Martínez Rivas's diurnal mural in which the green lawns of the United States become "los lozanos vastos / altos pastos del pánico" (the luxuriant vast / high pastures of panic)? The answer, according to Wolfgang Drost, lies in a double position assumed by the poet. Drost's commentary on the "Tableaux Parisiens" also illuminates the compositional technique of "Dos Murales U.S.A.":

> Baudelaire's position, then, is twofold. His "disgust with the real" is not so great as to compel the poet to reject the representation of the exterior world. Quite to the contrary, he demands reality, but [reality] full of vibrations, charged with ideas and emotions.[18]

In Baudelaire's poem "Les Aveugles," for example, the poet charges reality with his own particular emotions by carefully observing his subjects and penetrating not *their* psyches, but his own:

> on ne les voit jamais ver les pavés
> Pencher rêveusement leur tête appesantie.
>
> Ils traversent ainsi le noir illimité,
> Ce frère du silence éternel. . . .
>
> Je dis: Que cherchent-ils au Ciel, tous ces aveugles?

(One never sees them drop their heavy heads / toward the ground with the air of a dreamer. / They cross a limitless night, / that brother of eternal silence . . . / I ask: what do all these blind seek in the sky?)

Ultimately, the blind, as depicted by Baudelaire, conform to the poet's own limitations and aspirations. The metapictorial qualities of this common Parisian scene, however, transcend the individual poet as well as the so-called "real" aspects of the exterior world transformed by the poet into verse. Critic André Ferran addresses these traits of Baudelaire's approach to the creative process:

> We do not believe that he is inclined to realism. The painting of real life is worth nothing to him if it is not transformed by the temperament of the artist, animated by his imagination. For him, modernity is enriched by synthesis or by crystallizations that memories or the artist's personal sensibility incorporate there at the moment of creation.[19]

The inherently allusive and analogical powers of the poetic imagination give the "Tableaux Parisiens" as well as "Dos Murales U.S.A." the capacity to bridge not only the ostensibly different languages of poetry and painting, but also disparate civilizations and historical periods.[20] A canvas by Bruegel and a photograph by Brassai, for example, seem to emerge from and converge in these texts by Baudelaire and Martínez Rivas despite the barriers of time and space.

It is important to remember that the human figures populating these poems have a context—the city. The ruling poetics of space is the urban environment that shapes the texts. We have already mentioned the way that the verticality of the respective cities facilitates the elevated vantage point of the poet in certain poems by Baudelaire and sections of the long poem by Martínez Rivas. We have also addressed the importance of the horizontal plane of the urban landscape and how, with its congested streets, it affects the poet (as *flâneur*) who observes the multitude in their activities during the day and at night. The city itself is neither fixed nor unchanging. Like the people who inhabit it, the city, too, seems like a sentient being inseparable from the speakers' emotional states. One thinks, for example, of Baudelaire's personified city in "Le Crépuscule du Matin" (Morning twilight): "Et le sombre Paris, en se frottant les yeux, / Empoignait ses outils, vieillard laborieux" (And somber Paris, rubbing its eyes / clutched its tools, old worker). Paris and Los Angeles in the poems by Baudelaire and Martínez Rivas exert the same kind of horrific and charismatic influence as Joyce's Dublin, García Lorca's New York, and Durrell's Alexandria.

At the same time, however, the spirit of the city appears paradoxically independent from its affected inhabitants. Baudelaire, for example, witnesses the radical changes of the image of Paris wrought by Hausmann, when twisting medieval streets were transformed into wide modern boulevards. "Le vieux Paris n'est plus" (The old Paris is gone), remarks Baudelaire in "Le Cygne" (The swan). But the physical alterations of the city proceed with greater rapidity than humanity's capacity to adapt to the new space in which it will live: "(la forme d'une ville / Change plus vite, hélas! que le coeur d'une mortel)" (The shape of a town / changes more quickly, alas! than a mortal's heart). Indeed, as

Baudelaire goes on to say in the same poem, humanity, or at least the speaker in the poem, simply may be incapable of change that corresponds to a new urban environment:

> Paris change! mais rien dans ma mélancolie
> N'a bougé! palais neufs, échafaudages, blocs,
> Vieux faubourgs, tout pour moi devient allégorie,
> Et mes chers souvenirs sont plus lourds que des rocs.

(Paris changes! But nothing of my melancholy / has moved! new law-courts, scaffolding, blocks, / old suburbs, everything for me turns into allegory, / and my dear memories are heavier than rocks.)

Baudelaire likens the burden of memory to rock, the material that is destroyed and used to reshape the "cité pleine de rêves" (city full of dreams).

It is the absence of stone, as we have said, that Martínez Rivas laments in the second section of "Dos Murales U.S.A." This nocturnal mural subtitled "Aquí falta la piedra" (Here stone is lacking) describes a world that is constantly under construction ("STOP / ROAD CLOSED"), a false "simulacro / de piedrasobrepiedra" (simulacrum / of stoneonstone) that seems to be made of nothing more substantial than candy:

> Aquí, en cada esquina
> día a día
> todo el año
>
> al sol
> ensordecedor
>
> el taladro
> horada
> la cáscara
> de asfalto
>
> perfora
> buscando
> roca
>
> halla sólo
> turrón poroso

(Here, on every corner / day after day / all year long / in the sun / deafening / the jackhammer / drills / the shell / the asphalt / perforates / searching for / rock / finds only / porous nougat)

The contemporary U.S. city produces fear in the speaker precisely because of the impermanance of its composition and its subsequent inability to withstand even the aggressions of insects:

> Que de noche
> tenemos miedo porque falta
> la piedra. Y da pavor el cartón.
> La ciudad de cajas
> vacías. Su rumor
> solitario
> de papel carcomido por cucarachas.

(At night / we are afraid because / stone is lacking. And cardboard causes dread. / The city of empty / boxes. Its lonely / murmur / of paper gnawed by cockroaches.)

In their attempts to survive the shortcomings of the modern cities they inhabit, Martínez Rivas and Baudelaire imagine an ideal world linked with a classic or biblical architecture. Their utopia is not a natural, rural environment, but one constructed by human hands: arcades, fountains, and aqueducts. The combination of stone and water, associated with an elevated spiritual state, seems especially appealing to both poet-painters of modern life. The idealized world of Baudelaire in "Rêve Parisien" (Parisian dream) is a painting within a painting. The poet dreams his canvas in order to create a dynamic conflict between metapictorial perfection and pictorial horror:

> Et, peintre fier de mon génie,
> Je savourais dans mon tableau
> L'enivrante monotonie
> Du métal, du marbre et de l'eau.
>
> Babel d'escaliers et d'arcades,
> C'était un palais infini,
> Plein de bassins et de cascades
> Tombant dans l'or mat ou bruni . . .

(And, proud painter, / I savored in my painting / the intoxicating monotony / of metal, marble, and water. / Babel of arches and stairways, / it was an infinite palace, / full of artificial lakes and water / falling in dull or burnished gold . . .)

The brief finale of the poem's second part, set in a recent past, is sufficient to destroy the archaic world the poet has generated in his imagination:

En rouvrant mes yeux pleins de flamme
J'ai vu l'horreur de mon taudis,
Et senti, rentrant dans mon âme,
La pointe des soucis maudits . . .

(On reopening my eyes full of flame, / I saw the horror of my hovel, / and I felt, entering my soul again, / the object of my cursed anxieties.)

The fountains in the penultimate part of "Dos Murales U.S.A." express the metaphysical reality of the individual on the border of death. The stone of the world that does not exist is depicted by the poet in his canvas of an imaginary burial:

¡Y dormir! laja sobre bloque, dolmen
donde para morir ese segundo
hondo de nada y sueño de la vida.

En alianza con las secretas inextricables
apresuradas vertientes (aunque
espera: más bien lentas . . . ¡Sí! veneros
fluyendo apenas un poco más lentos que el tiempo),

piedra contra la piedra.
Puesto el oído en el profundo
callar de su corazón acueducto . . .

(And to sleep! slab on block, dolmen, / a place to die that deep second / of life's nothing and dream. / Allied with secrets, inextricable / hurried secrets, cascading (but / wait, rather slowly . . . Yes! fountains / flowing just a little slower than time), / stone against the stone. / The ear placed on the profound / silence of its aqueduct heart . . .)

The intangibility of the void of mortality is countered by the placing of human flesh against the hardness of stone. The moving water carried by the heart as aqueduct is the fluidity of being that transcends time.[21]

The city holds a fatal attraction for Martínez Rivas and Baudelaire because of its ability to mask mortality and to separate death and intimacy. For the speaker in section I, part 3 of Martínez Rivas's poem, the stoplight is no longer a harmless modern object used to control the flow of traffic. Instead, it emerges from the text as a dramatis persona with a terrible dimension that belies its apparently inanimate, utilitarian state:

Pero
no te conozco Máscara désta Muerte CARATULA
ESMERALDA
TOPACIO

> ¡huy, ROJA! ¿quién es eso? espectro para
> la fertilización del pánico.

(But / I do not know you Mask of this Death FALSE-FACE / EMERALD / TOPAZ / yikes, RED! Who is that? specter for / the fertilization of panic)

The stoplight is an expression of the same unknown quantity ("Pero no te conozco") (I do not know you) as the woman sleeping beside the narrator in the poem's following part ("Te desconozco") (I fail to recognize you). Similarly, in Baudelaire's "L'Amour du Mensonge" (The love of lies), a poem that may be read as an apostrophe to a personified city, the woman whose eyes allure "comme ceux d'un portrait" (like those of a portrait) is a secret oasis of morbidity and emptiness. The poet adores her beauty, despite her "bêtise" (silliness) and "indifférence" (indifference) because of what it occults: "Masque ou décor, salut!" (Mask or decoration, I greet you!). These literary manifestations recapitulate the esthetic difficulties of paintings in general, as defined by Octavio Paz in his essay on Baudelaire:

> Representation signifies the distance between the full presence and our gazing: it is the sign of our changing and finite being in time, the mask of death.[22]

The poetic text, like all aspects of language, signifies a removal from its subject that is more important for what it hides than what it reveals.

The female figure in "Dos Murales U.S.A." and "Tableaux Parisiens," as we have said, is linked to a powerful nether world in which being is simultaneously affirmed and negated. The narrator of Martínez Rivas's poem asks the woman, who forms part of a cubist canvas-poem à la Picasso and Reverdy with her "tres perfiles y cinco codos" (three profiles and five elbows), to convey him to the limits of mortality through the constriction of the sexual act:

> Aprieta
> las rodillas
> de cráneos de mellizas.
> Cierra las piernas
> cierra las tijeras
> de la Parca.
>
> Prénseme la trampa
> de tu hueso. Sienta
> la presión de tu muerte. Sepa
> el grado exacto de prensilidad de la
> muerte encarnada

de la carne descarnada
de tu esqueleto escarlata.

(Press together / the knees / of twin girls' skulls. / Close the legs / close the scissors / of Fate. / Let the trap of your bone / squeeze me. So I feel / the pressure of your death. So I know / the exact degree of prehensility of / death made flesh / of flesh unfleshed / of your scarlet skeleton.)

The speaker in Baudelaire's "Danse Macabre" explores the terrain of necrophilia with the same passion:

Pourtant, qui n'a serré dans ses bras un squelette,
Et que ne s'est nourri des choses du tombeau?
Qu'importe le parfum, l'habit ou la toilette?
Qui fait le dégoûté montre qu'il se croit beau.

(Still, who has not held a skeleton tight in his arms, / and who has not nourished himself on things from the tomb? / What good are perfume, clothes, and the dressing room? / The man who feigns disgust, shows that he thinks himself handsome.)

This presence of death (in its skeletal female incarnation) is desired by both poets and seems motivated by a profound misogyny. Consequently, the portrait of these women reflects an intense, though highly questionable, metapictorial reality.

Nevertheless, the characterization of women that reduces them to screens onto which the poets' own obsessions are projected is similar to the way the rest of the degraded figures are portrayed elsewhere in "Tableaux Parisiens" and "Dos Murales U.S.A." It is simply the result of the "particular emotions" of these two poets as they convert into art what critic Jean Starobinski calls the "spectacle extérieur":

The poet is left with the power to confront the unjustifiable and to speak in an allegorical way about his interior experience of the loss of sense, of disorientation, in other words, of grasping *within himself* and enlarging the non-sense of the exterior spectacle.[23]

While the dialectics of the interior and the exterior cannot justify an unjustifiable moral stance on the part of the poets, it does provide insight into their approach to the creative act. It also precipitates the breakdown of the facile and misleading labels of "exteriorism" and "interiorism" used to describe Nicaraguan poetry from the so-called Generation of 1940 to the present. One could say of the two principal poets of this generation that Carlos Martínez Rivas is as much of an exteriorist as Ernesto Cardenal. In the words of Nicaraguan poet and critic Alvaro Urtecho, "neither exteriorism nor interiorism exist in chemically pure states."[24] He goes on to characterize "Dos Murales U.S.A." as a poem that embodies both an epic and a lyric tradition.

Martínez Rivas, to a certain extent, is similar to Picasso, another twentieth-century artist who maintains many esthetic ideals from the previous century. In his book *The Success & Failure of Picasso*, John Berger paraphrases Ortega y Gasset in *Revolt of the Masses* and refers to Picasso as a "vertical invader," a primitive man, a barbarian whose artistic work always contains elements from the creator's own country and also from the past.[25] Martínez Rivas possesses many of the same savage qualities in his poetry that Baudelaire praises in Delacroix's painting.

Baudelaire and Martínez Rivas leave their readers with worlds painted with words that both register and transform into poetry modern urban life. The reader, in this context, is a spectator who, according to critic Gaeton Picon, "will receive space as if it were an exhalation of the surface. Life and space will no longer be represented, but present."[26] The coexistence of the pictorial and metapictorial elements of "Tableaux Parisiens" and "Dos Murales U.S.A." give these texts an immediacy that embraces both the ephemeral and the eternal as Baudelaire defines these terms in his essay "Le Peintre de la Vie Moderne." Indeed, the poems in their entirety possess the kind of well-conceived circularity that increases the longevity of a text. Baudelaire's series opens with "Le Soleil" (The sun), continues with the nocturnal reality of "Crépuscule du Soir" (Evening twilight), and concludes with "Le Crépuscule du Matin" (Morning twilight), in which Paris awakens for another day of fruitless drudgery. In a similar way, Martínez Rivas's poem begins with a "Mural Diurno" (Diurnal mural), continues with a "Mural Nocturno" (Nocturnal mural), and gives way to the treason of dawn, which offers no consolation. The final lines of "Dos Murales U.S.A.," with "el canto / del gallo" (the cry / of the cock), recall the betrayal of Christ by Peter, whose "amargos largos sollozos" (bitter long sobs) become a contemporary cry of existential anguish.

Part II

A Dialogue with France and the United States

4

The Eschatological Voyage in the Poetry of Joaquín Pasos, Vicente Huidobro, and T. S. Eliot

For the reader unfamiliar with the oeuvre of Nicaraguan Joaquín Pasos (1914-1947), it may seem presumptuous to mention his name in the same breath as the world-class poets Vicente Huidobro and T. S. Eliot. Pasos's obscurity certainly has a great deal to do with the fact that the poet was born in a small Central American country (which he never left, except to travel briefly to Costa Rica and El Salvador) and that he died at an early age without having published a book of his verse. Over the years, however, there has been a sustained critical interest in Pasos's poetry in Nicaragua.[1] Poets and critics from other Hispanic American countries also have written essays on Pasos and have included his poetry in anthologies. The Uruguayan Mario Benedetti, for example, believes that Pasos's most-accomplished poem "Canto de guerra de las cosas" (Warsong of the things) is of the caliber of verse by Vallejo, Neruda, and Parra.[2] As further evidence of the recognition of Pasos's contribution to literature, the Nicaraguan author was among fourteen Hispanic American poets represented in an anthology prepared for an issue of *Inti* by the noted critics Pedro Lastra and Luis Eyzaguirre.[3]

In this chapter we will investigate the theme of the eschatological voyage in three long poems: Pasos's "Canto de guerra de las cosas," Huidobro's *Altazor*, and *The Waste Land* by T. S. Eliot. In preparation for the analysis of the three texts, the chapter begins with a description of the voyage theme in Pasos's early poems and how it evolves from an exuberant naivete toward a preoccupation with death and mortality. The chapter continues by examining how the three poetic texts exemplify distinct similarities in terms of their use of the theme of the voyage, the metaphysical vastness of their spatial and temporal scopes, and their treatment of "last things," such as death and the possibility of redemption.

Pasos was intimately acquainted with both of the cited texts by Huidobro and Eliot. In an article on Huidobro entitled "Señoras y Señores, ¡Mucho Cuidado con Esta Poesía!" (Ladies and gentlemen, be very careful with this poetry!), Pasos recalls reading *Altazor* at some of the literary meetings of the Nicaraguan group that came to be known as the *Movimiento de Vanguardia* (Vanguard movement) in the early 1930s:

> I remember the evening meetings in the bell tower of La Merced church in Granada when, among swallows and bells, we read *Altazor* out loud. The tower was high: the poetry, higher.[4]

About Pasos's awareness of Eliot's great poem, Nicaraguan poet Pablo Antonio Cuadra says that Pasos prefaced a reading of "Canto de guerra de las cosas" with the following commentary:

> In principle, it is about the spent thing, *The Waste Thing*, as T. S. Eliot would say.[5]

Pasos had a legendary, intuitive command of English. According to Ernesto Cardenal, "he always knew English, ever since he was a child, without anybody having taught it to him."[6] Pasos even wrote at least eleven poems in English, which together form a group known as "Poemas de un joven que no sabe inglés" (Poems by a young man who does not know English).[7]

Pasos also had a firm grasp of the French language and a keen interest in avant-garde French poetry of the early twentieth century, which he translated into Spanish with his compatriots José Coronel Urtecho and Pablo Antonio Cuadra.[8] For the purposes of corroborating one of the theses of this chapter, namely that of Pasos's important intertextual dialogue with French avant-garde literary aesthetics, we will propose that Pasos also assimilated new poetry from France indirectly, by means of the verse of Chilean poet Vicente Huidobro. The categorization of Huidobro in this study as an example of a literary dialogue with France may strike certain readers as somewhat forced. My intent is not to negate intertextuality among poets from diverse areas of Hispanic America. Huidobro, however, as an active participant in the different groups of Parisian avant-garde artists and writers (beginning with his arrival in France in December 1916), composed no less than a third of his oeuvre in French, including initial versions of *Altazor*. On his extraordinary importance in this regard, Octavio Paz asserts that "the bridge between the French vanguard and the poetry of our language [Spanish] was, of course, Vicente Huidobro."[9]

Joaquín Pasos: The Imaginary Traveler

In contrast to the acute awareness of geographical and human limits evident in "Canto de guerra de las cosas," finished four years before the poet's untimely death in 1947,[10] Pasos's early travel poems demonstrate a faith in the power of the imaginary journey as a means of knowing a kind of paradise that exists on the border between a child's innocent Never-Never Land and an adolescent's world of burgeoning sensuality. While still a student at the Colegio Centroamérica in 1931,[11] the precocious poet wrote "Cook 'Voyages,'" an ecstatic "Invitation au Voyage" (Invitation to the voyage) addressed to a woman:

> Si tú estuvieras completamente a mi lado
> yo te diría sin mirarte: No tengo nada que hacer,
> Mariquita Primera.
> Mi lápiz no ha podido poner un punto fijo en todo
>   el mapamundi. . . .
> Estiro una pierna, y viendo mi zapato
> pienso en lejanías y en las puntas de los dedos del
>   mundo. . . .
> No son las 12 aún, y yo te aseguro que todavía
>   hay tiempo para que caiga un beso.
> Hablas despacio y la verdad es que tus ojos son otras
>   dos personas a quienes yo amo también.
> Tú y toda la bolit'el mundo.
>
> Mujer ¡qué tensa está la cuerda del mundo!
> ¡cómo mi amor la hace sonar de polo a polo!

(Poemas de un joven 26-30)

(If you were completely at my side / I would tell you without looking at you: I don't have anything to do, Mariquita Primera. / My pencil has not been able to put a fixed point in the entire globe . . . / I stretch out a leg, and seeing my shoe / I think about far-away places and about the fingertips of the world. . . . / It is not twelve o'clock yet, and I assure you there is still time for a kiss. / You speak slowly, and the truth is that your eyes are two other people whom I love as well. / You and the entire little ball of the world. / Woman, the world's string is so tightly-stretched! / How my love makes it resound from pole to pole!)

Just as a child marvels at the discovery of the limits of his body, the immense, unhostile otherness that is distinct from his being, so Pasos stretches his limbs and imagines distances that he wants to experience in the company of a woman that is more mother than lover.

These travel poems, twenty-one of which are grouped under the title "Poemas de un joven que no ha viajado nunca" (Poems of a young man who has never traveled), are usually narrated in the first person with a great sense of vivacious detail and humor:

He estado en el puente toda la mañana
y han pasado los carros de las pescaderías.
Una pequeña fábrica cariada de ventanas
lanza cada minuto el diávolo rojo del tranvía.

¡Oh! Esta es Noruega,
que tiene árboles de metal
y señoritas criadas en refrigeradoras.

(*Poemas* 25)

(I have been on the bridge all morning / and the carts of the fish merchants
have passed. / A little factory with windows like cavities / launches a red toy
streetcar every minute. / Oh! This is Norway, / which has metal trees / and
young women raised in refrigerators.)

Long Beach, Alhambra, South Pasadena,
flor y sol
qué fresco el aire, el viento,
el sol,
la vida está olorosa
las sonrisas, los autos,
el sol.

(*Poemas* 31-32)

(Long Beach, Alhambra, South Pasadena, / flower and sun / how fresh the
air, the wind, / the sun, / life smells wonderful / the smiles, the cars, / the
sun.)

Some early poems by Pasos share Huidobro's insatiable urge for
experimentalism (e.g. Pasos's concrete poem "Barco Cook" [Cook's
ship], undoubtedly a Nicaraguan homage to Huidobro's calligrammes
from more than a decade before). But more importantly, the visual
qualities of early poems by Pasos about imagined, distant places are
reminiscent of a Huidobrian capacity to reinvent with humor certain
stereotypes and cliches related to different nationalities in order to create
innovative poetry:

New York
          à quelques kilomètres
Dans les gratte-ciels
Les ascenseurs montent comme des thermomètres

Et près du Niagara
          qui a éteint ma pipe
Je regarde les étoiles éclaboussées

Le Cow Boy
    sur une corde à violon
Traverse l'Ohio

(*Vicente Huidobro: Obras Completas, Tomo 1* 258)

(New York / a few kilometers away / In the skyscrapers / the elevators rise like thermometers / And near Niagara Falls / which extinguished my pipe / I watch the sprinkled stars / The cowboy / on a violin string / crosses the Ohio.)

Pasos, however, seems unable to maintain the spirit of joy that was the impetus of the voyage. The recurring image of the shipwreck in Pasos's later travel poems (from the latter half of the decade of the 1930s) becomes a metaphor for the precariousness of life and for the metaphysical anguish of the individual:

Vivos abriendo los brazos.
Muertos tendidos en líneas.
Unos en la tierra muerta
y otros sobre el agua viva.
Unos de sonrisa ardiente
y otros de mirada fría.
Unos con deseos llenos
y otros con ansias vacías.

(*Poemas* 35-36)

(The living opening their arms. / The dead stretched out on the ropes. / Some on the dead earth / and others on the living water. / Some with a burning smile / and others with a cold look. / Some with full desires / and others with empty anxieties.)

el bote perdió la estela,
el barco perdió la vela,
el buque perdió la vida.

(*Poemas* 37)

(The boat lost its wake, / the vessel lost its sail, / the ship lost its life.)

In "Canción para morir" (Song to prepare to die), the sea bears the poet on his eschatological voyage (a quality that appears later in a more complex form in "Canto de guerra de las cosas"):

¡Qué oscuro mar
                sin velas
                sin sol
                sin agua!

¡Qué lejano recuerdo
                sin alas
                sin luz
                sin sangre!

(Poemas 39)

(What a dark sea / without sails / without sun / without water! / What a distant memory / without wings / without light / without blood!)

In the final poem of the section "Poemas de un joven que no ha viajado nunca," the poet exhorts his readers to prepare themselves for the inevitability of death. Here, prescience is synonymous with fatalism:

Dejadlo todo. . . .
que llegaremos tarde al naufragio que nos corresponde,
ese naufragio que nuestra familia se tiene señalado
        en el mapa
y en el cual el viejo criado tendrá a su cargo el
        trabajo de recoger los zapatos de los muertos.

(Poemas 52)

(Leave it all behind . . . / we will arrive late for the shipwreck that corresponds to us, / that shipwreck that our families point to on the map / where the old servant will be responsible / for gathering the shoes of the dead.)

Two Nicaraguan critics have offered partial explanations of the underlying motif of the voyage in Pasos's poetry. Ernesto Cardenal considers it an integral part of the Nicaraguan condition:

Poetry about travels and foreign themes is very characteristic of Joaquín, and also very Nicaraguan. The travelling spirit of the Nicaraguan is proverbial among us. Once, José Coronel told me that the Nicaraguan does not feel Nicaraguan if he has not travelled, and that the Nicaraguan's homeland is a foreign country.[12]

Julio Valle-Castillo places Cardenal's assertion in a larger literary context by pointing out that Pasos's obsession with travel is not endemic to Nicaraguan authors alone:

It responds to a fashionable theme that was hardly new in the continent. Vicente Huidobro, Carlos Pellicer, José Juan Tablada, and others, had developed it.[13]

One would have to add to this list of Hispanic American authors the names of certain French writers equally preoccupied with the voyage motif: indeed, Pasos was actively involved in the translation of poems by Apollinaire, Cendrars, Larbaud, Morand, and Supervielle.

Neither of these explanations, however, seems entirely satisfactory, given the logical fact that Pasos's psychology as an imaginary traveler would be conditioned by the poet's particular geographical perspective. In his discussion of Huidobro's poem *Ecuatorial* (Equatorial), Jaime Concha describes a complex spatial relationship between the cultural centers of twentieth-century Europe and the remote areas of the globe that were explored in the late eighteenth and nineteenth centuries. According to Concha, the artists of Huidobro's generation became aware of the limitations of Europe:

> What before was centripetal installation in a cultural obelisk, is now the consciousness of boundaries. Huidobro perceives in this instant the inner limits of the center, that becomes, in this way, a remote corner. For this reason, there is a leap to the periphery, in a prodigious, fleeting journey, surprising to those of us who believed ourselves in Europe.[14]

In his attempt to compose verse from an avant-garde European perspective, Pasos recapitulates Huidobro's spatial dilemma. An exterior space imagined by the poet becomes the interior space from which the poet writes. From an imaginary Europe, Pasos departs for equally unreal points in his travels from pole to pole. The joy of the journey diminishes with the increasing perception that, as Huidobro says in *Ecuatorial*, "Hombres de alas cortas / Han recorrido todo" (Men with short wings / have travelled everywhere) (*Antología* 238).

The terrifying extension of this hypothesis, as Jaime Concha suggests, is that global war may be the consequence of a "shrinking" planet thoroughly explored by humanity. It is as if the imagination, once deprived of a space to conquer, suddenly becomes aware of human limitations, feels inwardly claustrophobic, then outwardly belligerent. This psychological state, then, creates the necessary conditions for *Altazor* and *The Waste Land*, to a large degree products of World War I, and "Canto de guerra de las cosas," a poem composed before and during World War II. All three poems describe a protagonist's eschatological voyage toward the end of individual consciousness and, in the case of Pasos, the collective demise of humanity.

Prophetic Metaphysics in Altazor and
"Canto de guerra de las cosas"

The preface and seven cantos of Huidobro's *Altazor* form a text, according to René de Costa, "in discontinuous progress, suddenly brought to conclusion, frozen as an 'open work.'"[15] This is the result of unresolvable literary difficulties (the poem was begun in 1919 and was not published until 1931) that the poet transforms into a formidable definition of his new poetics. Pasos's "Canto de guerra de las cosas," on the other hand, is a more conventional, "finished" text that the poet composed in the comparatively brief period of time of perhaps four years. The other fundamental difference between the two long poems is that Pasos does not share Huidobro's fanaticism with regard to the systematic abandonment of the modes of poetic expression embodied in Symbolism, Modernism, Creationism, and Surrealism.[16] Nor is Pasos attracted in his poem to the kind of linguistic experiments that characterize *Altazor* in cantos IV-VIII. In "Canto de guerra de las cosas," the poet is more concerned with asserting traditional grammar and syntax to describe the reality of the physical destruction of the world than with the aesthetic possibilities of the text that self-destructs by means of a complete disarticulation of language. Nevertheless, despite these differences, the prophetic and metaphysical concerns central to both poems link them in an essential way.

Pasos, for example, joins the overall form and dramatic movement of "Canto de guerra de las cosas" to liturgical speech:

> It has the admonitory technique and the structure of a sermon. This poem imitates the classical rules of sacred oratory. The curious thing is that that same texture has given to its deliberateness the various parentheses of the priest in the pulpit.[17]

The poet as liturgist, then, accepts the responsibilities of his vocation: possessed with the uniquely human ability of forward dreaming, of engendering hope, he exhorts his listeners to heed his prophecies and hear his jeremiads. For this reason, "Canto de guerra de las cosas" begins with the epigraph from the Epistle to the Romans (8:18-23), since the poet, like the apostle Paul, knows "that the whole creation groaneth and travaileth in pain together." Pasos would instill the faith that we are waiting for "the redemption of our body."

A similar, though ultimately more pessimistic, concept informs Huidobro's *Altazor*, according to René de Costa:

> Evidently the early scheme for *Altazor* was religious and Rimbaldian, an anguished visionary poem in which the speaker's various personae were to beat their way toward redemption through the text.[18]

One of the personae in Huidobro's poem is a Christ-Yahweh figure called on to redeem language and to raise it from the dead by destroying it. In Canto III of *Altazor*, Huidobro speaks of the need for "cortacircuitos en las frases" (shortcircuits in sentences), "cataclismo en la gramática" (cataclysm in grammar), "aventura de la lengua entre dos naufragios" (adventure of the language between two shipwrecks), and a "catástrofe preciosa en los rieles del verso" (precious catastrophe on the tracks of lines of poetry). If the protagonist of *Altazor*, freefalling into infinity and convinced of the absence of God, cannot be saved, then perhaps the individual's only possible alternative is that of creating a new (or non-) language appropriate for the final primordial howl.

Huidobro's eschatological voyage in *Altazor* ("Cristal sueño / Cristal viaje / . . . cristal muerte" (crystal dream / crystal voyage / . . . crystal death) (Canto VI) results in despair and a perception of the emptiness of all ideals. Altazor, in addressing the plurality of readers who care to listen, longs for the same kind of death by shipwreck expressed at the end of Rimbaud's "Le Bateau ivre":

> Todo en vano
> Dadme la llave de los sueños cerrados
> Dadme la llave del naufragio
> Dadme una certeza de raíces en horizonte quieto
> Un descubrimiento que no huya a cada paso
> O dadme un bello naufragio verde
>
> Un milagro que ilumine el fondo de nuestros mares
>   íntimos
> Como el barco que se hunde sin apagar sus luces

> (*Vicente Huidobro: Obras Completas, Tomo I* 391)

(Everything in vain / Give me the key to the closed dreams / Give me the key to the shipwreck / Give me a certainty of roots on a still horizon / A discovery that does not flee at every step / O give me a beautiful green shipwreck / A miracle to illuminate the bottom of our intimate seas / Like the ship that sinks without extinguishing its lights)

Pasos uses the same rhetorical structure to recognize the supreme vulnerability of humankind as compared to the relative indestructibility of the instruments of war:

> Dadme un motor más fuerte que un corazón de hombre.
> Dadme un cerebro de máquina que pueda ser
>   agujereado sin dolor.

> Dadme por fuera un cuerpo de metal y por dentro
>   otro cuerpo de metal
> igual al del soldado de plomo que no muere

(Poemas 165)

(Give me a motor stronger than a man's heart, / Give me a robot's brain that can be murdered without pain. / Give me an outer body of metal and an inner body of metal / like the lead soldier's that does not die)

It is difficult to know if the image of the metallic, dehumanized warrior in Pasos's poem is a challenge to or a confirmation of the fascist Futurist manifesto of Marinetti on the Ethiopian colonial war in which the Italian poet objects to the branding of war as antiaesthetic:

> War is beautiful because it initiates the dreamt-of metalization of the human body. War is beautiful because it enriches a flowering meadow with the fiery orchids of machine guns.[19]

Perhaps it is a phenomenon rooted in the medieval psychology of war and armor, as in the bellicose poem "Be.m platz lo gais temps de pascor" (I like the happy time of Easter) by the troubadour poet Bertran de Born, or "Drogoman senher, s'ieu agues bon destrier" (Sir Dragoman, if only I had a good war horse)," in which the poet, Peire Vidal, speaks of "cors de fer o d'acier" (bodies of iron or steel). In any case, the soldier is a small but integral component of a larger military machine operating within a particular sociohistorical context. Pasos portrays this matrix directly in his index of metals in the liturgical opening of "Canto de guerra de las cosas":

> Recibiréis a los antiguos metales en el seno de
>   vuestras familias,
> trataréis al noble plomo con la decencia que
>   corresponde a su carácter dulce;
> os reconciliaréis con el zinc dándole un
>   suave nombre;
> con el bronce considerándolo como hermano del oro,
> porque el oro no fue a la guerra por vosotros,
> el oro se quedó, por vosotros, haciendo el papel
>   de niño mimado,
> vestido de terciopelo, arropado, protegido por el
>   resentido acero . . .

(Poemas 164)

(You will greet ancient metals in your homes, / you will treat noble lead with grace appropriate to its sweet character; / you will be reconciled with zinc, giving it a soft name; / with bronze, by considering it gold's brother, / because gold did not go to war for you. / Gold stayed, for you, playing the role of a spoiled child, / dressed in velvet, bundled up, protected by resentful steel . . .)

The young soldiers go off to fight the war, but the war-merchants' profits remain behind, secure, like an overindulged child of precious metal, protected by military armament.

In contrast to *Altazor*, "Canto de guerra de las cosas," as an extension of this militarism, is informed by the indelible knowledge of the nuclear holocaust of World War II. In its description of the ruins of Europe and Japan after the conflict, Pasos's poem prophesies a tragedy that lies beyond the limits of the human imagination:

> Asómate a este boquete, a éste que tengo en el
>   pecho,
> para ver cielos e infiernos.
> Mira mi cabeza hendida por millares de agujeros:
> A través brilla un sol blanco, a través un
>   astro negro.
> Toca mi mano, esta mano que ayer sustuvo un acero:
> puedes pasar en el aire, a través de ella, tus
>   dedos!
> He aquí la ausencia del hombre, fuga de carne, de
>   miedo,
> días, cosas, almas, fuego.
> Todo se quedó en el tiempo. Todo se quemó allá
>   lejos.

(*Poemas* 171)

(Look into this gap, the one I have here in my chest, / so you can see heavens and hells. / Look at my head. It has thousands of holes: / Through it shines a white sun, through it a black star. / Touch my hand, this hand that yesterday bore steel: / you can pass your fingers through it in the air! / Here is the absence of man, fleeing flesh, fear, / days, things, souls, fire. / Everything remained in time. Everything burned over there, far away.)

Pasos is a nuclear age descendent of the poet who declared "el Fin del Universo" (the End of the Universe) in the last line of *Ecuatorial* and the death of individual consciousness in *Altazor* (with no small amount of solipsism):

> Altazor morirás Se secará tu voz y serás invisible
> La Tierra seguirá girando sobre su órbita precisa

(*Obras* 385)

(Altazor you will die Your voice will go dry and you will be invisible / The Earth will keep spinning in its precise orbit)

Pasos is predicting a greater collective death ("el dolor supremo") (the supreme pain), the extinction of the human race. Ernesto Cardenal believes that Pasos describes death in "Canto de guerra de las cosas" in both personal and ecumenical terms:

> He himself became all the victims of the world, embodying them . . . in a communion of pain. . . . It would seem that he felt that death is not an individual act, but that each person's death becomes all the deaths of the earth, and that one ecumenically relives in one's own flesh the suffering of others.[20]

One might add to Cardenal's illuminating characterization of death and its relation to the narrator in "Canto de guerra de las cosas" that Pasos has constructed a complex conception of death that is based on the female principle. Here, Pasos's intertextual dialogue with *Altazor* seems particularly intense.

The phantasmal woman that appears in "Canto de guerra de las cosas" is associated with a kind of mystical ubiquity and irrevocable temporality:

> Subía, y luego bajaba en medio de la multitud y
>   besaba a cada hombre.
> Acariciaba cada cosa con sus dedos suaves de
>   sobadora de marfil.
> Cuando pasaba un tranvía, ella pasaba en el
>   tranvía;
> cuando pasaba una locomotora, ella iba sentada en
>   la trompa.
> Pasaba ante el vidrio de todas las vitrinas,
> sobre el río de todos los puentes,
> por el cielo de todas las ventanas.
> Era la misma vida que flota ciega en las calles
>   como una niebla borracha.
> Estaba de pie junto a todas las paredes como un
>   ejército de mendigos,
> era un diluvio en el aire.
> Era tenaz, y también dulce, como el tiempo.

(Poemas 167)

(She went up and then came down in the middle of the multitude and kissed each man. / She caressed each thing with the soft fingers of an ivory masseuse. / When a trolley car passed, she passed in the trolley car; / when a locomotive passed, she was sitting on the cowcatcher. / She passed—by all the shop windows, / upon the river of all the bridges, / through the sky of all the windows. / She was the same life that floats blindly in the streets like a drunken fog. / She was standing next to all the walls like an army of beggars. / She was a deluge in the air. / She was tenacious and sweet as well, like time.)

Pasos's potentially destructive divinity is a paired opposite of the female characterized (in the same enumerative style) as an archetypal goddess of creation in Canto II of *Altazor*:

> Eres el ruido del mar en verano
> Eres el ruido de una calle populosa llena de
>   admiración
> . . . .
> Nada se compara a esa leyenda de semillas que deja
>   tu presencia
> A esa voz que busca un astro muerto que volver a la
>   vida
> Tu voz hace un imperio en el espacio
> Y esa mano que se levanta en ti como si fuera a
>   colgar soles en el aire
> Y ese mirar que escribe el mundo en el infinito

(*Obras* 404)

(You are the sound of the sea in summer / you are the sound of a busy street filled with admiration . . . / Nothing compares to that legend of seeds that your presence leaves / to that voice searching for a dead star to return to life / Your voice makes an empire in space / And that hand that rises inside you as if it were going to hang suns in the air / And that look that writes the world in the infinite)

The female principle in Pasos's poem accompanies the narrator on his eschatological voyage (perhaps a simultaneous source of destruction and consolation) and offers him the possibility of transcending the conflagration of life "allá lejos" (far away). The association of transcendence with distance, in this case, mirrors the early travel poems in which the ideal world was located at some far point of the globe within reach of the poet's imaginary voyages.

Many Nicaraguan critics have attempted to demonstrate the underlying Christian spirit of "Canto de guerra de las cosas." Eduardo Zepeda-Henríquez, for example, speaks of how things are unconnected, isolated from each other, and dispersed in Pasos's poem and how the poet attempts to articulate "the spiritual disarticulation of humanity and the chaos of the modern world as a result of World War II." Zepeda-Henríquez goes on to say that beneath the perceived fragmentation is "a Christian sense of universal binding, of desired integration."[21] In a similar way, Pablo Antonio Cuadra characterizes the poem by Pasos as a Christian defense of man's dignity "in the sense that it assumes man's pain, exalts the nobility of that pain and raises what is human against war and everything that destroys us. He does this by putting the feeling of compassion and solidarity into language."[22]

It is possible, however, that, while the parameters of Pasos's poem are defined by Christianity, a coherent Christian formulation of redemption lies beyond its boundaries as a separate issue untreated by the poet: transcendence as lucidity facing death, rather than salvation. Chilean critic Walter Hoefler considers "Canto de guerra de las cosas" the prophetic sermon of a dying man:

> It is fitting for the moribund speaker to evade his lethal embargo and face his situation with lucidity. [Pasos's poem] is a sermon of augury ("Cuando lleguéis a viejos . . .") (When you reach old age); it is a sermon that serves as a testament, but whose sole legacy is an eschatological vision of destruction.[23]

In other words, how does the idea of resurrection fit in a panorama devoid of humanity ("Todos los hombres del mundo forman un solo espectro") (All the men of the world form a single specter) at the end of "Canto de guerra de las cosas," a poem that manifests such a strong nostalgia for life? Under such circumstances, one wonders if death possesses the strength to join God and the self, to be the integrating force that Pasos describes in his 1936 "Carta sobre la Muerte" (Letter about death), which he wrote after nearly dying of typhoid:

> The idea of death is the point of departure of all human love, beginning with the mysticism that is the love of God. And earthly love has its measure in it [mysticism]. . . . But what is born in a binding way from it is the love of oneself. Death teaches us our own self, it makes us come into life again, it glorifies us with a primordial pleasure.[24]

Perhaps Pasos is proposing that the new technological state facilitating nuclear warfare and human extinction negates the possibility of death being able to assume its role of linking the individual to "a primordial pleasure." In the absence of humanity, all sensuality as well as temporal conceptions are effectively erased.

While both "Canto de guerra de las cosas" and *Altazor* are testimonial, metaphysical poems, the relationship between their respective narrators and the prophesied future is quite different. In Pasos's poem, the reader senses a deep humility that is lacking in the poem by Huidobro. Pasos bears witness to the destructive forces of his time and envisions humanity's capacity for even greater destruction. According to Alvaro Urtecho, Huidobro's project, determined by the poet's new poetic language, is ultimately one of post-destructive creation:

> Huidobro wants to be both witness and judge of the universe. He contemplates all the social, moral and linguistic dislocation that he sees around him. From his nihilistic experience in *Altazor*, he attempts to create the world starting with its destruction. In order to do this, he resorts to the explosion of the phonic substratum of words. . . ."[25]

If it is true, as Julio Valle-Castillo believes, that what Pasos assimilates from Huidobro "is not only the concept of creationism, but the direct stimulus, the induction of Huidobro's words,"[26] then it is noteworthy in terms of the intertextual relationship between the two poets that Pasos is unwilling to engage in Huidobro's destructive experiments with the word itself.

Nevertheless, the global scope of the two poets' eschatological vision, full of apocalyptic imagery and prophetic warnings, is nearly identical—so much so, that Pasos's "Canto de guerra de las cosas" cannot be fully understood without being juxtaposed to *Altazor* by Huidobro. Shortly before he died, Pasos gave a remarkable conference on Huidobro in Managua in which he said:

> Over the last years, the world has made too much history. Perhaps poetry was too futile to concern it. It would seem that we have touched something too deep, grasped too much in the innermost part of human reality, and now the dream has surrendered its place to nightmare . . . We are more than frightened: we are empty and idiotic. . . . But there is something deeper and graver than being without poetry. It seems that we live in a time of such total transition, that we do not have the subsoil to produce [poetry]. We not only have no flowers: we fear that we have withered the roots and sterilized the earth.[27]

Pasos, after the unprecedented destruction of World War II and at the end of his own life, was considering the *impossibility* of poetry (not the destruction and subsequent recreation of language as in the case of Huidobro, but the *negation* of language) given the reality of a "waste land" that is simultaneously literary and literal.

Life and Death by Water in The Waste Land and "Canto de guerra de las cosas"

Like "Canto de guerra de las cosas," *The Waste Land* is a metaphysical meditation that attempts not to fill, but to describe a spiritual void. The two poems are an expression of an individual and collective loss of a moral identity that is the result of a general abandoning of ethical and religious values. The ravaged and infertile landscapes in both poems mirror and reinforce the psychological desolation of their inhabitants. Water, its presence and its absence, as well as its capacity to facilitate regeneration, to provide a means of transportation, and to destroy life, is a dominant eschatological symbol in the poems by Pasos and Eliot. It is important to remember, as Paul Ricoeur points out in *The Symbolism of Evil*, that "eschatological does not mean transcendent, heavenly, but final."[28] In the face of this End, whereas Eliot proposes an anachronistic recovery of lost values to create a contemporary spiritual wholeness, Pasos leaves the reader with the prophesied horror of the apocalypse brought on by warfare and the ultimate failure of humanity to survive as a species.

Stylistically, *The Waste Land*, because it resembles a cento (an early Christian form of composition based entirely on the "stitching together" of borrowed poetry), is more complex than "Canto de guerra de las cosas," a poem which does not strive for the highly-allusive density that characterizes Eliot's poem. Nevertheless, there is a similar breaking down of the world into smaller components—the fragmentation in Eliot's poem parallels the *cosificación del mundo* in the poem by Pasos. But instead of being a "heap of broken images," "Canto de guerra de las cosas" is a warsong, a convocation of the things of the world, a call for open rebellion, a testimony of human suffering. Nicaraguan poet Pablo Antonio Cuadra attributes the following words to Pasos with regard to "Canto de guerra de las cosas":

> In principle, it is about the spent thing, *The Waste Thing*, as T.S. Eliot would say. That thing, but in rebellion. The human pain produced by the moaning of the things.[29]

In a sense, part of Pasos's rebellion consists of a reevaluation of some of Eliot's basic, underlying assumptions about the world in 1922. In the famous opening lines of *The Waste Land*, the water of Spring represents the rebirth of everything except the spirit of humankind. Too, the poet is concerned with how an individual's finite consciousness adjusts to the life of a planet forever renewing itself. But in less than twenty-five years from the writing of *The Waste Land*, the world had changed irrevocably. "Canto de guerra de las cosas" reflects the post-Hiroshima/Nagasaki reality of nuclear weapons. In Pasos's poem, the biblical "deluge of liquid fire" is the water that not only burns, melts and reduces all things to rubble—it also smashes the wheel of the seasons so that nature loses its regenerative capacity:

> . . . hasta los insectos se equivocan en esta primavera
> sonámbula sin sentido.

La naturaleza tiene ausente a su marido.
No tienen ni fuerzas suficientes para morir las
    semillas del cultivo.

(Poemas 170)

(. . . even the insects make mistakes in this senseless, somnambulant spring. /
Nature's husband is not with her. / The seeds of the crop haven't the strength
to die.)

The primary navigator of these eschatological waters in Pasos's "Canto
de guerra de las cosas" is, as we mentioned in the previous section, the
feminine figure of death: "No había que buscarla en las cartas del naipe
ni en los juegos de la cábala. / En todas las cartas estaba, hasta en las de
amor y en las de navegar" (It wasn't necessary to look for her in the deck
of cards or in games of divination. / She was in all the cards, even in
those of love and navigation.). She represents a death that is omnipresent
and personal. In his personification of death, Pasos not only conjures
Eliot's "Madame Sosostris, famous clairvoyante" and her "wicked pack"
of tarot cards, but succeeds in creating a remarkable composite character
derived from the deadly feminine figure of Eliot's "Belladonna, the Lady
of the Rocks, / The Lady of situations" The Waste Land 31). Because of
the causal relationship between capitalism and war in "Canto de guerra
de las cosas," this female figure becomes particulary ironic and poignant
if the reader imagines her navigating below the gaze of Eliot's "man with
three staves," described in the Tarot Instructions in the following way:

> A calm, stately personage, with his back turned, looking from a cliff's edge
> at ships passing over the sea. Three staves are planted in the ground, and he
> leans slightly on one of them. Divinatory Meanings: He symbolizes
> established strength, enterprise, effort, trade, commerce, discovery; those are
> his ships, bearing his merchandise, which are sailing over the sea.[30]

The seawater and those who are borne by it are fundamental
intertextual links between The Waste Land and "Canto de guerra de las
cosas." The speaker in the "Madame Sosostris" part of The Waste Land's
first section is handed the card of the drowned Phoenician Sailor and is
told to "Fear death by water." Later, in section four of The Waste Land
("Death by Water"), the poet informs the reader that the corpse of
Phlebas the Phoenician has been floating on "the deep sea swell" for a
fortnight. The water that holds the promise of life throughout The Waste
Land destroys Phlebas's body. At the same time, however, he seems to
have achieved in death a greater peace, transcending "the profit and loss"
of his life as a merchant. In T. S. Eliot and Indic Traditions: A Study in
Poetry and Belief, Cleo McNelly Kearns considers Phlebas's death the
sacrifice of individual ego that is a prerequisite for enlightenment.[31] As

readers, we are asked to consider Phlebas's death (in relation to our own lives) as the possibility of a victory of spirituality over materialism. Here, the overriding question is one of *awareness* and the process by which the individual (all humanity, "Gentile or Jew") overcomes spiritual debilities.

A different interpretive approach to the "Death by Water" section yields the possibility of a reference to an ancient Egyptian fertility rite. Eliot may be alluding to rituals described in Sir James Frazer's *The Golden Bough* and Jessie L. Weston's *From Ritual to Romance*: at Alexandria, an effigy of the head of the fertility god was thrown into the sea at the end of the growing season; it was then carried by the current to Byblos (in the Nile Delta) where it was retrieved and worshipped as symbolic of the god (and nature) reborn. Whether Phlebas embodies the possibility of enlightenment or rebirth, his death by water represents a positive passage from this life to another.

The sailors stranded in the middle of their voyage in "Canto de guerra de las cosas" offer a frustrating, anguishing contrast to the dead Phoenician sailor. It is difficult for the reader to ascertain if they are more dead than alive. Pasos's sailors have no idea what is causing their doldrums, nor where they are headed, nor why they are lost in a sterile void in which "no hay peces, ni olas, ni estrellas, ni pájaros" (there are no fish, no waves, no stars, no birds). When the sailors address the captain of the vessel, he is singularly unhelpful. The sailors will know their destination as soon as they arrive. The captain has no control over the vessel (unlike the boat responding "to controlling hands" in the *Damyata* part of *The Waste Land*'s final section) or the natural elements that give the ship mobility. For the sailors, the events of life have been erased inexplicably forever: "No pasa nada. . . . Nunca volverá a pasar nada." (Nothing is happening . . . Nothing will ever happen again.) Trapped and immobile "en medio del viaje" (in the middle of the voyage), the sailors seem to inhabit a space in which life and death have ceased to define distinct realms. In *The Waste Land*, the living sailor/reader ("O you who turn the wheel and look to windward") is asked to think about the fact of death and the possibility of a "new" life. This alternative does not exist in Pasos's profoundly more pessimistic poem, which does nothing to resolve the existential quandary of the mute sailors becalmed on the sea for eternity.

The theme of the absence of water is another zone of intertextual convergence in *The Waste Land* and "Canto de guerra de las cosas." Poetry itself in certain sections of the two poems by Eliot and Pasos becomes a powerful desiccant that creates a particularly effective portrait of a moribund world. According to Walter Hoefler, "the imaginary term that serves to characterize death is 'dryness,' whose maximum efficacy as a poetic configuration of death can be found in 'Canto de guerra de las cosas.'"[32] In the absence of water, any sort of temporal continuity subject to the transformative powers of history (the lifespan of the individual as well as the successive generations of humanity) is impossible. Pasos focuses his intense longing for the future on the human body and the fluids it contains, similar to Eliot's "Sweat is dry" and "teeth that cannot spit":

> El agua es la única eternidad de la sangre.
> Su fuerza, hecha sangre. Su inquietud, hecha sangre.
> Su violento anhelo de viento y cielo,
> hecho sangre.
> Mañana dirán que la sangre se hizo polvo,
> mañana estará seca la sangre.
> Ni sudor, ni lágrimas, ni orina
> podrán llenar el hueco del corazón vacío. . . .
> y en medio del desierto los huesos en cruz pedirán en vano
>   que regrese el agua a los cuerpos de los hombres.

(Poemas 164-65)

(Water is the sole eternity of blood. / Its strength, made blood. Its disquiet, made blood. / Its violent longing of wind and sky / made blood. / Tomorrow they will say blood became dust, / tomorrow the blood will be dry. / Neither sweat, nor tears, nor urine / will fill the hollow of the empty heart / . . . and in the middle of the desert, the crossed bones will beg / the water to return to the bodies of men in vain.)

This collective phenomenon on a planetary scale in "Canto de guerra de las cosas" is the macrocosm of the microcosmic death of the individual Indian woman in Pasos's "India caída en el mercado" (Indian woman who fell in the market) (*Poemas* 114-15), whose "yugulares están secas" (jugular vein is dry) and whose blood "huyó secretamente" (fled secretly).

Alvaro Urtecho believes that water symbolizes not only the uninterrrupted flow of history in Pasos's poem, but also the possibility of transcending death, in that it guarantees the perennial nature of blood, life, and successive generations.[33] The search for this water leads both poets to the well. In *The Waste Land*, the uniform dryness of all sources of water produces a Bosch-like delirium with "voices singing out of empty cisterns and exhausted wells." The speaker in Pasos's poem, however, in his descent into the well and subsequent encounter with the sea, appears to achieve a kind of transcendent peace similar to that of Phlebas the Phoenician:

> Y en la puerta un cubo que se palpa
> y un camino verde bajo los pies hasta el pozo,
> hasta más hondo aún, hasta el agua,

y en el agua una palabra samaritana
hasta más hondo aún, hasta el beso.
Del mar opaco que me empuja
llevo en mi sangre el hueco de su ola,
el hueco de su huida
un precipicio de sal aposentada.
Si algo traigo para decir, dispensadme,
en el bello camino lo he olvidado.
Por un descuido me comí la espuma,
perdonadme, que vengo enamorado.

(*Poemas* 169-70)

(And in the doorway, a bucket someone gropes for, / and a green road beneath the feet down to a well, / down deeper still, down to the water, / and in the water a samaritan word, / down deeper still, down to the kiss. / From the opaque sea that pushes me, / I carry in my blood the hollow of its wave, / the hollow of its fleeing, / a precipice of chambered salt. / If I bring something to say, excuse me; / the beautiful road has made me forget. / I drank the surf through carelessness. / Forgive me. I'm in love.)

Nevertheless, in both poems, transcendence associated with water is less immediate than the drought linked to the impending catastrophe of war. In "Canto de guerra de las cosas," as a prelude to the poem's final, supreme conflagration, the soldier is willing to give back his blood to God in return for water. There is a similar structure in the final section of *The Waste Land*, in which the drought is related to the sequence of falling cities (Jerusalem, Athens, Alexandria, Vienna, and London). This suggests past collapses of civilizations, and prophesies—like Pasos (if on a less global scale)—future destruction: London during World War II, for example.

It is important to emphasize the *metaphysical* qualities of the three poems by Pasos, Huidobro and Eliot. The ontological questions raised by "Canto de guerra de las cosas," *Altazor*, and *The Waste Land*, though rooted in the individual, point to a collective spiritual crisis. Each of the poems is a pastiche of journeys subsumed in a greater eschatological voyage that confronts the poet (and the reader) with the major moral dilemmas of the twentieth century. As a testimony of violence, Pasos's poem creates a space that is categorically different from the poetic worlds of *Altazor* and *The Waste Land*. "Canto de guerra de las cosas" leaves the reader with the carnage of war as well as the possibility of humanity's self-inflicted extinction.

This chapter, like the others in this book, rejects the traditional generational groupings of Nicaraguan poetry in favor of a discussion of poetic "lineages." Having presented in previous chapters some of the ways that three Nicaraguan poets (Alfonso Cortés, Pablo Antonio

Cuadra, and Carlos Martínez Rivas) have engaged in a dialogue with certain French poets, the following chapters will examine a different group of poets (Salomón de la Selva, José Coronel Urtecho, and Ernesto Cardenal) whose work acquires a literary impact and a Nicaraguan identity as a result of its assimilation of North American literature. Because it incorporates the eschatological and some of the linguistic preoccupations of early twentieth-century poetry from both France and the United States, the oeuvre of Joaquín Pasos may be regarded as the transformational link between the two dominant lineages in modern Nicaraguan poetry.

Part III

A Dialogue with the United States

5

Salomón de la Selva: Testimonial Poetry and World War I

As a soldier in the British army, Nicaragua's Salomón de la Selva is the only Hispanic American poet to experience the unprecedented technological horror of mass-produced death during World War I.[1] His book that bears witness to this moment in history, *El soldado desconocido* (The unknown soldier),[2] published in Mexico in 1922 with a cover by Diego Rivera, has been overlooked unjustly by those who study and appreciate Hispanic American verse. For specialists in poetry of the First World War, de la Selva is a complete unknown. Mexican poet José Emilio Pacheco is one of the few critics outside Nicaragua to recognize the fundamental importance of de la Selva's *El soldado desconocido*. In an article entitled "Nota sobre la otra vanguardia" (Note on the other vanguard), Pacheco cites three lesser-known poets as the unacknowledged founders of a different kind of literature contemporary with the early poetry of Huidobro, Vallejo, and Neruda, the principle writers generally associated with Hispanic American avant-garde poetry. Perhaps, however, Pacheco's idea of "otherness" is simply an amplification of *vanguardia*, a bellicose, often vague, term assigned in retrospect by critics to quite divergent *poesías rupturistas* (poetry of rupture). Perhaps, again, the point of convergence between facile dichotomies such as realism-surrealism or traditional-experimental is the *experiential*. The reader must then distinguish between the experiences of the particular poet (e.g. as combatant or non-combatant) transformed into verse by a testimonial process of response and evaluation. In any case, Pacheco believes that Pedro Henríquez Ureña (1884-1946) from the Dominican Republic, Salomón de la Selva (1893-1956) from Nicaragua, and Salvador Novo (1904-1974) from Mexico should be recognized as precursors of the conversational "anti-poetry" that dominated Hispanic American poetry in the 1960s.[3] According to Pacheco, what these three poets share is a vital interest in the so-called New Poetry from the United States in the first decades of the twentieth century. Of especial interest to Pacheco is de la Selva's *El soldado desconocido*, a book which, "by incorporating the prosaic qualities of new poetry (in the U.S.), also

119

introduces the antiquities modernized by Pound and other poets of the
North American renaissance."[4] What Pacheco fails to address in his
otherwise excellent article is the highly-conflictive dialogue that de la
Selva maintains with North American verse in his evolution as a poet. In
this chapter we will investigate the intertextual complexities of a
Nicaraguan poet who wrote his first book, *Tropical Town & Other
Poems*,[5] in very traditional English verse forms, then rejected the English
language entirely to produce, in Spanish, *El soldado desconocido*, an
experimental, testimonial work that combines a variety of genres (the
chronicle, the diary, the letter, and the ballad) to produce a multi-faceted
description of a microcosmic experience of history that, ultimately,
becomes universal. As textual sources, we will compare poems in
English and Spanish by de la Selva, all of which have as their theme
World War I. In addition, for reasons both literary and historical that will
be explained later, we will analyze certain poems by de la Selva in
relation to texts by some *English* poets of the First War: Grenfell,
Brooke, and Sassoon.

Tropical Town & Other Poems: Nineteenth-Century Poetics and Politics?

De la Selva's first book, *Tropical Town & Other Poems*,
demonstrates the poet's attempt to perpetuate the esthetic standards of
the previous century, according to Henríquez Ureña:

> The majority of it corresponds to the norms of the nineteenth century. The
> truth is that, until now, one could say that Selva has not decided to break
> with the nineteenth century: the framework of his aspirations begins in Keats
> and Shelley and gets as far as Francis Thompson and Alice Meynell. Perhaps
> he hopes to master form before throwing himself completely into
> innovations.[6]

In a personal letter to Henríquez Ureña written prior to 1919, de la Selva
counts himself among writers such as Edna St. Vincent Millay and
Stephen Vincent Benét who "return to the traditional forms of English
poetry." De la Selva continues in the first person plural, saying, "we
represent the continuity that Alice Meynell asks for in her famous essay
'Decivilised.'"[7] Meynell's brief piece, published in 1896, is a thoroughly
colonialist and elitist diatribe against what she calls "colonial" America's
perversion of the English language:

> The difficulty of dealing—in the course of any critical duty—with
> decivilised man lies in this: when you accuse him of vulgarity—sparing him
> no doubt the word—he defends himself against the charge of barbarism.

Especially from new soil—transatlantic, colonial—he faces you, bronzed, with a half conviction of savagery, partly persuaded of his own youthfulness of race. He writes, and recites, poems about ranches and canyons; they are designed to betray the recklessness of his nature and to reveal the good that lurks in the lawless ways of a young society. He is there to explain himself, voluble, with a glossary for his own artless slang. But his colonialism is only provincialism very articulate. . . . Even now English voices, with violent commonplace, are constantly calling upon America to begin—to begin, for the world is expectant. Whereas there is no beginning for her, but instead a continuity which only a constant care can guide into sustained refinement and can save from decivilisation.[8]

It is surprising that no Nicaraguan critic has investigated the deepseated pro-English, anti-American conservatism contained in Meynell's piece (which de la Selva apparently considered a paradigm), and what this implies with regard to de la Selva's early poetry.

In the same letter cited above, de la Selva recognizes Masters, Amy Lowell, Frost, Robinson, Lindsay, Sandburg, and "others" as "today's poets." De la Selva, however, views the New American poetry they represent as an ephemeral trend that could disappear at any moment. According to de la Selva, who lived and taught in the United States, published his poems in English in important magazines such as *Harper's Monthly*, and was represented in Edwin Markham's major anthology of English-language poetry,[9] "the eruption of free verse is diminishing."[10] Henríquez Ureña considers de la Selva's traditional verse in *Tropical Town & Other Poems* with its "delicate images and verbal music" an anomaly in the context of poetry from the United States which, according to Henríquez Ureña, has a propensity "to realism, to concepts that are clear and without ornamentation." Henríquez Ureña offers the conclusion that de la Selva's first book of poems is a *rejection* of a North American cultural perspective in favor of that of England:

England is the country not only of great, imaginative poets, but great magicians of rhythm. Selva will find his own field for future development in England, then, with its proximity to Latin culture and tastes, rather than in North America.[11]

As we shall discover later in this chapter, the unadorned, prosaic, and brutally realistic sections of *El soldado desconocido* belie Henríquez Ureña's prediction. Nevertheless, de la Selva's penchant for traditional forms and lyricism in parts of *El soldado desconocido* and virtually all of his later works (all composed in Spanish) led Nicaraguan poet and critic José Coronel Urtecho to characterize de la Selva as "the most important neoclassical or neo-Greek poet of the [Spanish] language."[12]

Despite the rigid preoccupation with English rhyme and meter in the poems in *Tropical Town & Other Poems*, Coronel believes that "without a doubt, they were thought or felt in Spanish."[13] Coronel continues his occasionally hyperbolic piece on de la Selva with the idea that if Salomón had not given up the English language, he would have become "one of the most important North American poets of our time," and that he could have provided an important quality lacking in modern U.S. poetry, which was "the impregnation of the most Latin essences of French Symbolism and, above all, the experience of Hispanic American *modernismo* and its profound revolution in sensibility and in language."[14]

If what Coronel Urtecho says about de la Selva and French Symbolism is correct, what does this imply in terms of this study, which links de la Selva to poetry written in the English language and focuses on a single book by the Nicaraguan poet that does not represent his entire oeuvre? In addition to challenging the non-absolute critical categories proposed in this book, Coronel Urtecho's assessment of de la Selva's poetry raises complex questions regarding intertextuality in general. In each of these chapters, there are examples of both interlingual and intralingual intertextuality involving two or more authors. De la Selva, as a poet writing in two different languages and familiar with both literary traditions, embraces intertextuality between and within idioms. The distinction between tongues becomes, in a literary sense, nonexistent, if one accepts the idea that even works composed in one language may have been thought or felt in another. This phenomenon may be no less difficult to analyze (especially if one considers the profound political implications of language) than that of the Peruvian author José María Arguedas, who subverted the idiom of the oppressor (the Spaniard) by filling it with the vocabulary, the landscapes, the lives, and even the syntactic structures of the oppressed (the Quechua-speakers).

Coronel Urtecho surmises that de la Selva's motivations for rejecting the English language, but not certain characteristics associated with the literary traditions of the United States and England, were, indeed, political:

> Apparently, it was his anti-imperialism and his profound resentment of North American intervention that made him distance himself from the United States and stop writing his poetry in English.[15]

A spirit of Pan-Americanism, as well as anti-imperialism, permeates several of the poems in *Tropical Town & Other Poems*. The final poem of the book's first section (a series of Nicaraguan scenes entitled "My Nicaragua") has a long title that describes the poet's potential conflict with the United States: "The Dreamer's Heart Knows Its Own Bitterness (A Pan-American Poem on the Entrance of the United States into the War)." The poet creates a North-South dichotomy, characterizing the South as his Mother and the North as his Bride:

To the North I came, with a dream, with a song,
With a noise like the music of the rain in the Spring,
For I held the Vision and it ruled my tongue,
And North and South would hear me sing. . . .

"For this land I have blushed when its choice was shame;
For this land I have cheered with all my breath;
Sweet in my ears is its very name:
For its sake I would die the soldier's death.

"Not false to you, Mother; not false, my Mother!
It were not in my blood to be false to you!
You have I cherished above all other,
But I love this land, and my flags are two."

(*Tropical Town & Other Poems* 38-39)

The poet pledges his support to the United States in the war against "Belgium's wronger," yet urges the United States to be consistent in its sense of justice with regard to Latin America:

Will you let this thing be said of you,
That you stood for Right who were clothed with Wrong?
That to Latin America you proved untrue?
That you clamoured for justice with a guilty tongue?

Hear me, who cry for the sore oppressed:
Make right this grievance that I bear in me
Like a lance point driven into my breast!
So, blameless and righteous, your strength shall be
The power of God made manifest,
And I pledge the South shall never rest
Till your task is accomplished and the world is free.

(*Tropical Town* 43)

Despite a certain jingoism with regard to U.S. participation in World War I in this poem as well as others in *Tropical Town* that we will examine in a later section, one could say that Nicaraguan Salomón de la Selva was perhaps one of the most politically-aware poets of his time. His perception of the unjust political relationship between the United States and Latin America, especially in a poem such as "A Song for Wall Street," makes de la Selva unique among his contemporaries writing in the English language:

But for your dollar, your dirty dollar,
Your greenish leprosy,

> It's only hatred you shall get
> From all my folks and me;
> So keep your dollar where it belongs
> And let us be!

(Tropical Town 27)

Can one say, then, that, while it maintains nineteenth-century verse forms, de la Selva's early poetry in English treats political themes with a twentieth-century awareness? On the one hand, de la Selva's politicized verse is simply an extension of the English Romantic poets' conflicting attitudes toward patriotism and war. Jon Silkin, perhaps the most important critic and anthologist of poetry from the First World War, cites from Coleridge's "Fears in Solitude," Wordsworth's *The Prelude*, Byron's *Don Juan*, and Shelley's *Revolt of Islam* to demonstrate the extent to which each of these poets from the nineteenth century "anticipates in his poetry the positions of the First War poets."[16] But the questioning of and the violent struggle against the kind of political hegemony expressed, for example, in the Monroe Doctrine is primarily a twentieth-century phenomenon. That is to say, while de la Selva's *El soldado desconocido* may have much in common with *Drum-Taps* by Walt Whitman, the Nicaraguan poet would oppose Whitman's sincere, though ingenuous, support of Manifest Destiny in the time of William Walker's mercenary army in Nicaragua. One recalls, too, that Howard Taft began official, repeated U.S. intervention in Nicaragua by sending Marines to occupy the Central American republic in 1912. Henríquez Ureña reconstructs a legendary speech (in English) against U. S intervention in Nicaragua that Salomón de la Selva gave in February 1917 at the National Arts Club in New York. Despite much fervent applause, de la Selva's words caused one of the members of the audience, Theodore Roosevelt, to leave the auditorium in disgust:

> Nicaragua is small in extension, but powerful in its pride. My land is as great as its thoughts; as great as its hopes and its aspirations . . . To love the United States, as I do, requires a great deal of effort when my own country is outraged by the nation to the North. No true Pan-Americanism can exist until there is full justice for the weak nations.[17]

Speculations on a Ghost: A Missing Link

Because this study attempts to address diverse types of intertextuality, I have decided not to abbreviate the information in this section and relegate it to a note, despite its parenthetical nature. Although extensive searches have failed to locate the text, there still exists the possibility that

Salomón de la Selva published a group of poems in English entitled *A Soldier Sings* in London after the end of the war in 1919. In other words, there may be a missing link between *Tropical Town & Other Poems*, published in 1918, and *El soldado desconocido*, which appeared in 1922. Phantasmal publications such as this one, as the bibliographer of Latin American literature Hensley C. Woodbridge informed me in a letter, are known as "ghosts." Its alleged existence is the result of Nicaraguan poet Ernesto Mejía Sánchez[18] sending the bibliographical information (London: The Bodley Head, 1919) to Jorge Eduardo Arellano, who at the time was compiling an extensive bibliography of books and articles by and about de la Selva for the fundamental publication *Homenaje a Salomón de la Selva: 1959-1969*. To the best of my knowledge, no one has been able to locate the poems in *A Soldier Sings*. Nevertheless, given the successful publication of *Tropical Town*, it is not entirely improbable that Salomón would have continued to write poetry in English. After the war, he may have published a group of poems about his war experiences in an attempt to integrate himself into the poetry circles of England (where he lived until late 1919), perhaps using his friendship with Alice Meynell to facilitate the process. Was it a source of bitter disappointment to the poet that these poems in English were lost in the chaos of London after the war? In his memoirs, the well-known poet from the First World War Siegfried Sassoon describes this period when so many ex-combatants were writing poetry about their lives during the war. At the time, he was in charge of the literary page of the *Daily Herald*:

> By the end of April [1919], however, the accumulation of unreviewable volumes was becoming oppressive. . . . There was also a good deal of commonplace poetry, sent me by writers desirous of encouragement. Contemplating overcrowded shelves and their overflow on the floor, I felt inclined to pen a pungent literary note urging authors and publishers to cultivate continence. . . . I took to dumping weekly consignments [of books] into a taxi and depositing them with a stoical bookseller who dealt in discarded review copies. The profits went towards a summer outing for the office staff.[19]

Was *A Soldier Sings* a book announced by The Bodley Head, but never published? Were the poems published in a very limited private edition, or as a *separata* from some magazine? Did they appear under a pseudonym? For the time being, *A Soldier Sings* remains, as Arellano says in a personal letter, "a legend, one more myth in our literature rich in myths."[20] Nevertheless, it would be interesting to know if the text is an initial, perhaps partial, version in English of *El soldado desconocido*.[21] Are the poems written in traditional verse forms like virtually all the verse composed by the British poets of the First World War, or does de la Selva experiment with free verse in English as he does in the later version in Spanish? More interesting still is the possibility that de la Selva may have translated his traditional poems in English into non-traditional poems in Spanish.[22] For an intertextual study of this kind, the ramifications of *A Soldier Sings*, if the book does, in fact, exist, are extremely complex.

The Four Stages of War-Consciousness

Jon Silkin delineates four different stages of war-consciousness in his introduction to *The Penguin Book of First World War Poetry*.[23] These categories are a useful critical means of distinguishing between various kinds of war poetry. In addition, they aptly describe the evolution of Salomón de la Selva's verse, beginning with *Tropical Town & Other Poems* and continuing with *El soldado desconocido*. In this section we will compare texts in English and Spanish by de la Selva with texts by various English, rather than U.S., poets. As we explained previously, de la Selva's early poetry demonstrates a certain rejection of modern verse in the United States in favor of more traditional British poetry. Apart from these literary considerations, there are also historical realities that have determined the intertextual alternatives available for this chapter. In his introduction to *Doughboy Doggerel: Verse of the American Expeditionary Force 1918-1919*, Alfred E. Cornebise attributes the less serious verse written by the American expeditionary forces to the tardy entrance of the United States in the war. Furthermore, according to Cornebise, U. S. troops, unlike the British soldiers, "were largely spared the long, dreary, grinding punishment of trench warfare":

> To be sure, while divergent backgrounds explain some of the differences between the lighter American verse and that of the British soldier-poets, which in the late war years was characterized by disillusionment and morbidity, there was another most important factor to be considered, the relatively short time that Americans were actually engaged in combat on a large scale. Though they were there earlier, it was not until the spring of 1918 that there were Americans in sufficient numbers in the lines to have an appreciable effect on the course of the war. By the summer, the Germans were in retreat.[24]

With the exception of cummings, MacLeish, and Sandburg (each represented with a single, short poem in Silkin's anthology), there are virtually no American soldier-poets from which to choose.

The initial stage of war-consciousness, according to Silkin, is one of passive reflection on prevailing patriotic ideas. As we discussed in an earlier section, de la Selva's poetry in English occasionally takes a critical attitude toward blind patriotism, especially with regard to Latin

America. Nevertheless, this verse is often permeated by the rhetoric of those who favor war with a fervor that equals that of medieval troubadours such as Bertran de Born. In this respect, poems such as de la Selva's "The Knight in Gray," "A Prayer for the United States," and "Drill" from the section in *Tropical Town* entitled "In War Time" have a great deal in common with "Into Battle" by Julian Grenfell and "The Soldier" by Rupert Brooke. One could say, in general terms, that de la Selva's "war poetry" in English written in 1916 and 1917, prior to his experience in direct combat, corresponds to the verse written by the English poets in 1914 and 1915, before the war's grimmer turn after the Somme offensive in July 1916. The idealism, refined elegance, solemnity, and pastoral qualities of this poetry contrast sharply with the disillusioned, anti-heroic reportage from the trenches in later works such as de la Selva's *El soldado desconocido* and Siegfried Sassoon's *Counter-Attack*.

De la Selva's "Drill" (written in April 1917 when the poet was teaching Romance Languages at Williams College in Massachusetts) and Grenfell's "Into Battle" share what critic John H. Johnston calls the soldierly mystique of professionalism, a certain romantic delight and childish excitement about the possibility of warfare.[25] In de la Selva's poem, the potential of violence is a quasi-mystical source of ecstatic release that illuminates the world, increasing its natural beauty:

> *One! two, three, four! . . .*
>
> And the shuffle of six hundred feet
> Till the marching line is neat.
>
> Then the wet New England valley
> With the purple hills around
> Takes us gently, musically,
> With a kindly heart and willing,
> Thrilling, filling with the sound
> Of our drilling.
>
> Battle fields are far away.
> All the world about me seems
> The fulfillment of my dreams.
> God, how good it is to be
> Young and glad to-day!. . . .
>
> I will rise and I will go
> As the rivers flow to sea,
> As the sap mounts up the tree
> That the flowers may blow.—

> God, my God,
> All my soul is out of me!

(Tropical Town 74-75)

Although there is no first-person voice in Grenfell's poem, the lyrical speaker, as a combatant, draws sustenance from the landscape around him, a natural act that results in a transcendent life:

> The fighting man shall from the sun
>   Take warmth, and life from the glowing earth;
> Speed with the light-foot winds to run,
>   And with the trees to newer birth;
> And find, when fighting shall be done,
>   Great rest, and fullness after dearth.

(PBFWWP 83)

In attempting to explain the enthusiasm for the war, one must consider seriously sentiments such as those expressed by Grenfell in a 10 August 1914 letter in which he writes, "Isn't it luck for me to have been born so as to be just the right age and just in the right place—not too high up to be worried—and to enjoy it to the most!"[26] For the English elite such as Grenfell and Brooke, the war represented freedom from the dull constraints of aristocratic life. In August 1914, Brooke considered the war in chivalric terms: "Honour has come back like a king to earth."[27] On the participation of the working class in the war, Silkin wonders if they, too, were motivated by the confinement of their daily lives, hunger, an overriding national pride, or other selfless reasons that contradicted their interests as a social class excluded from the organization of the state by the ruling class.[28]

It would seem, however, that a moral fervor, no doubt taken advantage of by this ruling class, was as great a motivating factor as any. Cornebise writes of the American mood of exuberant patriotism in terms of a crusade. The "doughboy doggerel," according to Cornebise, reflected the belief that "the Allied cause was a moral and religious one and a manifestation of God's will—the advancement of the best of western civilization and Christendom. . . ."[29] The same moral laws, though in a more refined form, govern the early war poetry of the English elite. The following stanza of Grenfell's "Into Battle," for example, contains the cosmic equivalent of "God is on our side" in its images of bellicose constellations:

> All the bright company of Heaven
>   Hold him in their high comradeship,

The Dog-Star, and the Sisters Seven,
Orion's Belt and sworded hip.

(PBFWWP 83)

"A Prayer for the United States," composed by de la Selva in August 1917, echoes the sort of celestial solidarity in Grenfell's poem, but with less certainty as to the inherent virtues of battle:

> Apocalyptic blasts are ravaging over-sea.
> With lure of flag and conquest the harlot War is wooing.
> The horse John saw in Patmos its dread course is pursuing.—
> I pray the Lord He shelter the stars that shelter me.

(Tropical Town 71)

This short poem is a good example of the lack of literary-historical synchronization between de la Selva and the English poets of the First World War, whose verse, by August 1917, had become deeply morbid and disillusioned. Even so, de la Selva's poetry in English and Spanish from 1916-1922 reflects the poetic evolution of the principal English war poets from 1912-1918.

Given their initial concerns as writers associated with the group of Georgian poets before the war, one can understand the difficulties of English poets as individuals in assimilating the epic historical complexities of the First World War by means of the lyric poem. Robert Graves's daughter writes that by 1912 her father belonged to the group of Georgian poets under the maecenas Eddie Marsh, and that they sought a renewal of English poetry that had grown stagnant as a result of the legacy of Victorian puritanism, preferring in their verse a more accessible language with rural themes.[30] The inability of the Georgian poets to incorporate an objective historical reality in their verse, however, is precisely what John H. Johnston criticizes:

No previous body of poetry in English literature, inspired by momentous national events, has been marked by such limited knowledge and by such an excess of self-contemplation. . . . A tragic event which is understood only in terms of personal misadventure ceases to be tragic. Tragedy implies a relationship between the part and the whole, between man and the mysteries of the moral universe.[31]

Rupert Brooke's sonnet "The Soldier" is perhaps the best example of this kind of self-absorbed imperialism that characterizes Silkin's first stage of war-consciousness. According to Graves's daughter, the heroic death described in the poem by Brooke stimulated thousands of young people to enlist and spawned hundreds of imitators of his verse.[32] Not

coincidentally, the words "England" or "English" appear six times in the
famous fourteen-line poem that begins:

> If I should die, think only this of me:
>   That there's some corner of a foreign field
> That is for ever England. There shall be
>   In that rich earth a richer dust concealed;
> A dust whom England bore, shaped, made aware,
>   Gave, once, her flowers to love, her ways to roam,
> A body of England's, breathing English air,
>   Washed by the rivers, blest by suns of home.

(PBFWWP 81)

De la Selva's "The Knight in Gray," composed of eleven quatrains
with lines of varying length and an *a b a b* rhyme scheme, focuses on the
same passive, elemental qualities of the individual who acts in
accordance with a natural order in his role as a soldier:

> And if some hate, no hate have I
>   Who fought for love and love alone
> Returning to the earth and sky
>   Their elements I own.
>
> The songs I sang came to my lips
>   The way of seeds to fields afar,
> Shaken from trees whose budding tips
>   Were lances sharpening for war.
>
> My deeds were gestures in the wind,
>   I bent the way of a poplar bough,
> And if I fell, and if I sinned,
>   A larger breath shall lift me now.
>
> Where trampling armies melt the snow
>   And wounded men clutch withered grass,
> Torn from myself my self shall go
>   The way of rivers down a pass. . . .
>
> So, with the rush of summer rain
>   I shall have swept across the earth,
> And if it chance myself be slain,
>   My self shall have a richer birth.

(Tropical Town 83-84)

"The Knight in Gray" differs from Brooke's poem in terms of its content in one fundamental way: de la Selva refuses to engage in the promotion of a specific nationality as a result of his own ambivalence toward the United States.

The kind of verse in this first category of war poetry is particularly insidious in the way that it can be used to the advantage of the interests (and, of course, the individuals who represent these interests) promoting war. In the introduction to his anthology of war poetry from the twentieth century, Oscar Williams describes the underlying true nature of popular patriotic verse:

> The unpopularity of the true poem and, conversely, the popularity of the false poem, could much better be explained in psychological terms. In the case of war poems, patriotic bombast generally confirms the reader who likes it in a false concept either of himself or of social circumstances, or both. It eases him of responsibility and guilt in the matter of acquiescing in sending young men to death to protect himself. This kind of "escape" is also given by certain popular poetry which is accepted as "good" (such as Rupert Brooke's "The Soldier").[33]

De la Selva's poetry in English mirrors, for the most part, the kind of patriotic poetry composed by the English poets at the beginning of the war. But there are important exceptions that make the verse in *Tropical Town*'s "In War Time" section far from monolithic in tone and theme. Perhaps the best example of this is "December, 1916," a meditation on a frozen New England field covered with imaginary dead, which ends with the following stanza:

> But God is punctual and snow will come
> (*And peace will come*, the world's heart saith),
> And earth will hide her troublesome
> Face of despair, semblance of death.
> But this frozen horror that we know
> Shall be terrible still, under the snow
> (*Peace shall be terrible*, the world's heart saith).

> (*Tropical Town* 73)

Furthermore, the later work *El soldado desconocido* is not impervious to the sort of romantic, exuberant musings in the presence of death that characterize much of his earlier "war" poetry written in English. De la Selva, however, seems consciously intent on demonstrating the *evolution* of his own historical awareness in *El soldado desconocido*. Thus, the two poems, "Testamento" (Testament) and "La muerte afina su violín" (Death tunes her violin), from the book's first section entitled "Voluntario romántico" (Romantic volunteer), must be considered in the context of the entire book, whose narrative and visual qualities necessitate reading or viewing it as if it were a novel or a film. At the same time, these first two poems present the basis for the poet's formal evolution as well. That is to say, the alexandrines, hendecasyllables, rhyme schemes, and musicality of these initial poems, clearly linked to Darío's *modernismo*, give way to the free verse of a large part of "Jornada Tercera: Mêlée" (Third day's journey: conflict), the section of the book that concentrates on the physical horror of trench warfare.

In his use of colloquial language to depict the grotesque and to deflate elevated diction, Salomón de la Selva might be considered an inheritor of what Gwen Kirkpatrick has called "the dissonant legacy of *modernismo*" in her characterization of the poetry of Leopoldo Lugones and Julio Herrera y Reissig.[34] To what extent is de la Selva, a bilingual and bicultural writer, a "modernist" poet in *El soldado desconocido*? If we use the term in the Hispanic American sense in relation to Darío's literary revolution, one certainly detects, as Jorge Eduardo Arellano does, "a diluted *modernista* heritage in certain words and phrases."[35] If we consider the term in the Poundian sense, there is the prosaism of the "Carta" (Letter) poems, the Chinese presence in "La trinchera abandonada" (The abandoned trench), and the juxtaposition of the modern and the archaic in "Oda a Safo" (Ode to Sappho), in which the real battle is between elevated beauty ("Oh Safo, ¿tus rosas dónde se abren?") (Oh, Sappho, where do your roses open?) and its opposite ("En el dug-out hermético, / sonoro de risas y de pedos . . .") (In the airtight dug-out,/echoing with laughter and farts . . .).

This way of speaking is an essential characteristic of the poetry of Silkin's second stage of war-consciousness, which has to do with the description of war in the frankest, most realistic of terms. The epitome of this kind of poetry, in Silkin's opinion, is *Counter-Attack* by Siegfried Sassoon, a poet who "protests against the war variously: through the recreation of physical horror (he describes himself as a 'visually submissive' poet); through anger and satire; and through sardonic distancing" in an attempt to penetrate the uninformed civilian's "callous complacency."[36] There are many striking similarities between this work by Sassoon and de la Selva's *El soldado desconocido*.

To begin with, both authors successfully express the horror of war because of their highly-developed sense of battle narrative as actual participants in the conflict. Nevertheless, the nature of this war literature produced by the combatants themselves has sparked a polemic that distinguishes opposing attitudes toward testimonial poetry. For example, John H. Johnston is preoccupied with the English war poets' lack of what he calls "intellectual remoteness," a quality, says Johnston, necessary to give experience the proper artistic shape. In general, Johnston believes that, for fundamental formal reasons, the English soldier-poets were incapable of adequately describing their experiences using lyric poetry. Johnston focuses his study on epic and heroic poetry, which, in his opinion, the poets might have been able to cultivate if they had developed a more acute sense of duty, perhaps by means of a greater access to facts. He criticizes virtually all the verse by the English poets of World War I on the grounds that their poetry lacks both artistic rigor and an appropriate overall (epic) form. Worse still, according to Johnston, is their "failure to universalize their work" and their inability "to elevate it much beyond the level of vivid reportage."[37] To these observations, W. B. Yeats would add the nuance, as he did in his justification for not including the poetry of Wilfred Owen in the 1936 edition of *The Oxford Book of Modern Verse*, that "passive suffering" is not an appropriate theme for poetry.

On the other hand, one can argue that testimonial literature is a separate genre with different objectives. Given the increasing interconnectedness of a world in which wars can be broadcast live on television, ours is a century in which temporal and intellectual remoteness are simply physical and moral impossibilities. A work such as *El soldado desconocido* is destined to cyclical resonances coinciding with highly-technological and alienating conflicts. Too, de la Selva's testimonial work should be seen as an important antecedent to what John Beverley and Marc Zimmerman characterize as "the effort to reintegrate history and narrative with the new subjectivism and radical moralism" that one finds, for example, in the poetry of Ernesto Cardenal.[38] With regard to Nicaragua, for novelist and former Vice-President of Nicaragua Sergio Ramírez, de la Selva's *El soldado desconocido* is a key work in his country's literature in that it challenges traditional conceptions of the poet in terms of his or her relation to certain social commitments. Ramírez believes that the poem "Vergüenza" (Shame) provides an excellent definition of the militant term "cultural worker":

> Este era zapatero,
> éste hacía barriles,
> y aquél servía de mozo en un hotel de puerto . . .
>
> Todos han dicho lo que eran
> antes de ser soldados;
> ¿y yo? ¿Yo qué sería
> que ya no lo recuerdo?
> ¿Poeta? ¡No! Decirlo
> me daría vergüenza.

> (*El soldado desconocido* 23)

(This guy was a cobbler, / this one made barrels, / the one over there was a waiter in a hotel in a port . . . / Everyone has said what they did / before they

were soldiers; / And I? What did I do? / I can't even remember. / Poet? No!
I'd be / ashamed to say it.)

For Ramírez, there is an ethical urgency to participate both as artist and
as citizen, to imprint a praxis on artistic creation.[39] On the one hand,
then, testimonial literature serves to reinforce a collective spirit of
solidarity with shared ideological values. Under different historical
circumstances, it can function as an agent of information and
denunciation (as Nicaraguan verse did during the time of Somoza) as
well as an historical document of an ordinary individual's experience of
history that often is absent from the books of traditional historians.

Perhaps epic heroes, even with their evident, tragic flaws, are less
relevant to the interests of the modern poet, who is attracted to a different
sort of protagonist. The title of Salomón de la Selva's first book of
poems in Spanish, for example, is significant precisely because, as the
poet states with no small amount of irony in an introduction, "the hero of
the War is the Unknown Soldier. He's cheap and satisfies everyone. He
doesn't need to be given a pension. He has no name. No family. Nothing.
Only a country."[40] De la Selva, like the English war poets, was interested
in the unheroic human qualities of the individual combatant, unmitigated
by intellectual remoteness and unencumbered by the literary figure that
necessarily conforms to mythic models. In contrast to the epic poets who
describe a distant past by means of protagonists based on ancient oral
traditions, de la Selva and the British war poets are writing within an
urgent, immediate, overwhelming historical context: they are the first
poets to bear witness in verse to the devastating physical and spiritual
effects of modern technical warfare. Furthermore, not unlike the majority
of the poets anthologized by W. D. Ehrhart in *Carrying the Darkness:
American Indochina—The Poetry of the Vietnam War* (1985), they called
into question all the ancient values associated with epic poetry (e.g.
individual courage, strength, and intelligence) due to the very nature of
the war in which they fought.

De la Selva and Sassoon break with traditional poetic decorum by
presenting an individual experience that reflects the physiology of war as
if the battle itself were also an organism competing with other, weaker
beings around it. Sassoon's "Counter-Attack," for example, opens with a
first-person plural voice creating a personified dawn that mirrors the
grim portrait of each individual soldier:

> We'd gained our first objective hours before
> While dawn broke like a face with blinking eyes,
> Pallid, unshaved and thirsty, blind with smoke.

(Collected Poems 68)

The same poem continues with the truly gruesome description of the shallow trench that the soldiers are attempting to deepen in order to prepare for the inevitable German counter-attack:

> The place was rotten with dead; green clumsy legs
> High-booted, sprawled and grovelled along the saps
> And trunks, face downward, in the sucking mud,
> Wallowed like trodden sand-bags loosely filled;
> And naked sodden buttocks, mats of hair,
> Bulged, clotted heads slept in the plastering slime.
> And then the rain began—the jolly old rain.

(Collected Poems 68)

In an excellent exegesis of this passage, Silkin notes how Sassoon's characteristic "pre-lapsarian pastoralism" has been transformed, creating literary subtleties in a text whose surface possesses an overwhelmingly graphic directness and apparent simplicity. Silkin cites the interplay of gangrene and the natural forces that have lost their regenerative powers that is suggested by the use of "green." He highlights the metonymic power of "high-booted," which suggests the irony of arrogance in the face of mortality, as well as Sassoon's intense objectification of reality in his comparison of the human body with "trodden sand-bags." The phrase "the jolly old rain" is, according to Silkin, "an animating human response, with some relief, to a non-human phenomenon,"[41] a deeply ironic class-conscious derogation of a cliché.

Of great literary importance in this poem, which subsequently recounts the failure of the German counterattack and the absurd death of an officer, is the use of colloquial English exclamations such as "'Stand-to and man the fire-step!'" and "'O Christ, they're coming at us!'" In justifying the controversial nature of this poetic strategy by citing certain obvious precedents in English poetry, the British poet Edmund Blunden wrote of the necessity of "truthfulness," "common language," and a "powerful plainness":

> In respect of style or method, the poems in question may have upset the feelings of many faithful followers of the English Muse. Even after Robert Browning, and after the recognition of Thomas Hardy as a poet, the conversational approach to the poetic height was often distrusted. Siegfried Sassoon chose it as one of his styles.[42]

De la Selva also uses human speech in the context of war with great dramatic effect. The Nicaraguan poet translates not only the experience of war into his native language, but also the words of his comrades, as in "Mientras nos alistábamos" (While we were getting ready):

> ¡Infierno!
> con tal que no me mate,
> bienvenida es la bala
> que me dé una pensión toda la vida.

(El soldado desconocido 59)

(Hell! / as long as it doesn't kill me, / bring on the bullet / that will give me a pension for life.)

Like Sassoon, de la Selva is an astute observer of the horror around him, and makes an effort to record this inhumanity with great detail in the poem "Heridos" (Wounded):

> He visto a los heridos:
> ¡Qué horribles son los trapos manchados de sangre!
> Y los hombres que se quejan mucho;
> y los que se quejan poco;
> y los que ya han dejado de quejarse!
> Y las bocas retorcidas de dolor;
> y los dientes aferrados;
> y aquel muchacho loco que se ha mordido la lengua
> y la lleva de fuera, morada, como si lo hubieran ahorcado!

(El soldado desconocido 31)

(I've seen the wounded: / What horrible rags soaked with blood! / And the men who complain a lot; / and those who hardly complain at all; / and those who've stopped complaining! / And the mouths twisted in pain; / and the clenched teeth; / and that crazy young guy who bit his tongue / and left it sticking out, all purple, as if he had been hanged!)

Because the influx of detail is so overpowering in this poem, the poet is forced to create a poetic inventory that finally acquires a biblical, apocalyptic resonance.

De la Selva describes battle with a kind of eschatological awe that rarely enters Sassoon's more cynical, embittered verse. In "Comienzo de batalla" (The beginning of battle), for example, the poet recounts the mysterious, "majestuoso" (majestic) evil of the new technology of death, which the soldiers combat with the primitive "abanicos faraónicos" (fans of a Pharaoh):

> Todos enmascarados,
> iguales a demonios,
> vimos llegar rodar la amarillenta nube larga. . . .
> Nada perturba el majestuoso avance de la nube.
> Envolvió las defensas de alambre

y nos envolvió a todos
y se echó en la trinchera, dragón de humo,
entre un clamor de gongos y campanas
y de timbres eléctricos.

Batiendo con abanicos faraónicos
desalojamos al huésped mortal:
Fue trabajo de horas:
Allá irá, a las trincheras de segunda fila,
suavemente arrollado por el viento.

Echados en el lodo
hay muchos vomitando los pulmones.
Relinchan, presa de los estertores de la muerte.

(El soldado desconocido 44)

(All of us in our masks, / like demons, / we watched the long, rolling, yellow cloud arrive / . . . Nothing perturbed the cloud's majestic advance. / It covered the barbed wire defenses / and covered us all / and entered the trench, / dragon of smoke, / amidst the clanging of alarms and bells / and electric buzzers. / Flapping the fans of the Pharaoh, / we dislodged the fatal guest. / It took hours. / There it goes, toward the second line of trenches, / gently pushed by the wind. / Lying in the mud, / many [soldiers] are vomiting their lungs. / They rear up, prey caught in the throes of death.)

The poet's attempt to describe mustard gas highlights one of the most interesting characteristics of the poetry by de la Selva that belongs in Silkin's second category of war-consciousness. Due to the extremely alienating *foreign* qualities (in the geographical and experiential sense) of de la Selva's situation as a combatant in the First World War, the poet conjures consoling images of his native Nicaragua:

El gas que he respirado
me dejó casi ciego,
pero olía a fruta de mi tierra,
unas veces a piña y otras veces a mango,
y hasta a guineos . . .

(El soldado desconocido 49)

(The gas I inhaled / left me nearly blind, / but it smelled like the fruit of my homeland, / sometimes like pineapple and other times like mango, / and even like bananas . . .)

Other examples of the strange, syncretic presence of Nicaragua in this war poetry include the men in "Comienzo de batalla" "corriendo como iguanas" (running like iguanas) and "los chillidos de mono de las granadas" (the monkey screams of the grenades). In "Primera Carta" (First letter), the poet creates a fascinating metaphorical parallel between soldiers/rumble of war and Nicaraguan animals/earthquake:

> El cañoneo se oye como debajo de la tierra.
> Lo que sentimos es religiosidad bárbara,
> y lo que he visto sentir a las bestias
> cuando retumba el suelo en Nicaragua:
> Necesidad de mugir mirando al cielo
> y de volver y revolver los ojos

> *(El soldado desconocido* 29-30)

(The artillery sounds as if it's coming from below the earth. / What we feel is barbaric religiosity, / and what I've seen the animals feel / when the earth rumbles in Nicaragua: / the need to moo, watching the sky / and rolling their eyes.)

At least in terms of thematics, this phenomenon resembles the poet's preoccupation with Nicaragua (while he was living in the United States) in the first, and perhaps most convincing, section of *Tropical Town and Other Poems*. Nicaragua illuminates the poetic landscape of *El soldado desconocido*, however, only intermittently, like the "cohetes de luz" (flares) of the nocturnal battlefield.

There are, however, at least two fundamental differences between the poetry of de la Selva and Sassoon. With the exception of a few poems, de la Selva's verse is not marked by the profound antiwar sentiments that characterize virtually all of the poems in *Counter-Attack*. De la Selva, perhaps because of the relatively short time he was engaged in combat, did not seem to undergo the kind of deep philosophical transformations that sparked such relentless anger in Sassoon after his convalescence in Craiglockart Hospital in 1917 when he came into contact with the pacifist positions of Lady Ottoline Morrell and her husband. In fact, a prowar stance dominates much of de la Selva's book, despite the poet's horrific descriptions of battle and a momentary despair in one of his "Carta" (p. 69-70) poems in which he states in the simplest way: "lo único que creo / es que la guerra es mala" (the only thing I believe / is that the war is bad). In "El canto de la alondra" (The lark's song), for example, the poet praises his bayonet: "Mi bayoneta es bella por sobre las banderas; / tiene las rectitudes de mis ideales" (My bayonet is beautiful above the flags; / it has the rectitudes of my ideals). His dedication to the cause is complete to the extent that the poet establishes an intimate dialogue with the weapons of destruction in "La bala" (The bullet), in which the speaker says, "La bala que me hiera / será bala con alma . . ." (The bullet that wounds me / will be a bullet with a soul . . .).

Equally telling is the poet's remaking of one of the traditional symbols of poetry, Orpheus's lyre, in "La lira" (The lyre), so that it embodies the music of the war:[43]

> Yo quiero algo diferente.
> Algo hecho de este alambre de púas;
> algo que no pueda tocar un cualquiera,
> que haga sangrar los dedos,
> que dé un son como el son que hacen las balas
> cuando inspirado el enemigo
> quiere romper nuestro alambrado
> a fuerza de tiros.
> Aunque la gente diga que no es música,
> las estrellas en sus danzas acatarán el nuevo ritmo.

> (*El soldado desconocido* 41)

(I want something different. / Something made of this barbed wire; / something that not just anyone can play, / that makes the fingers bleed, / that makes a sound like the sound of bullets / when the inspired enemy / wants to break through our wire defenses / with gunfire. / Even though people might say it's not music, / the stars in their dances will respect the new rhythm.)

The other important difference between the two poets is their treatment of women. Like any ordinary soldier, de la Selva meditates on a real or imaginary *amada* (beloved) or *novia* (girlfriend) who, as an apparition of an Ideal, emerges, larger than life, from the cracks in the poet's living nightmare. In a strange inversion of Freudian symbolism, he associates her twice in *El soldado desconocido* with his bayonet. Sassoon, in his supreme cynicism and pessimism, is immune to such expressions of exuberance and idealizations of love. Women in the poems of *Counter-Attack* are simply another element of a selfish and uninformed public:

> You love us when we're heroes, home on leave,
> Or wounded in a mentionable place.
> You worship decorations; you believe
> That chivalry redeems the war's disgrace.

> (*Collected Poems* 79)

> Husbands and sons and lovers; everywhere
> They die; War bleeds us white.
> Mothers and wives and sweethearts—they don't care
> So long as He's all right.

> (*Collected Poems* 80)

In addition to the paradigmatic, virginal *novia* in many of de la Selva's poems, there is another image of women that does correspond to the portrait of women in Sassoon's poetry. On leave in London, de la Selva encounters myriad inquisitive women, whom he describes in "Las preguntas" (The questions):

> ¡Estas pobres mujeres preguntonas!
> Un hijo, un hermano, el amante,
> son razón suficiente para interminables preguntas.
> Yo no sé si decirles:
> —"¡Pues ya lo creo! lo conozco muy bien.
> Y está en lo rosadito de la vida:
> completamente lejos de peligro . . ."
> O si espetarles esto:
> —"Yo no conozco a nadie.
> Ni a mí mismo.
> ¡Nos mataron a todos
> y el diablo nos ha robado el cuerpo
> para llevarlas a ustedes al infierno!"

(El soldado desconocido 85)

(These poor women asking questions! / A son, a brother, the lover, / are reason enough for interminable questions. / I don't know if I should tell them: / "What a coincidence! I know him really well, / and he's in the pink of life: / completely out of danger . . ." / Or if I should skewer them with this bit of news: / "I don't know anyone. / Not even myself. / They killed us all / and the devil has stolen our bodies / in order to carry all of you to hell!")

On the subject of courage, de la Selva, unlike Sassoon, responds in the humble way of a person plagued by uncertainty and shame when confronted with words of patriotic praise from his *novia*:

> Dicen que me van a dar una medalla.
> Te la voy a mandar por si te gusta
> contar que eres mi novia. . . .
>
> Quiero, por si me muero,
> confesarte que casi
> todas las noches lloro,
> pero que sin embargo
> me estoy poniendo gordo,
> y ya nada me importa,
> quienes ganen o pierdan,
> pues, no sé cómo, ahora
> lo único que creo
> es que la guerra es mala.

Tus palabras hermosas
me avergüenzan por eso

(El soldado desconocido 69-70)

(They say that they are going to give me a medal. / I'll send it to you, in case you want / to tell people you're my girlfriend . . . / In case I die, I want / to confess to you that almost / every night I cry / but that nevertheless / I'm getting fat, / and that nothing matters anymore, / whoever wins or loses, / because I don't know how, but now, / the only thing I believe / is that the war is bad. / That's why your beautiful words / make me ashamed)

This excerpt from one of the "Carta" poems (there are five, excluding the rhetorical "Carta a Alice Meynell," which the poet could have refrained from including in *El soldado desconocido* with no loss whatsoever) highlights one of the interesting problems posed by the variety of genres that one finds in *El soldado desconocido*. Does published epistolary expression necessarily blur the distinction between private and public communication? These important poems form the book's narrative, novelistic spine. Unlike some letters written home from the front with the intention of concealing or embellishing negative aspects of reality, de la Selva's texts possess an undeniable immediacy and a strict forthrightness. In the context of the book, of course, the letters to different (imaginary?) recipients become published poems—and they are exemplary in the way the poet makes private truthfulness public. Together, the progression of letter-poems depict the contradictory qualities that make one human: arrogant, youthful ingenuousness and the savage, uncontrollable desire to enter battle; the shame, tears, and disillusion with heroism and the war; the intense desire to return not to the pleasures of an urban life or the rural, indigenous culture of his native country, but to the innocence of childhood; a Sufi-like mystical fixation on fire and mortality; the calling into question of the validity of the entire work in which the poem-letter is inserted:

Ya me curé de la literatura.
Estas cosas no hay cómo contarlas.
Estoy piojoso y eso es lo de menos.
De nada sirven las palabras.

(El soldado desconocido 71)

(I'm cured of literature. / There's no way to tell of these things. / I'm covered with lice, and that's the least of it. / Words aren't good for anything.)

Nevertheless, in a postscript to his "Ultima carta" (Last letter), the book's final poem, the poet leaves the reader with an incredibly optimistic prophecy of the literary and artistic future of Hispanic America, as if this were his definitive response to his conflict with the English language and U.S. literature:

> P. D.—La América tropical dará al mundo los mejores poetas, los mejores pintores y los mejores santos. Como tengo que hacer de centinela no me queda tiempo para dilatarme en explicaciones. Basta una: El Sol. ¡Me voy a ver la noche hasta que salga el sol!—VALE.

> (*El soldado desconocido* 154)

> (P. S.—Tropical America will give the best poets, the best painters, and the best saints to the world. Since I'm on guard duty, I don't have time to go into any explanations. Except one: The Sun. I'm going to see the night until the sun rises! —GOODBYE.)

If one had to summarize the nature of the literary experiment that takes place in *El soldado desconocido*, one would have to mention, as Nicaraguan poet Horacio Peña does in an article on de la Selva, the cinematic quality of the mixing of different documentary genres in the work: journalistic chronicles, a diary, letters, and ballads.[44] The net effect is not one of fragmentation, but of kaleidoscopic wholeness, with a clear narrative movement from beginning to end.

Although much of the verse in *El soldado desconocido* fits well in Silkin's second stage of war-consciousness, some cursory mention of other poems in keeping with the final two phases of Silkin's critical model would be fruitful. In the third stage, says Silkin, the combatant advances from anger and description into compassion. Taken as a whole, the poetry of Wilfred Owen is probably the most representative of this category, especially in a poem such as "Insensibility," in which the irony of lines such as "Happy are men who yet before they are killed / Can let their veins run cold" is hauntingly reminiscent of Rubén Darío's "Lo fatal" (The fatal). De la Selva is certainly a compassionate poet, but his compassion is more clearly linked to Silkin's final stage of war-consciousness, which is characterized by an intelligent merging of observation, rage and compassion in order to create an active desire for *change*. In this stage, a particular psychological state of being erases hatred and the very conception of "enemy." In de la Selva's "Curiosidad" (Curiosity), there is a puerile attraction on the part of the poem's speaker to the person who is supposed to be the target for the speaker's bullets. The narrator concludes: "Lejos de tenerle odio, / como que voy queriendo a mi enemigo" (Instead of hating him, / it's as if I'm beginning to love my enemy). In a similar way, the poet constructs a common cultural ground seemingly in the middle of no man's land when he says in "Prisioneros" (Prisoners) that at least one of the German P.O.W.s must have read "a Goethe; o será de la familia de Beethoven / o de Kant; o sabrá tocar el violoncelo" (Goethe; or be a member of Beethoven's family / or Kant's; or maybe he knows how to play the violoncello).

In the introduction to *El soldado desconocido*, written in New York in 1921, de la Selva also demonstrates a new kind of compassion for his fellow fighting comrades who have suffered the exploitation of the war's aftermath in an imperialist country. The poet's empathy has been hardened by his unequivocal political convictions. The typical veteran from the United States, according to de la Selva, is an "instinctive imperialist who hates other empires, which explains why he came to hate Germany so much and which augurs a future war with England or Japan." Furthermore, continues the Nicaraguan poet, the U.S. veterans to whom he refers are similar to the veterans of the other nations: "Deep down, the masses are the same everywhere."[45] The enemy of the First World War has been replaced by the greater enemy of imperialism. What bothers de la Selva deeply is the exploitative countries' dehumanization of *all* the people who fought in the war. The poet considers himself one of the anonymous, unknown soldiers "de carne y hueso, humano y muy humano" (of flesh and blood, human and very human)[46] to whom he dedicates his first book of verse in Spanish.

6

Translation and Intertextuality in the Poetry of José Coronel Urtecho

José Coronel Urtecho, the major poet, essayist, and translator was born in Nicaragua in 1906. Coronel was instrumental in revivifying Nicaraguan poetry, which, during the first several decades of the 1900s, had stagnated as a result of the proliferation of the unskilled imitators of Rubén Darío's *modernista* verse. This achievement depended a great deal on Coronel's obsessive, conflictive, and ambivalent dialogue with the literature and civilization of North America. In 1927, when Coronel returned to Granada, Nicaragua, after having spent three years in San Francisco, California, he brought with him poetry in English by Eliot, Pound, Moore, Sandburg, and many others published in magazines such as *The Dial* and *Poetry*. Along with Luis Alberto Cabrales (who had recently returned from France), Coronel founded the iconoclastic Nicaraguan literary group known as the *movimiento de vanguardia* (Vanguard movement) in the late 1920s and '30s. To a large extent, this literary project relied on translation as a means of creating its own linguistic and thematic innovations.

It may be true, as Nicaraguan critic Jorge Eduardo Arellano has suggested, that initially Coronel was "the poet of the protectorate,"[1] and that his primary goal as a translator was the transplanting of North American culture, which Coronel considered a "superior" civilization. Historically, the consolidation of Coronel's project coincided with the beginning of the Somoza dynasty, which continued Nicaragua's total subjugation to the political will of the United States. For some of the same reasons that attracted Pound to Mussolini and fascism in Europe, Coronel felt that what Nicaragua needed was a "healthy" dictatorship. Therefore, Coronel and other members of the *movimiento de vanguardia* signed a manifesto supporting the person who was at that time the young head of the army—Anastasio Somoza—in order to take power with him and thereby realize their cultural and political ideals.[2] Critic and novelist Sergio Ramírez describes the emergence of the *vanguardistas*, led by Coronel and supported by other youths from families that had consolidated their power "like an oligarchy," as a nationalistic, corporativist phenomenon that rebelled against the commercial spirit and bad taste of Nicaragua's bourgeoisie.[3] But perhaps the most important historical fact, in terms of Coronel's relationship with North American culture, is that this dialogue begins precisely during the years of Nicaragua's occupation by U.S. troops.

Nevertheless, Coronel gradually discovered that poetry in the United States tended to condemn certain negative qualities of U.S. culture. As a result, Coronel incorporated aspects of the poetry he translated into his own poetry in order to create a *Nicaraguan* way of understanding the world by means of the written word and, equally as important, of opposing the political and cultural domination of Hispanic America by the United States.

As a point of departure, we will consider Coronel, the author of two important anthologies of North American poetry,[4] as a translator seeking a substitute for a European cultural model in the visionary definition of the American continent that he discovers in poetry by Whitman and Sandburg. In translating the work of these and other poets into Spanish, Coronel recapitulates Pound's general approach to translation as a way of renewing language. We will also discuss in this first section three poems by Marianne Moore, Ezra Pound, and T. S. Eliot that Coronel translates and includes in his own book of selected poems as cultural and political manifestos that provide a concomitant definition of his own *ars poetica*. We will conclude with an analytical comparison of Coronel's poem "Paneles de Infierno" (Panels of hell) and "The Hill" (the first poem in Edgar Lee Masters' *Spoon River Anthology*) as an example of what is perhaps the culmination of Coronel's combative intertextual relationship with poetry from the United States in that Coronel makes use of the rhetorical structure of a quintessentially American poem by Masters to describe the Sandinistas' defeat of imperialism in Nicaragua.

The Translation as Poetic Manifesto

In his introduction to *Panorama y antología de la poesía norteamericana* (Panorama and anthology of North American poetry), published in 1949, Coronel summarizes the purpose of the anthology as one of "liberation from the European and adaptation to the American medium."[5] Coronel, although he seems to propose the anthology as a model or "guía" (guide), also recognizes the danger of exchanging European culture for the poetic expression of the United States, cautioning against an "excessive attachment."[6] Nevertheless, Coronel's initial enthusiasm toward North American poetry seems limitless. Walt Whitman and Carl Sandburg are the two poets who thoroughly captured Coronel's imagination as anthologist and translator. In his rejection of the European paradigm, Coronel discovers in Whitman nothing less than the creator of a continent, a true poet of the New World:

> Whitman, . . . the most "American" of the North American poets, perhaps the only poet who is 100% "American," inconceivable outside his country, is, nevertheless, simple and totally translatable. . . . I discovered Whitman's poetry in translations by Amado Nervo, and my impression was that of the sudden discovery of an unsuspected, marvelously new world with infinite possibilities and prodigious energies, full of life and happiness, youth and hope. . . . I imagined him as the bard of a continent, creating with the potency of his songs all the things confused in the heart of chaos, naming them, and shaping the new cosmos. In my moments of exaltation, I thought Walt Whitman was the creator of America.[7]

For Coronel, Sandburg is a natural extension of Whitman's realistic, libertarian, and multitudinous poetry. In addition, Sandburg's multiple proletarian professions manifested in his poetry make him a perfect reflection of life in the United States.[8] In his 1949 anthology, Coronel chooses nine poems by Sandburg, making him one of the most fully-represented poets. In *Antología de la poesía norteamericana* (Anthology of North American poetry), published in 1963, Coronel and co-translator Ernesto Cardenal include no fewer than thirty-one poems by Sandburg, a clear indication of how highly they regard Sandburg's verse. As a point of comparison, the editors of a standard compilation in the United States, *The Norton Anthology of Poetry*, select a mere two poems by Sandburg, including the obligatory "Chicago."[9] Perhaps what Coronel finds so appealing in a poem such as "Chicago" is its robust, direct, and emotional realism. Sandburg's poems praise but also unflinchingly indict "the American way of life." In explaining why Sandburg is his "favorite among the poets of the new poetry," Coronel declares that Sandburg offers a particularly valuable vision of the United States: "Not the ideal United States, or the spectacular United States, but the everyday United States."[10] For Coronel, then, the English and the Spanish idioms, transferred from Europe and subsequently transformed, are united in a fundamental way as the principal languages of the New World. Coronel assimilates Whitman's Adamic idealism and sense of rhythm as well as Sandburg's social realism.

Whitman and Sandburg may be Coronel's preferred "windows" on American life, but the great tower from which vistas of the entire world seem possible is Ezra Pound.[11] Perhaps Pound's most invaluable legacy to Coronel the translator is an understanding of how the translated word is capable of transforming the translator's own language. Translation is not simply a matter of gaining access to relatively unknown literatures (for example, Pound's translations from the Chinese, Latin, Anglo-Saxon, Provençal, Italian, and French). Literary translation may entail, at its controversial best, an experimental, transformative assault on the idiom into which the translator is working.[12] Throughout his literary essays, Pound develops the idea that great periods in the literature of a particular language are preceded by periods of translation in which literatures of other cultures and times become available in that language. According to Pound, perhaps the greatest translator-activist of this century, literature flourishes only when there is a free exchange between different cultures. Coronel is convinced that Pound's appearance was a vital necessity and occurred "at a time when North American poetry might possibly have disappeared or turned toward primitive, coarse forms."[13] According to Christoph de Nagy, Pound believes that change by means of translation should be "conditioned by more than a beneficial enthusiasm for a foreign literary work or period—it ought in fact to be guided and accelerated by those wishing to see a revival in the stagnating literature."[14] For Pound, this renewal, or renaissance, must be built by means of a systematic program of what he defines as conscious propaganda. Underlying Pound's translation project is something that Octavio Paz has called "a moral urge, a didactic impulse."[15] In other words, translation for Pound (as well as for Coronel) becomes a means to a greater end.

What was the intent of Coronel's didacticism? As we stated at the beginning of this chapter, Nicaraguan literature in the first three decades of the twentieth century was trapped in an empty, aristocratic admiration of Rubén Darío's *modernista* verse. Coronel himself was the author of what might be called the *vanguardia*'s banner against the falsifiers of Darío. In the legendary "Oda a Rubén Darío" (Ode to Rubén Darío), Coronel addresses the great Nicaraguan poet, saying, "soy el asesino de tus retratos" (I am the assassin of your portraits). Coronel satirizes Darío's "vestido de emperador" (emperor's clothes) as well as the poet's unrealistic preoccupation with the Classics: "enseñaste a criar centauros / a los ganaderos de las Pampas" (you taught the ranchers of the Pampa / how to breed centaurs). In many ways, "Oda a Rubén Darío " is a Nicaraguan version of Pound's early poem "A Pact" (*Selected Poems* 27), in which Pound recognizes, rejects, then makes a truce with Walt Whitman ("We have one sap and one root"). Nicaraguan critic Horacio Peña points out that "the two poems reveal the same attitude: a rebellion against the past and the acceptance of the necessity of that past."[16] Coronel's poem, less bitter and more humorous than Pound's, ends with a final iconoclastic liquidation of the modernist legacy in Nicaragua (a stance that the *vanguardistas* would later come to realize as exaggerated and misguided).

The strange, musical title of Coronel's first collection of poetry and translations *Pol-la d'ananta katanta paranta* is taken from Homer (*Iliad* 23, 116), and means, in Richmond Lattimore's translation, "They went

many ways, uphill, downhill, sidehill and slantwise."[17] The title is
especially appropriate given the many different literary directions
embraced in this book assembled by Jorge Eduardo Arellano in 1970 and
published by Nicaraguan poet Ernesto Gutiérrez. The book contains
selections from all the phases of Coronel's poetic production through the
1960s, and is composed of eleven sections, three of which include
translations. The majority of these translations are of North American
poets.

The Spanish versions by Coronel of Marianne Moore's "Poetry," Ezra
Pound's "Canto XLV," and T. S. Eliot's "Triumphal March" occupy a
central position in Coronel's own conception of the "new poetry" he
hoped would shake Nicaraguan verse from its doldrums. In the context of
Pol-la d'ananta katanta paranta, Coronel's translations become poems
by and about Coronel as a creator of poetry. If one were to define
Coronel's theoretical approach to the translation of specific poems, one
would necessarily distinguish him from Ortega y Gasset and the idea that
translation is an "impossible transubstantiation."[18] Nor does Coronel
share what might be termed the negative criticism of deletion of a
translator such as Pound, who considered the inviolability of the original
text subservient to his overall intent as a translator, especially in his
version of *Homage to Sextus Propertius*, in which Pound simply excised
in his translation a substantial amount of historical and mythological
material that he deemed unnecessary or superfluous. Although the
subtitle of Coronel's first collection of verse is "Imitaciones y
Traducciones" (Imitations and translations), one should not mistakenly
identify Coronel's approach to translation with that of his contemporary,
Robert Lowell, author of the controversial book *Imitations*, in which the
licenses of the poet-translator clearly transgress ethical norms with
regard to a basic respect the integrity of an original text. As an important
positive comparison, the idea of using the power of the word as a lawyer
might in order to achieve a certain outcome links Coronel's strategy as a
translator to that of Kenneth Rexroth. Rexroth believes that only a deep,
imaginative identification with the original text will enable the translator
to speak "with the veridical force of his own utterance, conscious of
communicating directly to his own audience."[19]

For Coronel, each translation is, at the same time, an act of criticism
not only in redaction, but in selection. The translations form an essential
component of Coronel's development as a poet. According to Carlos
Rafael Duverrán, Coronel's poetry and translations maintain a kind of
symbiotic relationship:

> Coronel's poetry is composed of two parallel sources: original poetry and
> translated poetry. Among both forms of creation (the created and the re-
> created), there is a secret thread that leads to the most intimate part . . . of the
> imaginative structure of his oeuvre.[20]

If his translations manage to remain very lively poems in Spanish, it is perhaps due to an idea that Coronel expresses in an interview: "I don't think the translator is always a traitor as the Italian saying goes, but, sometimes, a co-author in another language, in another medium, another situation."[21] When Coronel's translations appear in book form interspersed with his own poetry, they become integral parts of the author's *ars poetica*.

Pol-la d'ananta katanta paranta opens with the translation of Moore's "Poetry," a text that sets the tone of almost the entire book. One might consider the placement of the imported, appropriated text symptomatic of a cultural prioritization, a certain contempt for Nicaragua's national production of poetry. Coronel, in keeping with his purely literary approach to North American culture, defines the ambivalence that this value judgement produces in him as an individual in his 1962 essay "El americanismo en la casa de mi abuelo" (Americanism in my grandfather's house):

> I am not embarrassed to confess that I like North American literature better than that of our Latin America, and that, in many ways, I frankly consider it superior. The curious thing is that I do not like the United States, or at least, up until now, I have not been able to truly like North American reality, if it is not seen through its literature.[22]

Coronel has preferred to translate the thirty-eight-line 1935 version of Moore's "Poetry" rather than the earlier thirteen-line version and the later, three-line poem that appears in the poet's *Complete Poems* in 1967.[23] This poetic manifesto by Marianne Moore that Coronel has usurped is, for the *vanguardistas* who were tired of alexandrines, hendecasyllables, and a certain preciosity of language associated with Darío, a perfect antidote to the *modernismo* that the young Nicaraguan poets in the 1920s and '30s rejected:

> I, too, dislike it: there are things that are important beyond all this fiddle.
> Reading it, however, with a perfect contempt for it,
>   one discovers in
> it, after all, a place for the genuine.
>   Hands that can grasp, eyes
>   that can dilate, hair that can rise
>   if it must, these things are important not
>   because a
>
> high-sounding interpretation can be put upon them
>   but because they are
>   useful.

(Selected Poems 36)

The *vanguardistas*, however, were not rebelling against form and rhyme per se: one thinks, for example, of Coronel's innovative series of formal poems "Parques" (Parks), his "Sonetos de uso doméstico" (Sonnets for domestic use), and the satirical serial rhymes of his "poesía chinfónica" (chimphonic poetry). Rather, the writers of Nicaragua's *vanguardia* rejected a restricted thematic content for poetry as defined by the previous generation—a certain humorless, overly-solemn poetic diction and a Romantic conception of the poet as a divine, inspired being (such a poet obviously would not consider poetry with "perfect contempt"). The *vanguardistas* sought what Marianne Moore in "Poetry" calls "the raw material of poetry in / all its rawness." As Donald Hall declares in his assessment of Marianne Moore's "Poetry," "Imagination is placed in opposition to intellection. The raw material for poetry abounds, it is everywhere, is anything, but it must be imaginatively grasped."[24]

The poets of the Nicaraguan *vanguardia* transformed Darío's gardens populated with mythological creatures. For them, these metamorphosed gardens still were *literary* gardens; but, as Moore says, poets must be "literalists of / the imagination" capable of creating "imaginary gardens with real toads in them." In this redefined poetic cosmos, according to Moore (and also, of course, to her co-author in Spanish, Coronel), there is room for the "baseball fan" and "the statistician." The revolutionary quality of this manifesto consists of a redefining of acceptable themes for a poem. Hitherto "unpoetic" subjects suddenly have access to a literary world governed by a new order.

One could also link Moore's aesthetics in "Poetry" with the poetry of the *vanguardistas* in the way that their iconoclasm embraces ordinary speech and is also *moral*, a reaction against the symbolists and decadents of the nineteenth century. Donald Hall believes that an ethical sensibility underlies this new poetry in that "deliberate obfuscation is a species of immorality."[25] Stylistically, Coronel undoubtedly admired the colloquial tone in Moore's poem, a quality that he maintains in his translation. Pamela White Hadas delineates the implications of this "conversational state" in Moore's "Poetry":

> In the work of Marianne Moore we are reminded again and again that the abilities to communicate, to listen, to be interesting, to learn, and to be generally socially acceptable are moral abilities that show themselves nowhere as clearly as in one's conversation. For the poet who can say, offhand and sincerely, of poetry, "I, too, dislike it" ("Poetry"), style must aspire to the conversational state to be of use.[26]

The *vanguardistas*, in a desire to penetrate their social milieu and to challenge what they considered a pervasive false definition of poetry, wanted to be heard as much as they wanted to learn. For the sake of efficacy, Coronel's zeal for literary reform depended on a conversational style. After this definition of poetry that begins *Pol-la d'ananta katanta paranta*, Coronel introduces original poems stripped of all solemnity and decorativism such as "Oda a Rubén Darío," "Contrarrima" (Counter-rhyme), and "Obra maestra" (Masterpiece) that mark a fundamental change in Nicaraguan poetry.[27]

If the poem by Moore represents a sort of cultural manifesto for Coronel, Pound's "Canto XLV" ("With *Usura* . . .") embraces concerns of Coronel that are as sociopolitical as aesthetic. Pound's famous canto contains a sense of economics that, while curiously modern, cannot be explained entirely by Marxism or bourgeois materialism. According to Coronel, Pound is describing another era, late medieval civilization, which, to him, was a more dignified era for the creator, a healthier time for the arts, especially when compared to twentieth-century culture in the United States, which is founded on usury, greed, and the destruction of life's poetic meaning.[28] In a society dominated by commercialism, art is subservient to the whims of the supply and demand of the market, a situation at the heart of Pound's "Canto XLV":

> no picture is made to endure nor to live with
> but it is made to sell and sell quickly

(Selected Poems 136)

In *Tres conferencias a la empresa privada* (Three conferences to private enterprise), Coronel says that when culture is at the service of commerce, and commercialization assumes monopolistic characteristics, the result is a falsification and final paralysis of culture.[29]

When Coronel speaks of culture, he is referring to a totality of human values, all of which are adversely affected by commercialization. According to Lewis Hyde, Pound's poem is an explicit warning against the magnitude of the dangers of usury, particularly in a modern context:

> As with any scholastic analysis, Pound begins with the Aristotelian "usura, sin against nature" and, following the traditional natural metaphor, declares that if such "unnatural value" rules the market, all other spheres of value will decay, from human courtship and procreation, through craft, art and, finally, religion. . . . The poem may have a medieval argument, but it's a modern poem. . . . By "usury" Pound usually means an exorbitant rent on the loan of money; other times he simply means any "charge for the use of purchasing power." But Pound also connects usury to the life of the imagination . . .[30]

These ideas are crucial to an understanding of Coronel's relationship with North American literature—if one accepts, as Coronel does, that the majority of North American poets oppose the decadence of human values precipitated by commercialism. Furthermore, as we shall discover in the following chapter, Pound's "Canto XLV" also illuminates the poetics of Ernesto Cardenal.

The same is also true, though for different reasons, of Eliot's two-part poem "Coriolan" (1931), whose first section is entitled "Triumphal March." Although this poem is from Eliot's *Collected Poems 1909-1935*, it is not included in either of the two anthologies of North American poetry (published in 1949 and 1963) prepared by Coronel and Cardenal. "Triumphal March" may very well be a later discovery of the two Nicaraguan poets, corresponding to the development in the 1950s of what has come to be known as "la poesía exteriorista" (exteriorist poetry), an evolving concept we will define in greater depth in the next chapter.

Why would Coronel include in *Pol-la d'ananta katanta paranta* his own translation[31] of a single, relatively unknown poem by Eliot, when he had translated famous pieces such as "The Love Song of J. Alfred Prufrock" and "The Hollow Men"? One obvious possibility is the poem's enumerative precision in a particular section that is an imaginary inventory of what is perhaps a post-World War I European victory march syncretically linked to an imperial Roman celebration ("And so many eagles."; "And now they go up to the temple."):

> 5,800,000 rifles and carabines,
> 102,000 machine guns,
> 28,000 trench mortars

(Complete Poems and Plays 1909-1950 85)

In this fragment from Eliot's poem, the characteristic realism of North American poetry takes on an entirely different, super-objective, reportorial authenticity. Perhaps this poem, in a succinct way, is a definition of the objectification of reality that played such an important role in Cardenal's formulation of exteriorist poetry and Coronel's own experiments with exteriorism in poems from the early 1960s such as "Ciudad Quesada," a portrait of a city in northern Costa Rica near the farm where Coronel makes his home:

> 40.000 habitantes en 1961
> 8.000 km2 de extensión del Cantón
> 4.500 m.m. de precipitación pluvial por año,

(Pol-la d'ananta 159)

(40,000 inhabitants in 1961 / 8,000 sq. km. of the region / 4,500 mm of annual rainfall)

The poem continues its present-day inventory (which resembles Eliot's poem even in the typographical presentation of the statistics) in this manner for several pages. It then immerses the reader in an historical account of the founding of the city that includes the names of the individual members of the lineage. The poem concludes with lists of the flora and fauna that one encounters in the area around Ciudad Quesada. This collage of factual data and history in verse form has become a distinguishing feature of Nicaraguan poetry from the 1960s to the present.

Another factor that would call Coronel's attention to Eliot's poem is the clear contrast it provides between the new American poetry and the well-known, quintessentially *modernista* poem by Darío entitled "Marcha triunfal." Darío's poem, written in 1895, is an excellent example of the vibrant rhythmic innovations of the *modernistas*:

> ¡Ya viene el cortejo! Ya se oyen los claros clarines.
> ¡La espada se anuncia con vivo reflejo;
> ya viene, oro y hierro, el cortejo de los paladines!

> (*Antología poética* 79)

(Here comes the cortege! You can already hear the clear call of the bugles. / The sword is announced with vivid reflection; / gold and iron, here comes the paladins' cortege!)

Coronel uses Eliot's realistic antiwar poem in translation as yet another way to subvert the overblown rhetoric and the idealized themes of the *modernistas*.

A similar attempt to use Darío's poem as a point of contrast is an early poem by Cardenal, also entitled "Marcha triunfal," in which the poet rewrites Darío's diction in order to satirize Nicaragua's dictator more effectively:

> ya viene el General
> montado en su caballo blanco, rodeado
> de guardias y guardaespaldas y diputados y putas
> picadas

> (*Antología* 43)

(Here comes the General / riding his white horse, surrounded / by soldiers and bodyguards and congressmen and drunk whores)

Paneles de infierno: Intertextuality as Literary Weapon

Perhaps the most interesting example of Coronel's politicized verse is *Paneles de infierno* (Panels of hell), a book-length poem written in February 1980, some six months after the revolution that ended the Somoza dictatorship. Each long section of this poem begins with a question concerning the whereabouts of those who have exploited Nicaragua over the centuries: the Spanish conquistadors, William Walker, and the Somoza dynasty, which, as Coronel points out in *Paneles de infierno*, was "sustained for fifty years by Yankee imperialism." The answer to each similarly-phrased question is a variation on a refrain: "Todos están hundidos en el estercolero de la Historia" (They are all buried in the dunghill of History); "Todos ellos están en el fondo de las letrinas de la Historia" (They are all at the bottom of the latrines of History); "Todos todos están en el infierno de la Historia" (All all are in the hell of History).

This rhetorical structure (a series of questions answered with a refrain) which serves as the ordering principle in Coronel's poem, is a Nicaraguan rewriting of "The Hill," the first poem in Edgar Lee Masters' *Spoon River Anthology* which serves as an introduction to the dead narrators who will speak of their lives. "The Hill" is the only poem in Masters' *Anthology* not related by an individual in a first person voice. The speaker in "The Hill," translated by Coronel as "La colina del cementerio" (The cemetery hill) and published in both the 1949 and 1963 anthologies of North American poetry compiled by Coronel and Cardenal, assumes the role of the omniscient narrator observing and listening in the graveyard on the hill:

> ¿Dónde están el Tío Isaac y la Tía Emily,
> y el viejo Towny Kincaid y Sevigne Houghton,
> y el Mayor Walker que había hablado
> con venerables hombres de la Revolución?
> Todos, todos están durmiendo en la colina.
>
> A ellos les trajeron hijos muertos de la guerra,
> e hijas destrozadas por la vida,
> y sus chiquillos huérfanos, llorando.
> Todos, todos están durmiendo, durmiendo, durmiendo
>   en la colina.[32]

(Panorama y antología 168)

> Where are Uncle Isaac and Aunt Emily,
> And old Towny Kincaid and Sevigne Houghton,
> And Major Walker who had talked

With venerable men of the revolution?—
All, all, are sleeping on the hill.

They brought them dead sons from the war,
And daughters whom life had crushed,
And their children fatherless, crying—
All, all are sleeping, sleeping, sleeping on the hill

Is it possible that the initial impetus for using Masters' poem as a counterpoint for *Paneles de infierno* was suggested to Coronel by a rapid reading of words in his translation of "The Hill" that might be freely associated with the series of conflicts in Nicaraguan history: "Walker," "Revolución" (Revolution), "hijos muertos de la guerra" (sons killed in the war)? In any case, it is the refrain, "Todos, todos están durmiendo en la colina" (All, all are sleeping on the hill), that joins "The Hill" and *Paneles de infierno* in literature's intertextual continuum.

In Coronel's ongoing dialogue with North American literature, it is the voice of Masters that emerges from the mass of poets translated by Coronel for fifty years. "If the United States is our good neighbor, as Franklin D. Roosevelt would have it, the truth is that our best neighbors, our allies, are the North American poets,"[33] affirmed Coronel in the early 1960s. The type of intertextuality that manifests itself in *Paneles de infierno* produces a literary work that is intimately linked to what Coronel considers the best as well as the worst aspects of North American culture.

The series of 244 epitaphs in *Spoon River Anthology*, published in 1915, is a polemical, realistic, narrative, and psychological portrait of life in America that deals frankly with certain moral issues such as human sexuality, violence, and the failure of social justice.[34] For Coronel, Masters' book is a collection of frustrated ideals and dreams:

[Masters] accomplished one the most finished creations of North American realist poetry. In an ambience reduced to a monotonous, petty local level in which aspirations and generous ideals are frustrated in a pathetic way, he succeeds in giving life and universal meaning to an entire human community, just as it exists in reality, with no pseudoromantic idealization and false sentimentality.[35]

Paneles de infierno, like *Spoon River Anthology*, represents an example of the collapse of the mechanism that ensures justice in a particular society. Coronel's poem, in its recounting of the atrocities inflicted on Nicaragua by the United States beginning with the nineteenth-century Tennessee adventurer William Walker, is also a cultural revolt against extreme immorality:

¿Qué fue del frío filibustero paranoico robador de
    paises
el malaventurado aventurero de Tennessee . . .
el primer norteamericano que vio a Nicaragua
    el país el gobierno la tierra como negocio
    subsidiario de los negocios norteamericanos . . .
el primer norteamericano incendiario destruc-
    tor de ciudades nicaragüenses que las
    hubiera reducido todas a cenizas y dejado en
    escombros y sembrado la tierra de cruces de
    madera y cementerios desparramados y fosas
    comunes hasta entregarla desocupada a sus
    filibusteros esclavistas pero no pudo con la
    resistencia del pueblo de Nicaragua Costa
    Rica Honduras El Salvador y Guatemala

(*Paneles de infierno*, n.p.)

(Whatever happened to the cold paranoid filibuster stealer of countries / the unfortunate adventurer from Tennessee . . . / the first North American who saw Nicaragua the country the government the land as a business subsidiary of North American business . . . / the first incendiary North American destroyer of Nicaraguan cities that he would have reduced entirely to ash and left in ruins and planted the earth with wooden crosses and scattered cemeteries and mass graves and then handed it over to his filibuster slavers if it had not been for the resistance of the people of Nicaragua Costa Rica Honduras El Salvador and Guatemala?)

Too, Coronel's poem embodies many of the qualities of North American poetry that we have discussed previously in this chapter: Whitman's enumerative style, Sandburg's vituperative realism, the precise figures of war in Eliot's poem, and, especially Pound's money theories:

la banca legal oficial multinacional la de la banca convencional de Wall Street y los otros banqueros financieros usureros extranjeros del banco tradicional particular de la Empresa Privada la del banco fundado decía el fundador del Banco de Londres dice Pound "para sacar dinero de la nada" *to make money out of nothing*

(*Paneles de infierno*, n.p.)

(the legal official multinational bank the conventional bank of Wall Street and the other foreign bankers financiers usurers from the traditional private bank of Private Enterprise the banks founded according to the founder of the Bank of London says Pound "to make money out of nothing")

For Coronel, as we have seen throughout this chapter, the translation of North American poetry has meant a lifelong engagement with intertextuality. According to José Miguel Oviedo, Coronel "always copies, imitates, translates, smuggles the work of others into his own work: his profound originality consists of starting a dialogue with a context of texts."[36] Translation has been indispensable for Coronel in terms of his ambivalent relationship with the United States, a country with a compellingly attractive literature on the one hand and, on the other, a repulsive non-literary culture paralyzed by commercialism, mechanization, and dehumanization. The *vanguardistas*, then, had a specific mission that they hoped to accomplish, at least in part, through translation. One might say that the writers of Nicaragua's *vanguardia*, collectively translating works of literature, were a sort of minature version of the School of Translators of Toledo in thirteenth-century Spain,[37] with Coronel assuming the role of King Alfonso X, *el Sabio* (the wise). Coronel hoped to redirect and to change the course of the literature of his country by bringing into Spanish important works from other languages. By transforming his translations into emblems defining his own poetics, Coronel also used literary translation as a didactic method that would have a lasting impact on many Nicaraguan writers of later generations, especially Ernesto Cardenal.

7

Ernesto Cardenal and North American Literature: The Formulation of an Ethical Identity

Nicaraguan Ernesto Cardenal, born in 1925, is certainly one of the world's most widely-known contemporary poets. Intertextuality, the process by which a particular text establishes its (co)existence as a rewritten version of other texts, is an important determinant not only in the evolution of Cardenal as a poet, but in his continued widespread appeal to a culturally and linguistically diverse readership. One thinks, for example, of the symbiotic relationship that exists between the Book of Psalms and Cardenal's *Salmos* (Psalms), a recreation of a biblical text that becomes the vehicle for expressing the afflictions of the contemporary world. Too, there is the well-known correlation between Cardenal's *Epigramas* (Epigrams) (a work unique for its ingenuous, transparent union of amorous and political themes) and the poet's work as a translator of the Greek Anthology and the poetry of Catullus and Martial. In this chapter, we will discuss some of the ways that Cardenal's intertextual engagement with certain works of North American literature enables him to formulate a personal and collective ethical identity. The study will begin with a comparative analysis of historical figures that appear in works by Cardenal: Archibald MacLeish, William Carlos Williams, and Ezra Pound. We hope to demonstrate that these literary portraits, often in the form of the "persona" poem, are the basis for Cardenal's development of a definition of social and moral responsibility. The second section of the chapter will treat Cardenal's work with "primitive" poetry of the Amerindian culture (investigations that Cardenal began after leaving the Trappist monastery where Thomas Merton had been his Novice Master) and how this aspect of indigenous North America leads him to postulate a "new" ethics based on spirituality, antimaterialism, and agrarianism. Together, the two sections, in their more or less chronological approach to Cardenal's poetry, will examine the progression of certain rules of conduct (as expressed by means of the poetic word) governing local and global actions.

Ethics and the Literary Historical Figure

One of Cardenal's earliest poems, "Proclama del conquistador" (Announcement of the conquistador), written while the poet was in Mexico in 1946, is a clear indication of Cardenal's interest in historical themes as a point of departure for a literary work. This poem marks the beginning of what will develop into the principle concern of Cardenal that is both temporal and ethical: how does one utilize the past in a contemporary manner in order to create a moral platform for the prophetic?[1]

"Proclama del conquistador" undoubtedly receives its impetus, its theme, as well as certain aspects of its dramatic structure from the Pulitzer prizewinning, book-length series of poems entitled *Conquistador* (1932) by Archibald MacLeish. In the poems by MacLeish and Cardenal, the poets adopt a mask, a "persona," which enables them to speak in the first person as if they were the historical figure himself, a conquistador, resurrected from the dead. Later in this initial section, we will discuss the persona poem as it manifests itself in the poetry of Ezra Pound as well as its origins in the dramatic monologues of nineteenth-century poet Robert Browning. We will discover that Cardenal's early poems, with their objectively presented characters, whose personalities are less closely related to the poet's own, may have more in common with Browning than with Pound. The fundamental difference between subsequent experiments with this poetic technique by William Carlos Williams and Archibald MacLeish (even though they proceed from and are related to the transformation of Browning in Pound) has to do with historical perspective. Pound's cast of personae is predominantly European and Chinese, whereas MacLeish and Williams (especially in *In the American Grain*) select masks of figures prominent in the historical formation of the American continent. Similarly, in terms of the early poetry of Cardenal, "Proclama del conquistador" is Cardenal's attempt to extract poetry from a particular period of continental *American* history, an effort that clearly resembles MacLeish's, especially since the work of Bernal Díaz del Castillo is a primary source for both authors.[2]

In addition to the obvious thematic and technical resemblance between two poems that consist of a conquistador's monologue, there are also structural and tonal similarities. Cardenal's poem opens with the dramatic lakeside meeting of the conquistador and his troops with the indigenous prince and his entourage:

> Después de los terribles bosques cruzados con teas
>   encendidas . . .
> veremos junto a un lago violeta la casa del príncipe,

> y él, rodeado de sabios bajo una ceiba solemne,
> en la quietud de la tarde oirá el nombre de mi rey.

(*Nueva poesía nicaragüense* 443)

(After the terrible forests crossed with burning torches . . . / next to a violet lake, we will see the prince's house, / and he, surrounded by wise advisors beneath a solemn ceiba tree, / in the quiet evening, will hear the name of my king.)

A similar, though ultimately more hostile, encounter (between Cortés and Moctezuma) occurs in the eleventh book of Macleish's poem:

> And we marched down by the torches in dark way:
> And we found him under the garden trees and his
>   shoulders
> Shone in the torchlight in the leafy rain

(*Collected Poems* 243-44)

The speakers in both poems maintain a lofty, "unnatural" diction that Cardenal, as we shall soon discuss in greater depth, rejects in later poems. MacLeish's *Conquistador* seems to have given Cardenal a satisfying means of expressing historical drama in a first person voice, although Cardenal's conquistador (more a symbol than an actual human being) lacks a clearly-defined personality. Less satisfactory, however, is the conquistador's voice itself, which is reminiscent of the sensual abundance of Neruda's initial efforts as a writer.[3] Through MacLeish, Cardenal discovers an appropriate speaker (an historical figure linked to the history of the American continent) but not a suitable poetic voice.

MacLeish also reveals to Cardenal, especially in the tenth book of *Conquistador*, a spirit of eros that ultimately links history and the male desire to possess and to subjugate:

> And the girls they gave us for love with the scented
>   hair:
> The green light through the leaves: the slow awakening:
> How there were many and small birds in the air then. . . .
>
> We were like those that in their lands they say
> The steers of the sun went up through the wave-lit
>   orchards
> Shaking the water drops and those gold naked
>
> Girls before them at their dripping horns!
> And they ate the sea-doused figs with the salt taste:

And all their time was of kine and of sea and of
    morning:

So did we lie in that land in the long days:

(Collected Poems 235)

Cardenal's conquistador is a pretext to describe an exotic jungle
landscape with a sensuality that overflows into eroticism at the end of the
poem when the conquistador celebrates his new alliance by possessing
one of the daughters of the indigenous prince:

> Suenan flautas afuera, y tú, desnuda, brillas como
>   piedra de sacrificio,
> mientras sube el incienso negro de tu pelo, humareda de
>   los ídolos,
> y el olor de maderas resinosas de tus brazos que se
>   queman.
> Suenan flautas afuera, y tú me sabes a cacao y almíbar,
> y muchas avispas tengo que quitar en tu carne que gotea,
> tu carne que brota una leche alaste como los árboles
>   cuando se besa,
> y exhala la misma fiebre deliciosa de las flores
>   acuáticas.
> Y tomaré posesión de esta tierra jovial y disoluta,
> a la hora en que cante la luminosa oropéndula del alba,
> si antes al último sueño no lo estrangula la selva,
> si antes al último cuerpo no lo disipa la muerte.

(Nueva poesía nicaragüense 449-50)

(Flutes are playing outside, and you, naked, shine like a sacrificial stone, /
while the black incense of your hair rises, smoke-cloud of the idols, / and
your burning arms with their smell of resinous woods. / Flutes are playing
outside, and you taste like cocoa and sugar syrup, / and I have to pluck many
wasps from your dripping flesh, / your flesh from which sprouts a kind of
milk like the trees when someone kisses / and exhales the same delicious
fever of aquatic flowers. / And I will take possession of this jovial and
dissolute land, / when the luminous oriole of the dawn sings, / if the last
dream isn't strangled by the jungle, / if the last body isn't dissipated by
death.)

While "Proclama del conquistador" is certainly indicative of the
historical themes of future poems by Cardenal, perhaps the most striking
feature of this early work is the poet's inability to reveal the
psychological motivations of his character. This produces an absence of
an ethical framework in which the historical figure's actions may be

judged by the reader. At best, the reader is content with the description of an amicable meeting of two superficial racial types. At worst, however, the reader might believe that the poet, excessively identifying himself with the erotic movement of the poem's conclusion (curiously, it is the land that is "dissolute"), condones the cultural destruction wrought by the arrival of the Spaniards in the New World.

In the next series of historical poems undertaken by Cardenal in 1949, the poet appears to have discovered a plainer, less ornate system of linguistic expression than the one he uses in "Proclama del conquistador." "Raleigh," "Las mujeres nos quedaban mirando" (The women kept staring at us), "Omagua," and "John Roach, marinero" (John Roach, sailor), are the first examples of Cardenal's mature voice. Cardenal wrote them after studying new North American poetry at Columbia University in New York with writers such as Lionel Trilling, Karl Van Doren, and Babette Deutsch, from 1947-49, years that represents perhaps the most rapid period of evolution in Cardenal's career.[4] Paul W. Borgeson, Jr. asserts that Cardenal's experiments with a poetic language that is principally Poundian, combined with Nicaragua's formidable poetic tradition, produced the "hybrid hemispheric aesthetics"[5] that was later given the name *exteriorismo* (exteriorism) by Cardenal's Nicaraguan mentor José Coronel Urtecho.

Cardenal's "Raleigh" is a link between the overwrought abundance of "Proclama del conquistador" and the streamlined, documentary style of "Con Walker en Nicaragua" (With Walker in Nicaragua). "Raleigh," in keeping with the exteriorist tendency to include lists of names, contains an enumerative precision:

> y al norte del Orinoco los Wiriki
> y al sur de la boca de Orinoco los Arwaca
> y más allá los Caníbales

> (*With Walker in Nicaragua* 24)

(And to the north of the Orinoco, the Wiriki / and to the south of the mouth of the Orinoco, the Arwaca / and beyond, the Cannibals)

Because the poem is transitional, the reader discovers in the same text short lines and an "imagistic" approach (in the Poundian sense) to reality that resemble Japanese verse forms such as haiku: "y el rumor de unos remos, / el roce de unas hojas en el río" (the whisper of some oars, / some leaves in the river brushing past). This sort of poetic language coexists with the more extended lines and ornate diction we discussed in "Proclama del conquistador": Y vimos la Montaña de Cristal, la vimos lejos, / levantada sobre el horizonte como una iglesia de plata / y un río caía de su cima con el clamor de mil campanas." (And we saw the

Crystal Mountain, we saw it in the distance, / rising above the horizon like a silver church, / and a river was falling from its peak with the sound of a thousand bells.) The combination of languages, while possessing an adequate descriptive strength, lacks the capacity to give moral or immoral or amoral power to the speakers of the poems. "Raleigh," like "Proclama del conquistador" and other early poems, remains on the superficial, fragmentary level of a travelogue.

For comparison, one might consider a different treatment of the same subject in the influential work by William Carlos Williams entitled *In the American Grain* which, in 1925, was Williams' first commercially-published work. Reissued in 1939 with an introduction by Horace Gregory, *In the American Grain*, with its individualized portraits from American history based on original documentary sources, may very well have been a point of departure in Cardenal's initial process of assimilating North American literature. In his autobiography, Williams says that he began structuring *In the American Grain* in 1921:

> I had begun to think of writing *In the American Grain*, a study to try to find out for myself what the land of my more or less accidental birth might signify. I had made a few preliminary studies. The plan was to try to get inside the heads of some of the American founders, or "heroes," if you will, by examining their original records. I wanted nothing to get between me and what they themselves had recorded.[6]

Williams begins his prose work with Eric the Red, based on a translation of a Norse saga and continues with a chapter about the discovery of the West Indies that is derived from Columbus's journals. Part of the intent of the book, according to Williams, was to create a variety of mimetic literary styles, or voices (some of which speak in the first person):

> Raleigh was written in what I conceived to be Elizabethan style; the Eric the Red chapter in the style of the Icelandic saga; Boone in the style of Daniel's autobiography; Franklin was in Franklin's words; and John Paul Jones I gave verbatim. Thus I tried to make each chapter not only in content but in the style itself a close study of the theme.[7]

Cardenal chooses for his reduced, small-scale portrait of Raleigh a uniformly "modern" voice in accordance with the direct, unadorned poetics of new North American poetry:

> Y entramos en abril
> cuando las reinas del Amazonas se juntan en las
>   márgenes
> y danzan desnudas y untadas de bálsamo y oro
> hasta el fin de esa luna—
> Entramos en abril

> los barcos muy lejos de nosotros anclados en el mar,
> a la ventura—
> 100 hombres con sus balsas y sus provisiones para un mes

(With Walker in Nicaragua 24)

> (And we entered in April / when the queens of the Amazonians gather on the
> banks / and dance naked and covered with balsam and gold / until the end of
> that moon— / we entered in April / the ships anchored in the sea in the
> distance, / aimlessly— / 100 men in their small crafts with their provisions
> for a month)

Williams opens his depiction of Raleigh with a swirling overview of his subject's complex and contradictory life:

> Of the pursuit of beauty and the husk that remains, perversions and mistakes,
> while the true form escapes in the wind, sing O Muse; of Raleigh, beloved
> by majesty, plunging his lust into the body of a new world—and the deaths,
> misfortunes, counter coups, which swelled back to certify that ardor with
> defeat.

(In the American Grain 59)

More successfully than Cardenal (in Cardenal's pre-"Con Walker en Nicaragua" stage), Williams presents what Horace Gregory calls American history's "signs and signatures, its backward glances and, by implication, its warnings for the future."[8] Williams, unlike Cardenal, translates and reveals this link between the temporal and the ethical in his portrait of Raleigh.

Apart from the specific subject of their respective poems, perhaps the greatest similarity between "Raleigh" and "Sir Walter Raleigh" is a quest for the female principle, a similar preoccupation of the speaker in "Proclama del conquistador." According to Reed Whittemore, one of Williams' biographers, "always the earth discovered and explored was female with the consequence that the history of the exploration of the *Nuevo Mundo* became, throughout *In the American Grain*, a history of man chasing woman."[9] Given the inherently exploitative nature of this conception, however, it would be impossible for either Williams or Cardenal to build a satisfactory ethical framework based on such a principle.

Cardenal's early poetry, though flawed, does demonstrate an ethical progression that finally matures in "Con Walker en Nicaragua" (composed in 1950), a poem that defines—negatively—a moral position. Both "Proclama del conquistador" and "Raleigh" are persona poems that are unsuccessful in portraying even a fraction of the character-depth and historical scope of "Con Walker en Nicaragua," two qualities that are prerequisites for an establishment of acceptable and unacceptable modes of conduct. A juxtaposition of two fragments from MacLeish's *Conquistador* and Cardenal's "Con Walker en Nicaragua," a poem about the U.S. adventurer William Walker who took control of Nicaragua for several years in the mid-nineteenth century, might lead the reader to believe that the persona poem structure of Cardenal's poem is derived from MacLeish's:

> I: Bernal Díaz: called del Castillo:
> Called in the time of my first fights El Galán:
>
> I here in the turn of the day in the feel of
> Darkness to come now: moving my chair with the change:
>
> (*Collected Poems* 174)

> En una cabaña solitaria en la frontera,
> yo, Clinton Rollins, sin pretensión literaria,
> me entretengo en escribir mis memorias.
> Y mis pensamientos de viejo retroceden:
>
> (*Antología* 20)

(In a solitary cabin on the frontier, / I, Clinton Rollins, with no literary pretension, / entertain myself writing my memoirs. / And my thoughts of the old days come back:)

Both MacLeish and Cardenal, however, are creating literature from testimonial documents. MacLeish identifies the major source of the events chronicled in his poem as "the account given by Bernal Díaz del Castillo, one of the Conquerors, in his *True History of the Conquest of New Spain*."[10] Despite the similarity between these fragments by MacLeish and Cardenal, Jonathan Cohen has identified Cardenal's historical source as a serialized memoir by Clinton Rollins entitled "Filibustering with Walker: Reminiscences of Wild Days on the Pacific Coast," originally published in the *San Francisco Chronicle* in 1909-10. A translation of the piece was completed by a Nicaraguan, Guillermo Figueroa, and appeared in print in Managua in 1945.[11] The point is that MacLeish and Cardenal (and, as we said, Williams, too) have defined an *ars poetica* that entails consulting original sources and then artistically manipulating these sources to fictionalize history and thereby create works of literature. One could say that, in this particular comparison, the intertextuality between both poetic texts and their respective historical sources is reinforced by the intertextual correspondences between the two, similarly-generated poetic texts. Cardenal's use of the "foreign" text in his poetry, according to Pablo Antonio Cuadra, is a balance between the lyrical intimacy and/or epic vastness derived from the prose of the historian or the traveler.[12]

In Cardenal's "Con Walker en Nicaragua" (and even more so in "Hora 0"), there exists an area in which the self and the other overlap, a sort of ontological no man's land. Margaret Glynne Lloyd, in a statement concerning Williams' *In the American Grain*, defines what she calls "personal mythology," a concept that also applies to Cardenal's more mature historical poetry:

> In *In the American Grain* Williams reevaluates and recreates various myths of American history; yet it is significant that he deals primarily with episodes and characters which relate to his own interior tensions or with which he can particularly empathize or mold to his own purposes. Therefore, we are justified in speaking of Williams' "personal mythology." By "personal mythology" we are referring to the personal extension of a myth to such a degree that the interpretation becomes more important than the myth itself, as well as the conferring of mythical status on to personal elements by attaching these to ready-made myths.[13]

By adopting the sympathetic viewpoint of one of Walker's soldiers, Clinton Rollins, Cardenal transforms into literature the "tensions" of the crucial episode of Nicaraguan history that he has assimilated in a way that is deeply personal, given the fact that his family is from Granada, the city destroyed by Walker.[14] The poet submerges himself in the persona of Clinton Rollins and allows the filibusters to describe and, finally, to condemn themselves:

> Vi por primera vez a Walker en San Francisco:
> recuerdo como si lo viera su rostro rubio como el de un tigre;
> sus ojos grises, sin pupilas, fijos como los de un
>   ciego,
> pero que se dilataban y se encendían como pólvora en los
>   combates,
> y su piel de pecas borrosas, su palidez, sus modales de
>   clérigo,
> su voz, descolorida como sus ojos, fría y afilada,
> en una boca sin labios.
> Y la voz de una mujer no era más suave que la suya:
> la de los serenos anuncios de las sentencias de
>   muerte . . .
> La que arrastró a tantos a la boca de la muerte en los
>   combates.
> Nunca bebía ni fumaba y no llevaba uniforme.

Ninguno fue su amigo.
Y no recuerdo haberlo visto jamás sonreír.

(*Antología* 22-23)

(I saw Walker for the first time in San Francisco: / I remember as if I were seeing his face as fair as a tiger's; / his gray eyes, without pupils, staring like a blind man's, / but dilating and exploding like gunpowder in battle, / and his skin with faint freckles, his paleness, his clergyman's mannerisms, / his voice, colorless as his eyes, cold and sharp, / in a mouth without lips. / And a woman's voice was no softer than his: / the one that serenely announced the death sentences . . . / the one that dragged so many to the mouth of death in battle. / He never drank or smoke or wore a uniform. / No one was his friend. / And I never remember seeing him smile.)

This simple, though penetrating, portrait of Walker, together with the complete scope of the poem's vividly "recalled" historical presentation, succeed in creating a negative definition of ethics. Because of the poem's aura of journalistic objectivity, ostensibly presented by a witness other than the poet himself, it is not necessary for Cardenal in "Con Walker en Nicaragua" to define the moral character of his subjects as explicitly as he does in another, more predictable, poem (written more or less at the same time) "Los filibusteros" (The filibusters):

Hubo rufianes, ladrones, jugadores, pistoleros.
También hubo honrados y caballeros y valientes.
Reclutados por la necesidad y las ilusiones

(*Antología* 40)

(There were ruffians, thieves, gamblers, gunmen. / There were also honest, brave, gentlemen. / Recruited out of need and illusions)

Considered as a group, early poems such as "Con Walker en Nicaragua," "Los filibusteros," "Joaquín Artola," "José Dolores Estrada," "Greytown," "Squier en Nicaragua" (Squier in Nicaragua), and "Viajero del siglo xix en el río San Juan" (Nineteenth-century traveler on the San Juan River) form an integrated series that effectively encapsulates the landscape, culture, and history of Nicaragua in the nineteenth century. The unethical filibusters are juxtaposed with the highly ethical Nicaraguan heroes Artola and Estrada. Although the poet never intervenes in these poems directly as a first person speaker himself, Cardenal seems to have expanded his parameters to encompass his world in a way that resembles Stephen Tapscott's assessment of Whitman and Williams:

> What the modern writer can emulate . . . is Whitman's orientation toward the
> new world thus encountered: the poet identifies himself with his world,
> gigantically, then explores "himself". . . . From the first Vikings in America,
> through Christopher Columbus, Père Sébastian Rasles, and other early
> American visitors portrayed in *In the American Grain*, and even through
> George Washington . . . the consistently heroic gesture is this "turning
> inward," to suspend one's presumptions, so to let the American locality
> speak through the meditating self.[15]

Obviously, under these circumstances, a literary work exemplifies the
play between fabulae and fact (if such a thing as "fact" exists). In his
introduction to *In the American Grain*, Horace Gregory reminds the
reader of the traditional dialogue between the historical imagination and
poetry:

> The serious historian of the ancient world is careful never to forget his
> Homer. . . . There is a particular kind of reality alive within (Homer's
> fabulae) that will permit neither neglect nor violation: and in the reading and
> interpretation of history everything falls dead unless that reality is
> perceived.[16]

If this historical "reality" is always conjugated by means of the
writer's imagination, perhaps any notion of objectivity built into
definitions of literature advanced by Pound ("Imagism"), Williams
("Objectivism"), and Cardenal ("Exteriorism") is simply an illusion.
Nevertheless, it is this particular "artifice" that informs their art; the
common denominator of objectivity is critical in the creation and the
development of a moral position, which, when politicized, becomes
subject to different ideologies. Although we have discussed the historical
figures in Cardenal's early poems in relation to those that appear in
certain works by MacLeish and Williams, it is important not to forget
that Ezra Pound's seminal theories and poems enabled all three of these
poets (as well, of course, as countless others) to come into their own as
writers. Cardenal explains this in his frequently-cited 1970 interview
with Mario Benedetti:

> In terms of my own poetry, I think that the primary influence . . . is that of
> Ezra Pound. From Pound comes almost all North American poetry. Eliot is
> derivative of Pound, as he himself recognizes. And so is e.e. cummings,
> William Carlos Williams, Archibald MacLeish, Hart Crane.[17]

Perhaps the area of greatest similarities and differences between the
poetry of Pound and Cardenal is that of the persona poem. At the
beginning of their careers, both poets entered the literature of cultures
other than their own by means of translation and the creation of

personae. K. K. Ruthven explains this strategy, as it relates to Pound, as a form of apprenticeship:

> Lacking a poetic personality, the poet experiments with personae until he eventually discovers the "sincere self-expression" that gives an individual quality to his verse. In practice Pound's personae turn out to be somewhat browningesque, although this was perhaps inevitable.[18]

It was inevitable because, as James F. Knapp explains, "Pound believed Browning's dramatic monologue to be the most interesting form in Victorian poetry, and he admired the older poet's concrete individuality of style."[19] N. Christoph de Nagy has delineated three important differences, however, between Browning's dramatic monologue and Pound's persona poem that will prove useful in our analysis of Cardenal's poetry. According to de Nagy, Browning's monologues retain a higher degree of objectivity than Pound's personae. Browning does not assume any ethical responsibility for the opinions expressed by his speaker. Additionally, Browning's characters are generally involved in a localized conflict, whereas Pound's speakers do not concentrate on any given dramatic situation. Finally, unlike Pound, Browning uses the presence of a silent listener to justify and sometimes to direct the words of his speaker.[20] In these ways, we might consider Cardenal's "Proclama del conquistador," given the closeness of the poet to his mask, more Poundian, despite the poem's lack of Pound's technical characteristics. And, "Con Walker en Nicaragua," marked by Pound's unrhetorical "new" language, is certainly more Browningesque in terms of the relationship between poet and speaker.

Both poets, however, use personae as a way of ordering the past: Pound begins by shaping a literary history (drawing from European and Asian cultures) and Cardenal begins by giving form to a political history (revolving around the American continent). The question that must be addressed by each poet becomes one of selection. Pound's choice of speakers and subjects (with the exception of Jefferson, Adams, and Mussolini) are predominantly literary figures (Cino da Pistoia, Rihaku [Li Po], Guido Cavalcanti, Sextus Propertius, etc.). Cardenal, on the other hand, consistently chooses to bring historical figures (William Walker, Sandino, Somoza, etc.) back to life in many of his poems. For Pound, politics is the equivalent of hero-worship: what Jefferson and Mussolini (as they are portrayed in the so-called "Jefferson Nuevo Mundo Cantos" [31-41], published in 1934) have in common is that they are, in critic William M. Chace's words, "men concerned with order, with new ways to envision society. [Pound] sees them—one might almost say perversely—not as men primarily concerned with power, but as artists."[21] Both individuals as brilliant leaders, according to Chace's assessment of Pound's views, willed the births of their respective nations, Italy and the United States. Chace explains how Pound's populist, anti-Marxist fascism evolved from his elevation of the "artistic" politician:

> Pound's reliance upon the creative power of single individuals leads quite naturally to his belief that democratic procedures are inefficient and anti-artistic.[22]

Chace calls Pound an "Imagist of politics": "the task was once again, and now with greater fervor, to search for and isolate the particular."[23] Consequently, Pound chose to single out the Jews and specific financiers. Pound attacked the abuse of capitalism, not the system itself (see Pound's Canto XLV); nor, as an elitist, did Pound view his as being a struggle against hierarchy. Unlike Cardenal, whose poetry manifests the ways that social being determines consciousness, Pound remained convinced that each individual's consciousness determines being. Nevertheless (and this is important common ground), both poets are acutely aware of how political and economic developments have the power to condition all aspects of life. Furthermore, both poets realize that solutions to the exploitative situation in which humanity finds itself must be, above all, *ethical*. In comparing Cardenal with another author motivated by and plagued with moral obsessions (the Peruvian César Vallejo), José Miguel Oviedo finds in both poets "an internal discipline and implacably rigorous ethical exercise."[24] In the 1930s, Pound, like the writers of Nicaragua's *movimiento de vanguardia* (vanguard movement)[25] (the literary generation preceding Cardenal's), embraced Mussolini-style fascism as a means of creating moral and social order. Cardenal, searching for a political system that would be capable of establishing a just code of conduct on a national (and even global) level, came to regard (in the early 1970s) Cuba's experiments in Marxist socialism as an admirable, revolutionary point of departure.

The evaluation of the intertextual relationship between the poetry of Pound and Cardenal must be undertaken not by entering into the problematic area of literary rankings and categorical judgments. Peter Brooker, in a statement that applies not only to Pound but to Cardenal as well, believes that "the important point . . . lies not in questions of artistic worth, but in Pound's method and object, in his choice of sources and in his selection from these in the making of a poem which seeks to master and control history for its own purposes."[26]

It is this underlying moral urge to manipulate history that most critics have ignored in their assessments of Pound's "influence" on Cardenal. Critics such as Borgeson, Veiravé, and Oviedo[27] trot out the obligatory three rules that Pound, H.D., Richard Aldington, and F. S. Flint used to define the Imagist literary movement in 1912:

1. Direct treatment of the 'thing' whether subjective or objective.
2. To use absolutely no word that does not contribute to the presentation.
3. As regarding rhythm: to compose in the sequence of the musical phrase, not in sequence of a metronome.[28]

In his study of Cardenal, Borgeson mistakenly limits Cardenal's debt to Pound to a technical inventory without considering areas of philosophical agreement:

> Concrete but suggestive images; limited but productive use of the adjective . . . ; an innate musicality that refers to the content and not to a manifest metrics; and the opening of the poetic language to presences, vocabularies and linguistic layers hitherto excluded from Hispanic American verse. These elements are important, and reveal Cardenal's debt in terms of technique. But they are no more than that . . . Cardenal's philosophy, on the other hand, in no way reflects Pound's.[29]

While it is certainly valid to interpret Cardenal's poetry according to Pound's rules, which one supposes would embody what Borgeson calls "technique," a reader would never confuse any of Cardenal's poems (not even the most "Imagistic" poems from *Gethsemani, ky*) with the classic Imagist poems (e.g. Hulme's "Autumn," Flint's "The Swan," Pound's "In a Station of the Metro," Williams' "The Red Wheelbarrow," Lowell's "The Pond," and Sandburg's "Fog") composed in keeping with the tenets of these dicta. More important factors in the Pound-Cardenal intertextual dialogue include the source of these images, their selection, the way these images are grouped, and the historical implications of such a compositional method.

Cardenal has explained how Pound's work increased the parameters of previous definitions of poetry:

> Statistical data, fragments of letters, editorials from a newspaper, historical chronicles, documents, jokes, and anecdotes (things that used to be considered elements of prose and not poetry) all fit in a poem.[30]

The selection of images from these sources, at least for Pound, and quite possibly for Cardenal as well, has to do with Pound's notion of "Paideuma," derived from the thought of the German anthropologist Leo Frobenius. Pound defines "Paideuma" in the following way:

> The active element in the era, the complex of ideas which is in a given time germinal, reaching into the next epoch, but conditioning actively all the thought and action of its own time.[31]

When Cardenal multiplies the number and variety of sources from which he creates his poems, especially in "Hora 0" (Zero Hour) and "El estrecho dudoso" (The dubious strait), he is attempting to gather the elements (isolated fragments that do not reflect but *are themselves* the "complex of ideas" of which Pound speaks) that condition a particular period in Nicaraguan history. Pound groups these clusters of details in a dynamic way by means of what he calls the "ideogrammic method." According to James F. Knapp, Pound uses this technique "to construct individual passages, in which the juxtaposed details might be as brief as single words—as well as to construct the larger form of his poem, where images may fuse into pattern only over the space of hundreds of pages."[32] One of the advantages of the ideogrammic method (as true for Pound as it is for Cardenal) is that the poet can write extensive poems without completely giving up Imagism as a method of composition.[33]

The rapid movement from source to source and scene to scene by means of "collisional montage" in Cardenal's "Hora 0" has prompted Robert Pring-Mill to coin the term "documentary poems" in a study in which he describes the historical implications of Cardenal's "filmic" technique. Pring-Mill cites film critic James Monaco's discussion of Kracauer's documentary cinematic style:

> Ethics must replace esthetics, thereby fulfilling Lenin's prophecy . . . that "ethics are the esthetics of the future."[34]

Pring-Mill goes on to explain that Cardenal's documentary version of history ultimately redeems reality in a religious sense:

> Cardenal's recording of the present or the past is aimed at helping to shape the future—involving the reader in the poetic process in order to provoke him into full political commitment, thus fostering the translation of the poet's more prophetic visions into socio-political fact.[35]

Ironically, Pring-Mill, in a scholarly article devoted exclusively to Cardenal's filmic technique in the second episode of "Hora 0," questions the historical imagination of the poet in this poem (when the poet creates poetic fiction and modifies history) and reminds Cardenal of an overriding moral responsibility:

> Narrative engaged poetry has a certain testimonial character for the majority of its readers, which imposes certain extrapoetic responsibilities on the people who write it.[36]

Here, Pring-Mill takes a somewhat high-handed, altruistic stance as historian-critic, and demands perhaps a higher degree of "accuracy" than the rich interplay between fact and fabulae in poetry will bear.

For Pring-Mill, historical accuracy in "engaged" poetry is of paramount moral importance. Can one assume, then, that the method of composition of the poem also demands equally high ethical standards? In "Hora 0," for example, Cardenal collects bits of material from songs, telegrams, and historical works as a way of simultaneously defining a new ethics and aesthetics. But can this form of creation include the almost verbatim use of sources by authors who *have already consciously fictionalized* a particular historical event? Consider, for example, the striking resemblance between the following two texts. The first is part of a chapter from the 1936 work *Sailing South American Skies*, by James Saxon Childers, a U.S. journalist and travel writer who visited Managua shortly after Sandino was assassinated on 21 February 1934:

> Four soldiers were digging a grave, taking turns with the pick and shovel.
> "Who's dead?" one of them asked.
> "Nobody," said the officer.
> "Then what are we digging a grave for?"
> "Never mind. Just dig it."
> A quarter of a mile away the American Minister to Nicaragua was entertaining guests at the American Legation. Tompkins, an ex-marine, was bowing to General José Moncada, former president of Nicaragua. "Will you have coffee, sir?" he asked.
> The general was looking out of the window. Tompkins moved nearer. "Will you have coffee, sir?" he asked.
> "It's a very good coffee, general," the American Minister said.
> "What?" The general turned from the window quickly and looked up at the butler. "Oh, yes. Yes, I'll have coffee." He smiled. "Certainly."
> Later that afternoon five men were talking in a room with sentries on duty outside the doors and windows. One of the men had only his left arm. They were talking rapidly but quietly when the door opened and a man in uniform came in.
> "Well?" one of them asked.
> "Yes," the newcomer said.
> The men got up and went out of the room.
> About dark in a house in another part of Managua, the capital of Nicaragua, the man for whom the grave was being dug—but who thought he was only going out to dinner that night—said to his friends: "It's time we were going." He and his father and their friends went out and got into the automobile that was waiting.
> They drove to the Casa Presidencial and had dinner with the president of Nicaragua. About ten o'clock they left the president's house, got in the same car and started down the hill toward the city. They had driven only a short distance when they saw a company of soldiers blocking the road. When the car stopped, the soldiers closed in around it and took the men out of it.
> They put the two elderly men in one car and sent it in one direction. They put the other three men in another car and drove to an open field near where the soldiers had dug the grave.
> "But where are we going?" asked the man who was on his way to the grave.

No one answered.

Then the car stopped and an officer said, "Get out."

The three men got out. They were led in front of a firing squad. One of them, the leader, begged for his life.

The man with only a left arm was in command of the firing squad. He listened to the man begging for his life, then walked close to him. He held out the stump of an arm. "Look at that," he said. "Do you remember how you took your machete and cut my arm off. Do you remember?" He stepped nearer and with the arm-stump struck the man in the face. "I'll save your life, you son-of-a-bitch. It'll be my greatest pleasure."

Then he stepped back and half turned to the firing squad: "Fire," he said.

(Sailing South American Skies 13-15)

The second text is a fragment from Cardenal's "Hora 0" followed by an English translation:

Cuatro presos están cavando un hoyo.
"¿Quién se ha muerto?", dijo un preso.
"Nadie", dijo el guardia.
"Entonces, ¿para qué es el hoyo?"
"Qué perdés", dijo el guardia, "seguí cavando".

El Ministro Americano está almorzando con Moncada.
"Will you have coffee, sir?"
Moncada se mantiene mirando a la ventana.
"Will you have coffee, sir?
It's a very good coffee, sir".
"What?" Moncada aparta la mirada de la ventana
y mira al criado: "Oh, yes. I'll have coffee".
Y se rió: "Certainly".

En un cuartel cinco hombres están en un cuarto
     cerrado
con centinelas en las puertas y las ventanas.
A uno de los hombres le falta un brazo.
Entra el jefe gordo con condecoraciones y les dice:
     "Yes".

Otro hombre va a cenar esa noche con el Presidente
(el hombre para el que estuvieron cavando el hoyo)
y les dice a sus amigos: "Vámonos. Ya es hora".
Y suben a cenar con el Presidente de Nicaragua.

A las diez de la noche bajan en automóvil a Managua.
En mitad de la bajada los detienen los guardias.
A los dos más viejos se los llevan en un auto
y a los otros tres en otro auto para otro lado,

a donde cuatro presos estuvieron cavando un hoyo.
"Adónde vamos?"
preguntó el hombre para el que hicieron el hoyo.
        Y nadie le contestó.

Después el auto se paró y un guardia les dijo:
"Salgan". Los tres salieron,
y un hombre al que le faltaba el brazo gritó: "¡Fuego!"

(Antología 66-67)

(Four prisoners are digging a grave. / "Who's dead?" asked a prisoner. / "Nobody," said the soldier. / "Then what are we digging the grave for?" / "Never mind," said the soldier. "Keep digging." / The American Minister is eating lunch with Moncada. / Will you have coffee, sir?" / Moncada is looking out of the window. / "Will you have coffee, sir? / It's a very good coffee, sir." / "What?" Moncada turned from the window / and looked at the butler: "Oh, yes. I'll have coffee." / And he laughed: "Certainly." / In a barracks, five men are in a closed room with sentries at the doors and windows. / One of the men was missing an arm. / The fat chief with medals comes in and says, "Yes." / Another man is going to eat that night with the President / [the man for whom the grave was being dug] / and he says to his friends, "Let's get going. It's time." / And they went up to eat dinner with the President of Nicaragua. / At ten o'clock they drove down to Managua. / When they had gone half way, the soldiers stopped them. / They took away the two elderly men in one car / and the other three [went] in another car somewhere else, / to the place where the four prisoners were digging a grave. / "Where are we going?" asked the man for whom they made the grave. / And no one answered. / Then the car stopped and a soldier told them: / "Get out." The three men got out, / and a man missing an arm shouted: "Fire!")

At the very least, the resemblance between these two texts raises questions about Cardenal's compartmentalization of ethics in terms of his attempt to use original poetry as a way of creating an inspiring ethical identity.

Apart from any doubts that might arise regarding the legitimacy or originality of Cardenal's verse, the portrait of the primary historical figure in "Hora 0" is the means by which a moral code is established. Whereas in "Con Walker en Nicaragua," the definition was negative, in "Hora 0," Sandino becomes perhaps the most ethical figure in any of Cardenal's verse, a star by which future revolutionaries can orient their conduct:

¿Qué es aquella luz allá lejos? ¿Es una estrella?
Es la luz de Sandino en la montaña negra.[37]

(Antología 64)

> (What is that light in the distance? Is it a star? / It's the light of Sandino in the black mountain.)

Victor Farías describes the death and resurrection of this mythical, immortal, Christ-like hero as a transcendent ethical event that prepares the way for the future revolutionary struggle and historical salvation.[38] Cardenal, in a poem such as "Hora 0," may possess the historical focus of Neruda, but, unlike the Chilean poet, Cardenal casts a moral light on reality that is endowed with a particularly Christian spiritual sense.

Given this highly developed ethical framework that is both personal and collective in Cardenal's poetry, a quality he assimilated from Pound, it is not exactly accurate to insist as many critics (such as Pring-Mill) have on summarizing the intertextual relationship between Cardenal and Pound as one that is based on "an extreme cult of poetic objectivity: a conscious and deliberate suppression of subjective elements."[39] Objectivity in Cardenal's poetry, based on an objectification of a language that expresses the things outside the self in the external, empirically-perceived world, expresses intimate moral values that are personal, mysterious, urgent. Furthermore, the creative act of constructing a poem implies choice, selection—conscious inner actions that belie any sort of true, pure "objectivity" or "exteriorism."

Perhaps Cardenal's "exteriorism" can be seen as a linguistic simplification of Pound (more reminiscent of the transfiguration of everyday American speech in William Carlos Williams' poetry) that approaches Williams' dictum "No ideas but in things," yet fails to embody it because of ethical, spiritual and, later, political considerations. Stephen Tapscotts' explanation of the double objectivity behind Williams' "No ideas but in things" applies to, but only partially defines, Cardenal's poetics:

> When Williams summarizes this first necessity for modern writing, he is talking about the need for two kinds of objectivity, both toward the world and toward words. His belief in the power of words when they're used objectively, that is, stems from a fundamental belief in the power and significance of objective things in the physical world.[40]

There is, however, a third part of this definition of "Objectivism," proposed by the Objectivists (Williams, Zukofsky, Reznikoff, and Oppen) in the 1920s, that does include the moral, sometimes didactic, urge in Cardenal's poetry. Tapscott points out that originally the Objectivists "stressed the importance of the objective world, of the poet's personal 'objectives,' and also of the mediating, 'objective' properties of the word."[41] Cardenal's *objectives* as a poet are unequivocally ethical, even when he presents the reader with a negative definition of morality as he does in the two persona poems "Con Walker en Nicaragua" and

"Somoza desveliza la estatua de Somoza en el estadio Somoza" (Somoza unveils the statue of Somoza in Somoza stadium).

This poem about the elder Somoza (Somoza García) was composed, along with the rest of the *Epigramas*, between 1952 and 1956 (presumably before Somoza was gunned down by the poet Rigoberto López Pérez at a party in León in 1956). Although the *Epigramas* circulated widely (and anonymously) in mimeographed form, the poems were not published as a collection until 1961. "Somoza desveliza la estatua de Somoza en el estadio de Somoza" is a particularly effective satiric attack (against the extraordinarily cynical conduct of a tyrant) that the poet achieves by letting the political figure condemn himself in his own words:

> No es que yo crea que el pueblo me erigió esta
>   estatua
> porque yo sé mejor que vosotros que la ordené yo
>   mismo.
> Ni tampoco que pretenda pasar con ella a la
>   posteridad
> porque yo sé que el pueblo la derribará un día.
> Ni que haya querido erigirme a mí mismo en vida
> el monumento que muerto no me erigiréis vosotros;
> sino que erigí esta estatua porque sé que la odiáis.

(Antología 16)

(It's not that I think the people erected this statue / because I know better than you that I ordered it myself. / Nor do I pretend to pass into posterity with it / because I know the people will topple it over someday. / Not that I wanted to erect to myself in life / the monument you never would erect to me in death: I erected this statue because I knew you would hate it.)

This parodic poem by Cardenal countervails Pound's praise (in Canto XLI) of Mussolini, "the Boss," the one who drained marshes to plant crops, put in a water supply, and built a million rooms in which people could live. Pound's alliance with a political system that provides social benefits mirrors the poetry Cardenal published after the Sandinista revolution in *Tocar el cielo* (To touch the sky).

Ultimately, any similarities between Pound and Cardenal on technical and/or philosophical grounds are less important than the obvious differences in the voices of the poem's personae. Cardenal does not imitate Pound; he assimilates and simplifies what Pound has to offer and creates a "new" poetic language, highly influential in its own right, within the Spanish idiom. It is difficult to accept, as Isabel Freire has suggested, that "where Pound seems to spring up disconnected from his own contemporary cultural scene and to be working against it, putting his roots through books into the past, Cardenal is born into a ready-made cultural context and shared political conscience."[42] Both poets, although from opposite ends of the ideological spectrum, are engaged in an intense dialogue with the past, and hope to manipulate history in order to create a more ethically-sound future.

Toward a "New" Ethics: Ernesto Cardenal and the Amerindian Culture

Cardenal's interest in North American poetry, however, is not confined to the usual writers from the nineteenth and twentieth centuries that one finds in a standard poetry anthology. Cardenal and co-translator José Coronel Urtecho begin their excellent *Antología de la poesía norteamericana* (1963) with a selection of thirty-six native American poems and songs in Cardenal's Spanish translation. Later, Cardenal expands this section to include more indigenous material from the American continent as well as "primitive" poems from around the world in *Antología de poesía primitiva* (Anthology of primitive poetry) (1979). Cardenal's research on the American continent's indigenous cultures is due, in large part, to the encouragement he received from Thomas Merton, Cardenal's Novice Master from 1957-59, at the Trappist monastery Our Lady of Gethsemani in Kentucky.

Merton was a key figure (a kind of spiritual father when one considers the title of Cardenal's "Coplas a la muerte de Merton" an echo of Jorge Manrique's "Coplas a la muerte de su padre")[43] in the formation of Cardenal's religious thought, especially in the rejection of the mystic/ascetic/contemplative's traditional *contemptus mundi* to favor a more "engaged" relationship with the world outside the monastery walls. Initially, Cardenal embraced Merton's Zen-like pacifism, though Cardenal later abandoned Merton's principles of nonviolence when he expressed his solidarity with the armed insurrection in Nicaragua, justifying his position theologically not on the basis of Thomas Aquinas' just-war doctrine (as did Nicaragua's Catholic bishops) but on certain biblical precedents such as David and Goliath, and Holofernes' sword wielded by Judith.[44] Merton was also instrumental in convincing Cardenal to establish the contemplative community in Nicaragua that came to be known as Solentiname.[45]

To the best of our knowledge, critical material on Cardenal's poetry has not addressed the specific ideas concerning Native American culture that Merton and Cardenal (known in the monastery as Fr. Lawrence) no doubt discussed when they were able. In an unpublished letter (in Spanish) to Pablo Antonio Cuadra, written in December 1958, while

Cardenal was still at Our Lady of Gethsemani, Merton forges a synthesis of traditional Indian religion and Christianity:

> Man, image of God, should be a creator, not only as an individual, but as a brother of other creators. Let us continue creating and struggling for the truth and the kingdom of God. We have a tremendous and marvelous vocation, the vocation of being *Americans*, that is to say, of being and of forming the true America that is the Christ of the Americas: the Christ that was born among the Indians already many centuries ago, who manifested himself in the Indian culture, before the coming of official Christianity: the Christ that has been crucified for centuries on this great cross of our double continent; the Christ that is agonizing on this same cross; when will the hour of the Resurrection of our Christ of the Americas come?, the Christ of the united, free America, emancipated from "the liturgy of the lie and of the pontificate of the infallible ignorance" which is modern politics; many years will pass, and we will not see the true America that still has not been born. We can and should be prophets of its advent . . .[46]

This fragment of Merton's letter contains virtually all the important themes in Cardenal's post-Trappist poetry: history and prophecy, the ethics of Christian and indigenous traditions, even liberation theology in an embryonic form.[47] The work by Cardenal that undoubtedly represents a culmination of this thematic content is *Homenaje a los indios americanos* (Homage to the American Indians), first published in 1969 then expanded in later editions.

Cardenal's poem "Kentucky," from *Oración por Marilyn Monroe y otros poemas* (Prayer for Marilyn Monroe and other poems) (1965), is an important transitional piece and prelude to the social concerns addressed by the *Homenaje* poems. In "Kentucky," as in earlier poems, Cardenal uses an historical figure to create a contrast in ethics. In the first line of "Kentucky" is a quote from Daniel Boone's autobiography: *"Kentucky es un segundo paraíso dijo Daniel Boone"* (Kentucky is a second paradise, said Daniel Boone). The Edenic world that Boone inhabits with a lifestyle resembling that of his Native American neighbors is compared to the modern Kentucky with its materialistic suburban life and its pollution:

> Desde una ventana abierta se eleva un high fidelity . . .
>
> Y ahora en el Ohio desembocan todas las cloacas,
> desperdicios industriales, sustancias químicas.

(*Antología* (Educa) 113)

(From an open window, the sound of high fidelity soars . . . / And now all the sewage flows into the Ohio, / industrial waste, chemical substances.)

With regard to "Kentucky," Henry Cohen believes that Boone represents a paradigm for all that contemporary society has lost and destroyed:

> Cardenal's Daniel Boone is *le bon sauvage*, living in balance with nature, more Indian than European. Conserving natural resources, religiously respectful of his surroundings and in tune with their rhythm, Boone is naive, good, untainted by the preoccupation with property, and ruggedly self-sufficient, in short, a foil for everything that the poet finds distasteful in modern U.S. society.[48]

Daniel Boone is also the subject of one of the chapters in William Carlos Williams' *In the American Grain*. In one sense, Williams' "The Discovery of Kentucky," though it does not juxtapose pioneer and contemporary life, is a more revolutionary interpretation of Boone than Cardenal's. Williams portrays not only Boone's lifestyle as compatible with that of the Native Americans but also Boone's *solidarity* with the Indians in their struggle against the encroachment of the white man:

> Too late the American Congress did follow him [Boone] with some slight recognition. But that was by then to him really a small matter. He had already that which he wanted: the woods and native companions whom, in a written statement of great interest, he defends against all detractors and in that defense establishes himself in clear words: the antagonist of those of his own blood whose alien strength he felt and detested, while his whole soul, with greatest devotion, was given to the New World which he adored and found, in its every expression, the land of heart's desire.

> (*In the American Grain* 139)

What the two portraits of Boone by Cardenal and Williams share is a use of the historical figure as a positive role model, in this instance a white man who adopts the ways of the Indians in order to lead a more spiritually-enriched life.

Spiritual fulfillment is also the subject of the long speech by Tahirassawichi in "Tahirassawichi en Washington" (Tahirassawichi in Washington) from *Homenaje a los indios americanos*. It is an extension (perhaps an even more appropriate one) of the persona poem, a literary technique that we discussed earlier. Boris de Rachewiltz's analysis of some of the pagan and magic elements in Pound's various poetic guises (or personae) also defines Cardenal's verse in *Homenaje*:

> A mask, by virtue of its function, may be said to have a certain wavelength over which its wearer is attuned to and in communication with the character of the person or deity it represents and so acts as both transmitter and receiver. This applies no less to the immaterial masks of poetry than to real masks, the function of which has been the subject of ethnological study.[49]

In this way, Cardenal, by assuming the mask of Tahirassawichi, is possessed by the spirit of the indigenous figure he resurrects. The poet becomes an intermediary, receiving signs, transforming these signs and transmitting them as meaningful speech in a poem. Like Cardenal's *Salmos*, in which the poet adopts the voice of a contemporary Hebrew prophet,[50] *Homenaje a los indios americanos* can be read as a book-length persona poem. According to José Miguel Oviedo, each poem contributes to the reaffirmation of "agrarian communism, the nonexistence of bourgeois freedom, and the synthesis . . . of a religion and a politics."[51] Individually, Tahirassawichi embodies the moral values of an entire indigenous culture that Cardenal projects both as an antidote to present ills and as a paradigm for the future.

In *Homenaje*, Cardenal continues to include the kinds of sources that he used in prior documentary verse in order to create an historical veracity. In addition, Cardenal weaves native songs and prayers into these poems with indigenous themes in such a way as to create *mythical* verisimilitude. In "Tahirassawichi en Washington," for example, Cardenal merges a "Canción de los indios pawnees" (Song of the Pawnee Indians) into the text of Tahirassawichi's speech:

> Mira cómo suben, cómo suben
> sobre la línea donde el cielo se junta con la
>   tierra:
> ¡Las Pléyades!
> ¡Ah! Ascendiendo, vienen para guiarnos,
> para irnos cuidando, que seamos uno;
> Pléyades,
> enseñadnos a estar, como vosotras, unidos.

> (*Antología de la poesía norteamericana* 25)

(Look how they rise, how they rise / above the line where the sky meets the earth: / the Pleiades! / ah! ascending, they come to guide us, / to take care of us, so that we become one; / Pleiades, / teach us to be like you, united.)

> Y cantamos en la noche cuando salen las Pléyades.
> Las siete estrellas están siempre juntas
> y orientan al que está perdido, lejos de su aldea
> (y enseñan a los hombres a estar unidos como ellas).

> (*Homenaje* 86)

(And we sing in the night when the Pleiades come out. / The seven stars are always together / and they guide the one who is lost, far from his village / and they teach men to be united like they are.)

Tahirassawichi also informs the Department of State in Washington in 1898 that an integral element of the indigenous way of life, the buffalo, no longer exists:

> Y cantamos a los búfalos, pero no en las praderas
> el *Canto de los Búfalos* lo cantamos en la choza
> porque ya no hay búfalos.

(Homenaje 84)

(And we sing to the buffalos, but not in the prairies, / we sing the "Song of the Buffalo" in the hut / because there are no longer any buffalos.)

The song remains, however, as a way of preserving the past and appealing to Tirawa for a renewed future:

> Visión de los búfalos del pasado
>
> ¡Ah, ah, ah!
> ¡Mira! Allá lejos en el pasado. ¡Mira! Un punto . . .
>
> ¡Ah, ah, ah!
> ¡Mira! Ahora en el presente. ¡Mira! Muchos puntos.

(Antología de poesía primitiva 117)

(Vision of the buffalos of the past / Ah, ah, ah! / Look! Far away in the past. Look! A point . . . / Ah, ah, ah! Look! Now in the present. Look! Many points.)

Gordon Brotherston, author of *Latin American Poetry: Origins and Presence*, believes that Cardenal's *Homenaje* is "a verse collection which incorporates whole passages of (indigenous) poetry as a vindication of cultures widespread over the original America."[52] Brotherston criticizes Cardenal for not going to the poems in their original languages and for relying on flawed secondary sources. However, when Cardenal successfully creates an intertextual balance between his own poetry and the indigenous verse the result, according to Brotherston, is "the striking effect of 'emptying' his Spanish and creating resonance between his voice and that of the ransomed text."[53] For Cardenal, "primitive" poetry has a great deal in common with what he himself has attempted to define as *exteriorismo*:

In general, primitive poetry has neither consonant nor assonant rhyme. . . . Frequently, however, there is "rhyme" based on parallelism or repetitions. In

many cases, the rhythm is highly-accentuated, and among the North
American Indians, the rhythm of the verse is that of the drum. . . . And one
characteristic of primitive poetry of all times is that it is made not with
abstract ideas, but concrete images.[54]

In addition, however, primitive poetry contains a ritual function and its
authors, in Jerome Rothenberg's words, must be considered "technicians
of the sacred." Rothenberg, one of a number of poets in the United States
who began to embed anthropological concerns in poetry in the 1960s (the
same decade that produced Cardenal's *Homenaje*), agrees with Cardenal
that so-called primitive poems have a great deal in common with what
many American (in the continental sense) writers were trying to achieve
in their work two decades ago. The differences, however, according to
Rothenberg, are fundamental:

> What's missing are the in-context factors that define them more closely
> group-by-group: the sense of the poems as part of an integrated social and
> religious complex; the presence in each instance of specific myths & locales;
> the fullness of the living culture. Here the going is rougher with no easy
> shortcuts through translation: no simple carry-overs. If our world is open to
> multiple influences & data, theirs is largely self-contained. If we're
> committed to a search for the "new," most of them are tradition-bound.[55]

This functional spiritual quality, above all, accounts for the vital
attraction that Native American culture held for Cardenal: the poet, in
this traditional sense, chronicles his culture's history and interprets the
divine signs in order to guide his people within an ethical framework that
reflects a political and religious order.

With regard to signs and their ritual use, "Tahirassawichi en
Washington" also contains a variation on Pound's use of the Chinese
ideogram in many of his *Cantos*. Pound proceeds to define Imagism on
the mistaken assumption (based on what he learns from Fenollosa) that
the ideogram is the equivalent of a pictogram and that, therefore, the
individual components of the Chinese language are inherently visual and
poetic. The "primitive" graphic symbol in "Tahirassawichi" is much
closer to the essentially visual poem that Pound imagines to exist in each
Chinese character. Cardenal's sign, drawn in blue water and earth on the
face of the children, represents the God Tirawa, that is, the blue bend in
the river where Tirawa lives. The river is a mirror of a particular
indigenous culture over the course of time and subsequent generations.
The child becomes perfectly integrated into his world by simultaneously
wearing Tirawa's face and perceiving Tirawa's face in the surface of the
river into which he stares. Like so much of Cardenal's poetry, the scene
is marvelously, transparently simple yet complex:

Con el agua azul pintamos el signo de Tirawa
(un arco y en su centro una recta que baja)
en el rostro de un niño.
    El arco en la frente y las mejillas
    y la línea recta, en la nariz.
(el arco es la comba azul donde vive Tirawa
y la línea recta su aliento que baja y nos da vida).
El rostro del niño representa la nueva generación
y el agua del río es el pasar de las generaciones
y la tierra azul que mezclamos es el cielo de Tirawa
(y el dibujo azul así trazado es el rostro de Tirawa).
Después hacemos al niño mirar el agua de río
y él al mirar el agua ve también su propia imagen
como viendo en su rostro sus hijos y los hijos de sus
    hijos
pero está viendo también el rostro azul de Tirawa
retratado en su rostro y en las futuras generaciones.

(Homenaje 86)

(With blue water we paint the sign of Tirawa / (an arch and in its center a descending line) / on the face of a child. / The arch on the forehead and the cheeks / and the straight line on the nose. / (the arch is the blue dome where Tirawa lives / and the straight line his breath that descends and gives us life). / The face of the child represents the new generation / and the riverwater is the passing of generations / and the blue earth that we mix is Tirawa's sky / (and the blue drawing drawn like this is Tirawa's face). / Later, we make the child watch the riverwater / and he, watching the water, sees his own image as well / as seeing in his face his children and his children's children, / but he is also seeing Tirawa's blue face / portrayed in his face and in the future generations.)

Thomas Merton, in an essay entitled "The Sacred City," defines "primitive" humanity in terms of a childlike contact with the exterior world. Merton's use of "narcissism" (in terms of the word's mythological origin) is especially interesting in comparison with the boy in Cardenal's poem who considers the meaning of the reflection he perceives in the surface of the water:

The primitive, like the child, remains in direct sensuous contact with what is outside him, and is most happy when this contact is celebrated in an aesthetic and ritual joy. He relates to things and persons around him with narcissistic play. Our narcissism has been increasingly invested, through intellectual operations, in the money, the machine, the weaponry, which are extensions of ourselves and which we venerate in our rituals of work, war, production, domination and brute power.[56]

Cardenal, too, believes that peace in the modern world is incompatible with the profit-oriented objectives of capitalism. Against the materialism and spiritual emptiness of contemporary society, Cardenal opposes the communitarian economics of indigenous culture that existed in the past. Indeed, one of Cardenal's most important contributions as a poet is his ability to envision historical parallels and to use the past as a source of guidance for the future.[57] Past historical moments also form the basis for the prophetic mode in Cardenal's poetry—a force intimately linked with moral clarity, according to Paul Ricoeur in *The Symbolism of Evil*:

> Prophecy, then, consists in deciphering future history by giving it in advance a meaning relative to the ethical life of the people.[58]

To a large extent, Pablo Antonio Cuadra's summary of *Homenaje a los indios americanos* as a revival of "the neoclassical concept of the paradisiacal Indian (the 'good savage')"[59] is correct. This assessment, however, does not take into account Cardenal's balanced perception of the past in *Homenaje*, a work that embraces the horrendous as well as the ideal. One thinks, for example, of the poem "Mayapán," in which the poet encounters a parallel between the cruel dictatorship of the Cocom family and the dynasty of the Somozas in Nicaragua. With a certainty that comes from his knowledge of history (almost a Mayan vision of temporality: cycles continuing to repeat, though never exactly in the same way), the poet also projects the successful rebellion of Ah Xupán into a revolutionary future: in 1979, a decade after Cardenal wrote his poem, the Sandinistas were victorious in Nicaragua. For Cardenal, history is a series of revolutionary experiences as certain ethical figures struggle against unjust governments to replace them with just ones. Cardenal's ethical system is based on a merging of Christian and Marxist principles in order to apply an understanding of history to social inequality.[60]

Nevertheless, to the extent that Cardenal's *Homenaje* poems idealize the past and project it as a paradigm for the future, Cardenal's verse with indigenous themes more closely resembles Poundian than Marxist critiques of capitalism, despite Cardenal's second "conversion" (to Marxism) after his 1968 visit to Cuba. David Murray points out a fundamental difference between Pound and Marx and their relationship to the past:

> While both Marx and Pound are opposed to this domination of money-values, Marx differs from Pound in his refusal to idealize what preceded it. He did not look back to an ideal agrarian medieval society as an alternative to capitalism because . . . he saw in feudalism the whole basis of the capitalist alienation of man from his labour.[61]

This attempt to create a paradigm of a particular historical moment, as we discussed in the previous chapter on the poetry of José Coronel Urtecho, is precisely the spirit underlying the poetry of Ezra Pound. To develop the theme of the "backward-look" in Pound and Cardenal, an issue that lies beyond the scope of the present work, one would need to investigate the relationships that exist between Pound's ideal medieval society and Cardenal's perfect indigenous way of life as the two erudite poets envision them. The differences between European and "primitive" American cultures are legion, yet perhaps a fundamental comparison is possible on the basis of "good" economics versus the kind of "bad" economics that destroys a culture's social, political, and spiritual fabric. Too, both Cardenal (in *Homenaje*) and Pound (at least in Canto XLV) simplify very complex economic issues in a masterly, forceful way and convert them into poetry that carries essentially the same warning.

One assumes, finally, that Cardenal would share Merton's conviction that it is pointless to idealize indigenous society on the basis of the spiritual and material benefits that each *individual* member derived from society:

> There would be no point in merely idealizing primitive men and archaic culture. There is no such thing as a charismatic culture. Though the life of an Indian was much more individualistic than we have imagined, it was integrated in the culture of his tribe and in its complex rituals. "Vision" was perhaps more often a deepening of the common imagination than a real breakthrough of personal insight.[62]

For this reason, the personal actions of the moral figures that constantly appear in Cardenal's poetry (in opposition to the immoral actions of other individuals) must eventually be fulfilled or redeemed in the collective actions of an entire population. This is especially true in the later poems by Cardenal, in which, for example, there are individuals such as Leonel Rugama in "Oráculo sobre Managua" (Oracle on Managua):

> Por eso vos Leonel Rugama poeta de veinte años
> te metiste a la guerrilla urbana.
> Ex-seminarista, marxista, decías
> en la Cafetería La India que la revolución
> es la comunión con la especie.

(*Antología* 214)

(That's why you, Leonel Rugama, twenty-year old poet / joined the urban guerrillas. / Ex-theological student, Marxist, you used to say / in the Cafetería La India that the revolution / is the communion with the species.)

The "communion with the species" is complete when the actions of ethical individuals transform the people of a country into a revolutionary force (in which the poet includes himself) as in "Barricada" (Barricade), a poem written after the Sandinista victory:

> Esto fue una tarea de todos.
> La verdad es que todos pusimos adoquines en la gran barricada.
> Fue una tarea de todos. Fue el pueblo unido.
>   Y lo hicimos.

(Antología 268)

> (It was the work of everyone. / The truth is that we all put paving stones in the great barricade. / It was the work of everyone. The people united. / And we / did it.)

Cardenal's consistent preoccupation with the establishment of a guiding moral code is so overriding that it eclipses and suppresses any mystical impulse that attempts to surface in his work. Despite the faint trace of mystical inclinations in *Gethsemani, ky* and a certain "cosmic" consciousness in other works, Cardenal, as a poet, is essentially a moralist. In a prologue to Cardenal's *Vida en el amor* (Life within love), Merton distinguishes between the moralist and the mystic:

> For the moralist, human life is a complicated system of virtues and vices, and in the middle of this is love, which is only one of the virtues. But for the mystic, that complicated system does not exist, and love is all.[63]

Cardenal's formulation of an ethical identity for Nicaragua that possesses the capacity to set a global standard is based, to a large extent, on the intertextual relationship between his verse and literature from the United States. As we have seen, the impetus for Cardenal's poetry is derived from his assimilative dialogue with works of MacLeish, Williams, and Pound, as well as the songs/prayers of the Amerindian culture. The portraits of the historical figures in Cardenal's poetry, from the early conquistador to the contemporary urban guerrilla, are all related to the historical evolution of Nicaragua and all define an ethical framework—either negatively, for example, in the case of Walker, or positively, in the case of Sandino—that achieves its maximum definition in the Nicaraguan revolution of 1979.

Notes

Introduction

1. See Octavio Paz, "El caracol y la sirena," in *Cuadrivio* (Mexico: Joaquín Mortiz, 1965), pp. 9-65.

2. See Fidel Coloma, "La imitación como base del proceso creativo en *Azul* . . . ," in *Azul . . . y las literaturas hispánicas* (Managua: Biblioteca Nacional "Rubén Darío"; México: UNAM, Instituto de Investigaciones Bibliográficas, 1990), p. 165. See also Gwen Kirkpatrick, *The Dissonant Legacy of Modernismo: Lugones, Herrera y Reissig, and the Voices of Modern Spanish American Poetry* (Berkeley: University of California Press, 1989), p. 7.

3. Rubén Darío, *Rubén Darío: poesía*, ed. with an introduction by Pere Gimferrer (Barcelona: Planeta, 1987), p. xx. For the reader's benefit, all sources have been rendered in English. The translations of these texts as well as the poems cited in French and Spanish are mine, unless otherwise indicated.

4. Gérard Genette, *Palimpsestes: La littérature au second degré* (Paris: Editions du Seuil, 1982), p. 8.

5. Michael Riffaterre, *Text Production*, trans. Terese Lyons (New York: Columbia University Press, 1983), p. 250.

6. See the discussion at the beginning of chapter 5 in this study.

7. Some of this material appears in *Encendidos oros: antología de la poesía nicaragüense del siglo xx*, ed. Steven F. White (Madrid: Orígenes, 1993).

8. There are, of course, other exceptions to consider. One thinks, for example, of José Coronel Urtecho's brief incursion into Surrealism as a result of a personal mental crisis in the 1940s. "Retrato de la mujer de tu prójimo" (Portrait of thy neighbor's wife), however, is less characteristic of the poet's oeuvre than "Pequeña biografía de mi mujer" (Brief biography of my wife).

Chapter 1. The Journey Toward God in the Poetry of Cortés, Baudelaire, Rimbaud, and Mallarmé

1. Alice Coléno, *Les Portes d'ivoire* (Paris: Librairie Plon, 1948), p. 16.

2. See Francisco Fuster, *Alfonso Cortés: Vida e ideas*, published in its entirety as the "Libro del Mes" in *Revista Conservadora del Pensamiento Centroamericano* 20.101 (1969): pp. 39-40. Fuster cites the complete text of this poem composed by Cortés in French. A translation of this poem into Spanish appears in Alfonso Cortés, *Poemas eleusinos* (León, Nicaragua: Talleres Hospicio San Juan de Dios, 1935), p. 65.

3. See Fuster, *Alfonso Cortés*, p. 42. Fuster lists the specific poems that were translated by Cortés then later published in the first issue of the magazine *Ventana* (León, Nicaragua) in 1964.

4. See José Varela-Ibarra, *La poesía de Alfonso Cortés* (León, Nicaragua: Editorial Universitaria, 1976), pp. 30-31.

5. John Beverley and Marc Zimmerman, *Literature and Politics in the Central*

American Revolutions (Austin: University of Texas Press, 1990), p. 59.

   6. See Julio Valle-Castillo, introduction, *Poetas modernistas de Nicaragua (1880-1927)* (Managua: Colección Cultural Banco de América, 1978), pp. xiv-xv; See also Ernesto Cardenal, introduction, *30 Poemas de Alfonso* by Alfonso Cortés (Managua: Editorial Nueva Nicaragua, 1981), p. 13. Here, Cardenal seems to confuse symbolist and surrealist poetry.

   7. Hans Jonas, *The Gnostic Religion* (Boston: Beacon, 1963), p. 45.

   8. Oliver Sacks, *Awakenings* (New York: Dutton, 1983), p. 221. In this chapter I have chosen not to dwell on the biographical fact of the poet's mental illness, diagnosed as paranoid schizophrenia. In a later study I will take a pathological/psychoanalytical approach to Cortés's poetry, a strategy used by James L. Rice in his study of Dostoevsky entitled *Dostoevsky and the Healing Art: An Essay in Literary and Medical History* (Ann Arbor, Mich.: Ardis, 1985). In his work, Rice delineates the highly complex relationship between Dostoevsky's epilepsy and his oeuvre: "In every regard Dostoevsky's greatness lies not in the denial of illness but in its acceptance and mastery, and in the discovery (and invention, to be sure) of polymorphous and polyphonic values precisely within his pathological condition, which he consciously and ingeniously negotiated through art." (234). Rice later concludes that "Dostoevsky perceived that it was his *right* to use illness defensively and creatively, metaphorically and hyperbolically, as a therapeutic mode of being." (279).

   9. See, for example, François Mauriac, "Charles Baudelaire the Catholic," in *Baudelaire: A Collection of Critical Essays*, ed. Henri Peyre (Englewood Cliffs, N.J.: Prentice, 1962), p. 37; Pierre Messiaen, *Sentiment chrétien et poésie française: Baudelaire, Verlaine, Rimbaud* (Paris: Les Editions Marcel Daubin, 1947), p. 7; Joseph Melançon, *Le spiritualisme de Baudelaire* (Montreal and Paris: Editions Fides, 1967), p. 112; and Marcel A. Ruff, *L'esprit du Mal et l'esthétique baudelairienne* (Paris: Librairie Armand Colin, 1955), p. 333.

   10. It is interesting to note a variant in the text of the opening of "La canción del espacio" in which the poet has written "yo no he alcanzado" (I have not succeeded) instead of "Dios no ha alcanzado" (God has not succeeded) The manuscript version of the poem's first two stanzas (after which is written "etc., etc.") in Cortés's own handwriting was shown to me by the late Nicaraguan poet Ernesto Mejía Sánchez during my visit to México City in August 1982. The long lines of the manuscript version undoubtedly precede Cortés's subsequent creation of three, eight-line stanzas.

   11. Joseph Frank, *The Widening Gyre* (New Brunswick, N.J.: Rutgers University Press, 1963), p. 10.

   12. Gaston Bachelard, *The Poetics of Space*, trans. María Jolas (Boston: Beacon, 1969), p. 184.

   13. Ibid., p. 218.

   14. Alfonso Cortés, "La Belleza Perfecta," cited by Fuster, *Alfonso Cortés*, pp. 51-52.

   15. Lawrence LeShan and Henry Margenau, *Einstein's Space and Van Gogh's Sky* (New York: MacMillan, 1982), pp. 108-9.

   16. Messiaen, *Sentiment*, p. 244.

   17. Cf. Stéphane Mallarmé, "Toute l'âme resumée . . . ," in *Oeuvres complétes* (Paris: Librairie Gallimard, 1945), p. 73. The poem is a kind of playful *art poétique* in which poetry itself is no more than a puff of smoke (from Mallarmé's cigar) that contains the entire soul.

   18. Bachelard, *Poetics of Space*, p. 217-18.

   19. Sacks, *Awakenings*, p. 210.

   20. Varela-Ibarra, *Poesía de Cortés*, p. 96.

   21. Alfonso Cortés, "Proemio," in *El poema cotidiano* (León, Nicaragua: Editorial Hospicio, 1967), p. 5.

   22. Cf. Richard M. Restak, M.D., *The Brain: the Last Frontier* (New York: Warner

Books, 1979). Of no small import in Mallarmé's poem is the subject's perception that the river exudes a powerful perfume. Recent research on the brain has shown that the sense of smell is particularly potent, profoundly affecting the human psyche, because the olfactory fibers synapse directly with the hippocampus and amygdala, two loci in the brain associated with the storage of spatial and emotional memory. Cf. also Joaquín Pasos, "Un libro con ojos, nariz y boca" (A book with eyes, nose and mouth), in *El Diario Nicaragüense* (Granada, Nicaragua), 14 enero 1935, p. 1+. In his review of Cortés's *Tardes de oro*, Pasos says that Cortés "did not want to forget any of his five bodily senses, even those he has not fully developed, such as taste and touch." Pasos praises the aural imagery in Cortés's poetry: "And that, in truth, is what life is for this poet of monstrous auditory nerves, capable of interpreting, as a musician would, all the feelings in all the sounds." Nevertheless, Pasos concludes by pointing out the limitations of empiricism: "For the people tired of the small sensorial human world nothing remains except to long, like Alfonso, for a world 'beyond the senses,' the mystery of unknown sensations, whose existence is scarcely suspected and calculated, like the invisible stars."

23. Eduardo Zepeda-Henríquez, *Alfonso Cortés, al vivo* (Managua: Imprenta Nacional, 1966), pp. 3-4.

24. Beryl Rowland, *Animals with Human Faces: A Guide to Animal Symbolism* (Knoxville: University of Tennessee Press, 1973), p. 100.

25. George Cattui, "Mallarmé et Les Mystiques," in *Orphisme et prophétie chez les poètes français: 1850-1950* (Paris: Librairie Plon, 1965), p. 118.

26. John Porter Houston, *The Design of Rimbaud's Poetry* (New Haven: Yale University Press, 1963), p. 135.

27. Fuster, *Alfonso Cortés*, p. 28.

28. Ibid., p. 28.

29. Octavio Paz, *The Bow and the Lyre (El arco y la lira)*, trans. Ruth L. C. Simms (Austin: University of Texas Press, 1973), p. 222.

30. Elaine Pagels, *The Gnostic Gospels* (New York: Random House, 1979), p. 118.

31. Ibid., p. 144.

32. Ibid., p. 126.

33. James S. Robinson, ed., *The Nag Hammadi Library* (New York: Harper & Row, 1977), p. 126.

34. Kenneth Rexroth, "Gnosticism," in *Assays* (New York: New Directions, 1961), p. 141.

35. Dante Alghieri, *Paradiso*, trans. Allen Mandelbaum (New York: Bantam, 1986), pp. 272-73.

36. Max Pulver, "Jesus' Round Dance and Crucifixion According to the Acts of St. John," in *The Mysteries: Papers from the Eranos Yearbooks*, ed. Joseph Campbell (Princeton: Princeton University Press, 1955), p. 177.

37. Thomas Merton, introduction, *Las rimas universales* by Alfonso Cortés (Managua, Nicaragua: Editorial Alemana, 1964), p. 11. Merton wrote this introduction toward the end of his life at a time when he was expanding the parameters of his interpretation of Catholicism to include Marxism and Zen Buddhist philosophy. Also, in a 22 May 1962 letter to Ernesto Cardenal, Thomas Merton says the following:

> Yesterday your essay on Alfonso arrived and last evening I read the first few pages. It is most impressive. I will probably add to the poem on Alfonso about which I told you in my letter of a few days ago, on the basis of the extraordinary picture you give of him. I think he is a most absorbing and wonderful figure, in some sense prophetic.
> The thing that strikes me most about his poems, and you may yourself have said this in pages which I have not yet reached, is his extraordinary ontological sense, his grasp of objective being. He is much more than a surrealist. Indeed he is the only true surrealist, for instead of going like them to the heart of a subjectivity which is at the same time all real and all unreal, he plunges to the heart of a transobjective subjectivity which is the purely real, and he expresses it

in images as original and as eloquent as those of Blake. He is one of the most arresting poets of the twentieth century, and in my opinion certainly one of the very greatest.

38. David Bohm, interview, *About Time*, ed. Christopher Rawlence (London: Jonathan Cape, 1985), p. 161.

39. Cf. Jalal al-Din Rumi, *Mystical Poems of Rumi*, trans. A. J. Arberry (Chicago: University of Chicago Press, 1968). The majority of the mystical poems by the great thirteenth century Persian Sufi poet Rumi end with a call for silence. Cf. also Cattaui, *Orphisme*, p. 119: "Toute la poésie de Mallarmé tend au silence."

40. See Amelia Barili, "Borges on Life and Death," *New York Times Book Review*, 13 July 1986, p. 29.

41. Varela-Ibarra, *Poesia de Cortés*, p. 157.

42. See Octavio Paz, *Sor Juana Inés de la Cruz o Las trampas de la fe* (México: Fondo de Cultura Económica, 1982), p. 490. In addition to certain French writers, one should consider an important Hispanic American antecedent. Sor Juana's conflictive relationship with Christian precepts, her intellectual rather than emotional approach to divinity, and her image of the individual as a spark from a divine being link her work, especially the *Primero sueño*, to Gnosticism and the poetry of Cortés.

43. Pablo Antonio Cuadra, "Alfonso, discípulo del centauro Quirón," *Revista Conservadora del Pensamiento Centroamericano* 20.101 (1969): 24-25. Cuadra calls Cortés a disciple of Quirón, the metaphysical centaur in Rubén Darío's "Coloquio de los Centauros" (Colloquium of the centaurs), *Darío: antología poética* (Managua: Editorial Hospicio, 1966), p. 98. In this poem, Quirón says:

> Las cosas tienen un ser vital: las cosas
> tienen raros aspectos, miradas misteriosas;
> toda forma es un gesto, una cifra, un enigma.

(Things have a vital being: things / have strange aspects, mysterious looks; / every form is a gesture, a cipher, an enigma.)

Cortés echoes the ideas expressed by Baudelaire in "Correspondances" (and reiterated by Quirón) in the poem "Me ha dicho el alma" (The soul has told me):

> ¿No ves cómo te arroja miradas misteriosas
> lo que puede llamarse "los ojos de la cosas"?

(Can't you see the way that what might be called "the eyes of things" / are throwing you mysterious looks?")

44. Bachelard, *Poetics of Space*, p. 193.

45. Harold Bloom, *Agon: Towards a Theory of Revisionism* (New York: Oxford University Press, 1982), p. 8.

Chapter 2. Pablo Antonio Cuadra and Jules Supervielle: Utopia, National Identity, and History

1. Ezequiel Martínez Estrada, "El nuevo mundo, la isla de *Utopía* y la isla de Cuba," *Cuadernos Americanos* 2.127 (1963): 90.

2. See Martin S. Stabb, "Utopia and Anti-Utopia: The Theme in Selected Essayistic Writings of Spanish America," *Revista de Estudios Hispánicos* 15.3 (1981): 377-93. See also Claudia Schaefer, "A Search for Utopia on Earth: Toward an Understanding of the Literary Production of Ernesto Cardenal," *Crítica Hispánica* 4.2 (1982): 171-79.

3. Pablo Antonio Cuadra, "Sobre Jules Supervielle," in *Torres de Dios* (Managua: Ediciones El Pez y la Serpiente, 1986), p. 48.

4. Ibid., p. 48.

5. *Cuaderno del sur* is a collection of a dozen poems written between 1934-35 while Cuadra accompanied his father on a trip to South America. The poems remained unpublished until they appeared in *Revista del Pensamiento Centroamericano* 177 (1982): 9-24.

6. Jorge Eduardo Arellano, "Los *Poemas nicaragüenses*," *La Prensa Literaria*, 20 julio 1985, p. 6.

7. José Coronel Urtecho, Pablo Antonio Cuadra, and Joaquín Pasos, trans. "Traducciones de poesía francesa del movimiento de vanguardia" *El Pez y la Serpiente* 24 (1981): 139-183. In many of these translations, the theme of the voyage is a predominant one, such as "Torre" (Tower) by Apollinaire, "Far-West" by Blaise Cendrars, an ample selection from Valery Larbaud's *Poèmes par un riche amateur* (Poems by a rich dilettante), (a book in which Larbaud's fictional protagonist, A. O. Barnabooth, a gluttonous South American millionaire, travels from port to port in Europe), "Nueva York" (New York) and "Globo-Panorama" by Paul Morand, and there is also the long poem by Jules Supervielle "La Pampa," the title of which in French, at least as it appears in Supervielle's *Choix de poèmes* (Paris: Gallimard, 1947), p. 13, is "Le Retour" (The return).

8. William Nelson, introduction, *Twentieth Century Interpretations of Utopia*, ed. William Nelson (Englewood Cliffs, N.J.: Prentice Hall, 1968), p. 8.

9. Christian Sénéchal, *Jules Supervielle: Poète de l'univers interieur* (Paris: Librairie Les Lettres, 1939), p. 91.

10. See Ester de Caceres. *Significación de la obra de Jules Supervielle en la cultura uruguaya* (Montevideo: Instituto de Estudios Superiores de Montevideo, 1943), p. 65. According to Ester de Caceres:

> Lautréamont and Laforgue—born in Uruguay—have no place in our literary process; they are essentially French poets, whose relation to our country is only circumstantial and of limited importance. Supervielle has lived for many years in France, was raised there, and writes in French; yet, nevertheless, he continues to be our writer; our landscape, our people and our way of life persist in the themes of his work.

11. Sénéchal, *Supervielle*, p. 138.

12. James A. Hiddleston, *L'univers de Jules Supervielle* (Paris: Librairie José Corti, 1965), p. 83.

13. Frank E. Manuel and Fritzie P. Manuel, *Utopian Thought in the Western World* (Cambridge: Harvard University Press, 1979), p. 61.

14. Mircea Eliade, *The Myth of the Eternal Return, or, Cosmos and History* (Princeton: Princeton University Press, 1954), pp. 10-11.

15. Cf. Miguel León Portilla, *Trece poetas del mundo azteca* (México: Universidad Nacional Autónoma de México, 1972); and also Edmundo Bendezú Aybar, ed., *Literatura Quechua* (Caracas: Biblioteca Ayacucho, 1980).

16. Yves-Alain Favres, *Supervielle: La rêverie et le chant dans Gravitations* (Paris: Librairie A.G. Nizet, 1981), p. 22.

17. Jacques Robichez, *Gravitations de Supervielle* (Paris: Societé D'Edition D'Enseignement Supérieur, 1981), p. 36.

18. George Steiner, *After Babel: Aspects of Language and Translation* (New York: Oxford University Press, 1975), p. 204.

19. Ibid., p. 124.

20. Arellano,"Los *Poemas nicaragüenses*," p. 6.

21. Sénéchal, *Supervielle*, p. 57.

22. Robert Vivier, *Lire Supervielle* (Paris: Librairie José Corti, 1971), pp. 109-10.

23. Favres, *Supervielle*, p. 27.
24. Eliade, *Myth of the Eternal Return*, p. 20.
25. Pablo Antonio Cuadra, *Poemas nicaragüenses* (Santiago, Chile: Editorial Nascimento, 1934), p. 124.
26. Sénéchal, *Supervielle*, p. 98.
27. Tatiana W. Greene, *Jules Supervielle* (Genève: Librairie E. Droz, 1958), p. 26.
28. Manuel and Manuel, *Utopian Thought*, p. 62.
29. Cf. Garcilaso de la Vega, "Egloga I," in *Renaissance and Baroque Poetry of Spain*, ed. Elias L. Rivers (New York: Scribners, 1966), pp. 61-62.
30. Dennis Tedlock, trans. and ed., *Popol Vuh* (New York: Simon & Schuster, 1985), p. 63.
31. Cf. Pablo Antonio Cuadra, *Obra poética completa*, 8 vols. (San José, Costa Rica: Editorial Libro Libre, 1983), 1:114. The author has included the following introduction to *Poemas nicaragüenses*:

Poemas nicaragüenses is the first book published by Pablo Antonio Cuadra. It was written between 1930 and 1933 and published by Editorial Nascimento in Santiago, Chile in 1934. It contained 34 poems, among them six *cantos* (songs) and *romances* (ballads) that belonged to a previous book: *Canciones de Pájaro y Señora* (Songs of bird and lady). The author revised almost all of *Poemas nicaragüenses* in 1935 for a second edition that was never published. These revised poems are the ones that have appeared in anthologies authorized by the author from that time to this day . . . The poet, furthermore, eliminated seven poems in this new version: "Stadium" (Stadium), "Sombras y distancias" (Shadows and distances), "Sabana atardecida" (Savanna at dusk), "Barco" (Ship), "El valle de las rosas" (The valley of the roses), "Luna" (Moon), and the long poem "Lucha" (Struggle), that years later became the short story "Agosto" (August).

32. Carlos Tunnermann Bernheim, "La poesía nicaragüense y universal de Pablo Antonio Cuadra," *Revista del Pensamiento Centroamericano* 177 (1982): 71.
33. Edelberto Torres, *Sandino y sus pares* (Managua: Editorial Nueva Nicaragua, 1983), p. 335.
34. Jorge Eduardo Arellano, personal interview, 22 November 1986. Arellano comments on the parallel works in poetry and prose produced by Cuadra in the early 1930s during Sandino's struggle against foreign intervention:

Pablo Antonio Cuadra finished two great works in 1933: *Campo* (Countryside), which was the original title of *Poemas nicaragüenses*, and a novel about Sandino's struggle. The 200-page manuscript of the novel was lost. Pablo Antonio lost the chance to begin a successful literary career. I always told him that he lacked audacity, that it is never too late, that he could reconstruct it. But there isn't time, because Pablo Antonio is a person consumed by the demands of journalism. For this reason, he has a ferocious conflict with his work as a journalist. The problem is more serious than anyone can describe in an interview. He deposited one of his greatest enthusiasms in that novel. But it got lost. In Nicaragua everything has gotten lost and has been destroyed. Destruction is part of our history and identity as Nicaraguans. If Pablo Antonio had published the novel in 1933, before or after Sandino's death, he would have established himself in Latin America as a novelist. Pablo Antonio was a Sandinista, a fresh and pure young man, twenty-one years old, who was describing his hero, transforming him into myth. In addition, the novel contained the traditions of that time as well as the stories, the ambushes, and the demonstrations in support of Sandino in Granada's park.

35. José Román, *Maldito país* (Managua: Ediciones El Pez y la Serpiente, 1983), p. 129.
36. Martínez Estrada, "El nuevo mundo," p. 117.
37. Gerhard Ritter, "*Utopia* and Power Politics," in *Twentieth Century Interpretations of Utopia*, ed. William Nelson (Englewood Cliffs, N.J.: Prentice Hall, 1968), p. 48.

38. See Genesis 2:7 and also Tedlock, *Popol Vuh*, 79-80. The Mayan gods in *Popol Vuh* seem more fallible than the God of Judeo-Christian tradition: The Mayan Maker, Modeler, Bearer, and Begetter fail in their attempts to fashion humanity (first from mud, then from wood) until they discover the perfect substance of ground corn.

39. See Román, *Maldito país*, pp. 143-44. Román quotes Sandino on the military strategy of the Sandinistas as compared to that of the North American soldiers:

> The motorboats that the Marines used, even the smallest ones that had outboard motors, turned out to be very impractical for this war in such narrow rivers between mountains since the noice of the motor amplified by the echoes of the mountains betrayed their position way in advance. Besides, it was difficult to get them around rapids and whitewater. When the crews of our dugout canoes (which were totally silent) heard the sound of a plane or motorboat . . . they simply went to the shore, got in the water, and hid in the jungle with their canoe. Everything disappeared without a trace.

40. Alvaro Urtecho, "Pablo Antonio Cuadra o la vuelta de los tiempos," *La Crónica Literaria* 29 (31 mayo 1989): 1.

41. Eliade, *Myth of the Eternal Return*, p. 42.

42. Ibid., p. 162.

43. See Román, *Maldito país*, pp. 152, 162. Román quotes Sandino recounting the difficulties faced by the Sandinistas themselves, who had to deal with a landscape that was both benevolent and extremely hostile.

44. See Guillermo Yepes Boscán, "Hacer el poema con el aliento del mito y el lodo de la historia" (introduction), in *Siete árboles contra el atardecer* by Pablo Antonio Cuadra (Caracas: Ediciones de la Presidencia de la República, 1980), pp. 7-22.

45. José Emilio Balladares, *Pablo Antonio Cuadra: La palabra y el tiempo, secuencia y estructura de su creación poética* (San José, Costa Rica: Editorial Libro Libre, 1986), p. 11.

46. Gloria de Guardia Alfaro, "Visión del mundo o centro espiritual de Pablo Antonio Cuadra a través de su evolución temática," *Revista del Pensamiento Centroamericano* 177 (1982): 38. The article is an excerpt from her book *Estudio sobre el pensamiento poético de Pablo Antonio Cuadra* (Madrid: Editorial Gredos, 1971).

Chapter 3. Carlos Martínez Rivas and Charles Baudelaire: Two Painters of Modern Life

1. Octavio Paz, "Baudelaire as Art Critic: Presence and Present," in *On Poets and Others*, trans. Michael Schmidt (New York: Seaver, 1986).

2. Ibid., p. 52.

3. Charles Baudelaire, "Le Peintre de la Vie Moderne," in *Sur le dandysme*, ed. Roger Kempf (Paris: Bibliotèque 10/18, 1971), p. 205.

4. Originally published in *Cuadernos Hispanoamericanos* 181 (1965): 20-28.

5. Charles Baudelaire, *The Mirror of Art: Critical Studies*, ed. and trans. Jonathan Mayne (London: Phaidon, 1955), p. 306.

6. During a March 1979 visit with Carlos Martínez Rivas in Granada, Nicaragua, the poet allowed us to examine in a cursory fashion an impressive pile of notebooks which contained commentaries on expositions in Europe and the United States.

7. Carlos Martínez Rivas, interview, *Culture & Politics in Nicaragua: Testimonies of Poets and Writers*, ed. and trans. Steven White (New York: Lumen, 1986), pp. 48-49.

8. Julio Valle-Castillo, "Carlos Martínez Rivas o la soberbia verbal," *Nuevo Amanecer Cultural* 517 (16 junio 1990): 2.

9. Paz, "Baudelaire," pp. 54-55.

10. Lois Boe Hyslop, *Baudelaire, Man of His Time* (New Haven: Yale University Press, 1980), p. 42.

11. André Ferran, *L'Esthétique de Baudelaire* (Paris: Nizet, 1968), p. 479.

12. Cf. Carlos Martínez Rivas, "En la carretera una mujerzuela detiene al pasante" (On the highway a strumpet detains the passerby), in *La insurrección solitaria* (Managua: Nueva Nicaragua, 1982), p. 115-16. In this poem, Martínez Rivas rewrites Baudelaire's idea of rebirth with striking literalness:

> En su vientre lo conservaba
> cada mujer. No encinta
> de un hijo de él sino preñada
> dél.

(In their wombs, each woman / kept him. Not pregnant / with a child by him, but pregnant / with him.)

13. Baudelaire, *The Mirror of Art*, pp. 37-38.

14. See Martínez Rivas, interview, 52-53:

". . . In 1955, when I was at a department store called Bullock's, I saw death enter—that woman in the poem ["Dos Murales U.S.A."]. So I wrote down on a little card: 'The woman I saw at Bullock's. Don't forget. Write a possible poem to be entitled "Reflections on a Passerby".'"

15. Ibid., pp. 126-27.

16. Paz, "Baudelaire," p. 57.

17. Jean Starobinksi, "De la critique à la poésie," *Preuves* (Mai 1968): 18.

18. Wolfgang Drost, "De la critique d'art Baudelairienne," *Baudelaire: Actes du Colloque de Nice (25-27 mai 1967)* (Monaco: Annales de la Faculté des Letres et Sciences Humaines de Nice, 1968), p. 87.

19. Ferran, *L'Esthétique de Baudelaire*, p. 480.

20. See Paz, "Baudelaire," p. 59.

21. Cf. Charles Baudelaire, "Le jet d'eau" (The fountain). The metaphysical links between fountain, soul and heart in this poem strongly resemble the metaphorical structure of Section II, part 5 of "Dos Murales U.S.A."

22. Paz, "Baudelaire," p. 53.

23. Starobinski, "De la critique à la poésie," p. 22.

24. Alvaro Urtecho, interview, *Culture & Politics in Nicaragua: Testimonies of Poets and Writers*, ed and trans. Steven White (New York: Lumen, 1986), p. 117.

25. See John Berger, *The Success & Failure of Picasso* (London: Writers & Readers, 1980), p. 40.

26. Gaeton Picon, "La Qualité du Présent," *Preuves* (Mai 1968): 25-26.

Chapter 4. The Eschatological Voyage in the Poetry of Joaquín Pasos, Vicente Huidobro, and T. S. Eliot

1. See, for example, Pablo Antonio Cuadra, "Prólogo a *Breve suma*," Ernesto Cardenal, "Joaquín Pasos," and Jorge Eduardo Arellano, "Esbozo biográfico de Joaquín Pasos," in *Joaquín Pasos: 1914-1947* (León, Nicaragua: Cuadernos Universitarios, 1972), pp. 27-35, 13-26, and 46-52, respectively. See also Julio Valle-Castillo, introduction, in *Poesías escogidas* by Joaquín Pasos (México: Comunidad Latinoamericana de Escritores, 1974), pp. 7-41. It is important to add that this critical interest has been augmented by new editions of Pasos's *Poemas de un joven* published by

Editorial Nueva Nicaragua in 1983 and by Fondo de Cultura Económica in Mexico in 1984. Too, Carlos Martínez Rivas's "Canto fúnebre a la muerte de Joaquín Pasos" is surely one of the most moving elegies in Hispanic American poetry.

2. See Mario Benedetti, "Joaquín Pasos o el poema como crimen perfecto," in *Joaquín Pasos 1914-1947* (León, Nicaragua: Cuadernos Universitarios), p. 36. Originally published in *Letras del continente mestizo* (Montevideo: Arca, 1967).

3. See Pedro Lastra and Luis Eyzaguirre, eds., "Catorce poetas de hoy," *Inti* 18-19 (Otoño 1983-Primavera 1984). This issue also includes an article on Pasos by George Yúdice, "Poemas de un joven que quiso ser otro," (pp. 1-10).

4. Joaquín Pasos, "Señoras y Señores, ¡Mucho Cuidado con Esta Poesía!," *Ya!* 12 (1941): 13. We would like to express our thanks to Huidobro scholar and University of Chicago professor René de Costa for providing a copy of this infrequently-cited article.

5. Pablo Antonio Cuadra, "Prólogo a *Breve suma*," in *Joaquín Pasos: 1914-1947* (León, Nicaragua: Cuadernos Universitarios, 1972), p. 33. Originally appeared as the prologue to Pasos's posthumously-published *Breve suma* (Managua: Nuevos Horizontes, 1947).

6. Ernesto Cardenal, "Joaquín Pasos," in *Joaquín Pasos: 1914-1947* (León, Nicaragua: Cuadernos Universitarios, 1972), p. 24. Originally appeared as the prologue to Pasos's *Poemas de un joven* (México: Fondo de Cultura Económica, 1962).

7. See Alberto Ordóñez Argüello, "Poemas de un joven que no sabe inglés," *La Nueva Prensa* (Managua), 5 agosto 1937, n.p. Ordóñez quotes at length from an unpublished prologue that Pasos wrote in 1937 for a group of eleven poems in English which were not published until they appeared in *Breve suma* and *Poemas de un joven*. In this prologue, Pasos theorizes about the absolute autonomy of poetry:

> Poetry is independent even from language. It simply is. If I write poems with English words, it does not mean that I wanted to write them with English words, but that the poems wanted to be that way. They have the right to their independence as *criaturas* (creatures, babies). . . . The English of these poems is, in terms of grammar, very censurable. They have forms and expressions that are inadmissable in academic English which were set forth by a poetic logic that does not recognize canons or grammars.

8. See José Coronel Urtecho, Pablo Antonio Cuadra, and Joaquín Pasos, trans., "Traducciones de Poesía Francesa del Movimiento de Vanguardia," *El Pez y la Serpiente* 24 (1981): 139-183.

9. Octavio Paz, "La Palabra Edificante," in *Cuadrivio* (México: Joaquín Moritz, 1965), p. 175.

10. In a letter to Pablo Antonio Cuadra dated 27 March 1943, Pasos says that the "Canto" "is ready." The fragment Pasos eliminated from "Canto de guerra de las cosas" that begins "Dicen que vais a la guerra" (They say you're going to war) (see note 19 in this chapter) clearly indicates that Pasos had a version of his important poem before the events of Pearl Harbor in December 1941.

11. One of Pasos's teachers at this time (a Jesuit) made the following comment about his student on a report card dated 15 September 1931: "A correct, well-educated young man: he takes advantage of his studies, but he would be better off if he didn't waste so much time writing poetry, etc." The poet's personal papers and manuscripts are now in the care of his brother, Luis Pasos Argüello, a prominent lawyer in Managua. We had access to this material, much of it unpublished, in January and February 1984, during a visit to Managua. The material is more or less well-ordered because an effort had been made to publish Pasos's complete prose together with some unpublished poems that the poet wrote during his adolescence. Unfortunately, this project has been totally abandoned.

12. Ernesto Cardenal, introduction, in *Poemas de un joven* by Joaquín Pasos (Managua: Editorial Nueva Nicaragua, 1983), p. 19.

13. Julio Valle-Castillo, introduction, in *Poesías escogidas* by Joaquín Pasos (México: Comunidad Latinoamericana de Escritores, 1974), p. 27.

14. Jaime Concha, *Vicente Huidobro* (Madrid: Ediciones Júcar, 1980), p. 73.

15. René de Costa, *Vicente Huidobro: The Careers of a Poet* (Oxford: Oxford University Press, 1984), p. 146.

16. See de Costa, *Vicente Huidobro*, p. 155. De Costa believes that Canto III of *Altazor* represents "the cyclic death of poetry from Modernism to Creationism, from Symbolism to Surrealism."

17. Cuadra, "Prólogo a *Breva Suma*," p. 33. Perhaps this sermon-like quality is felt most strongly in the poem's opening direct address to "vosotros." It is interesting to compare this first section of the poem to a supressed fragment that began "Canto de guerra de las cosas" in earlier drafts of the poem. The deleted fragment has a wholly different, mystical conception of life's struggles and uncertainties:

> Grande, alto, fuerte, de enorme músculo encendido,
> el día se levanta y alza la mano en busca del
>   rostro del Señor.
> No hacen un día todas las vidas de los hombres,
> ni todas las guerras juntas hacen tanta lucha.
> Es triste el hombre vivo que ensaya el pobre
>   aliento
> en su pierna, en su caballo, en su mujer.
> Ni todas las piernas del mundo hacen la carrera del
>   día,
> ni todos los caballos pueden arrastrar un ayer.
> Pero este día arrastra al otro y al otro día,
> perfectos y redondos modelos del trabajo del sol
> ante el hombre de manos inútiles que ha dejado
>   escapar el milagro
> ante las barbas del hombre el brazo del día se alza
>   día a día
> hasta tocar las barbas del Señor.
> ¡Las espantosas barbas del Señor!

(Great, high, strong, with enormous burning muscle, / the day rises and lifts its hand in search of the Lord's face. / All the lives of humanity do not make a day, / nor do all the wars together make for so much struggle. / It's sad, the way the living man rehearses his poor breath on his legs, on his horse, on his wife. / Nor do all the legs of the world equal the race of the day, / nor can all the horses drag back a single yesterday. / But this day drags another and another day, / perfect and round models of the work of the sun / while man, with such useless hands, has let the miracle escape, / right in front of man's beard, the day's arm rises, day after day / until it touches the Lord's beard. / The awesome beard of the Lord!)

18. de Costa, *Vicente Huidobro*, p. 150.

19. F. T. Marinetti cited in Walter Benjamin, "The Work of Art in the Age of Mechanical Reproduction," in *Illuminations*, ed. Hannah Arendt, trans. Harry Zohn (New York: Schocken Books, 1969), p. 241. Also see Julio Valle-Castillo, "Joaquín Pasos: El poeta de la vanguardia," and Ileana Rodríguez, "Poetas y Poesía," *Nuevo Amanecer Cultural* (24 enero 1987), pp. 1+ and 3+, respectively. These two articles reflect a recent Marxist valorization of Pasos (as well as the foray into fascist politics of his generation's *vanguardia* movement) on the occasion of the fortieth anniversary of Pasos's death. Valle-Castillo, in his search for "an ideological impulse" in Pasos's "Canto de guerra de las cosas," says: "I have always thought that this poem is Joaquín Pasos's lamenting of the defeat of fascism and Nazism in World War II. He laments the death and definitive failure of his generation's political project." Luis Alberto Cabrales published a relevant supressed fragment from "Canto de guerra de las cosas" in *Política de Estados Unidos y*

poesía de Hispanoamérica (Managua: Publicaciones del Ministerio de Educación Pública, 1958). According to Cabrales, "Pasos does not believe, and many others would agree with him, that the citizens of the United States are fit for war. He considers [North Americans] weakened by comfort and the good life, incapable of confronting the spartan youth of Germany and Italy" (p. 9).

> Dicen que vais a la guerra.
> ¡Qué vais a ir!
> Dicen que partís al alba.
> ¡Qué vais a partir!
> Dicen que sois fuertes, dicen que sois altos,
> dicen que vais a luchar.
> Dicen que anheláis la lucha.
> ¡Qué va!
> Dicen que daréis la sangre
> además
> de viejos tubos de dentífrico y de jabón de afeitar
>
> Dicen que vais a acabar
> con el hambre de los pueblos,
> pero después de cenar.
>
> Dicen que pondréis las cosas en su lugar,
> pero hay mucho lugar sin cosas y muchas cosas sin lugar.
>
> Os esperan esas cosas
> enfurecidas, allá;
> ¿y vais a partir? ¡Qué va!
> Allá sólo el bronce tiembla
> y lo hace para cantar.
> Y vosotros, ya tembláis!
> Tembláis de miedo a morir,
> y dicen que vais a la guerra . . .
> ¡Qué vais a ir!

(They say you're going to war. / That you're going to go! / They say that you're leaving at dawn. / That you're leaving! / They say that you're strong, they say that you're tall, / that you're going to fight. / They say that you long to fight. / How absurd! / They say that you will give your blood / in addition / to old tubes of toothpaste and shaving cream / They say that you will end / the hunger of the people, / but after dinner. / They say that you will put things in their place, / but there are many places without things and many things without places. / Those furious things / await you, over there; / and are you going to leave? How absurd! / Over there, only bronze trembles / and does so in order to sing. / And you, you're already trembling! / You tremble because you're scared of dying, / and they say you're going to war . . . / That you're going to go!)

For Valle-Castillo, this fragment is not only anti-North American and anti-imperialist, but also an attack against a country fighting fascism. He concludes his article by saying that "the excellence of 'Canto de guerra de las cosas' and of the poetry of Joaquín Pasos in general transcends its ideological aberrations and, as art, is irreducible to it."

20. Ernesto Cardenal, "Joaquín Pasos: un joven que no ha viajado nunca," *Cuadernos Americanos* 6.4 (1947): 229-30.

21. Eduardo Zepeda-Henríquez, "Joaquín Pasos: sabiduría y temporalidad," *Joaquín Pasos: 1914-1947* (León, Nicaragua: Cuadernos Universitarios, 1972), p. 143.

22. Pablo Antonio Cuadra, interview, *Culture & Politics in Nicaragua: Testimonies of Poets and Writers*, ed. and trans. Steven White (New York: Lumen Books, 1986), p. 22.

23. Walter Hoefler, "Algunos temas en la poesía de Joaquín Pasos," diss., Universidad Austral de Chile, 1971, p. 33.

24. Joaquín Pasos, "Carta sobre la muerte," *Los Lunes de la Nueva Prensa* (Managua), 27 enero 1947; p. 2. Also, cf. Joaquín Pasos, "La vida es muerte: juguete trágico," *La Prensa Literaria* (Managua), 5 mayo 1984, p. 8, the original of which was given to me by Jorge Eduardo Arellano. An excerpt on love and death from these notebook sketches (composed toward the end of the poet's life) is more characteristic of the pessimism in "Canto de guerra de las cosas":

> Love? What good is love in places like these? It only serves to bring more people into the world, more men going toward death, more women who wait, crying on tombs, their own tombs. Each swelling womb is a nascent grave, each look of love is a memory toward the end. No. Love is death.

25. Alvaro Urtecho, "La tierra baldía de Joaquín Pasos," *Nuevo Amanecer Cultural* (Managua), 24 enero 1987, p. 1.

26. Julio Valle-Castillo, "Joaquín Pasos: El poeta de la vanguardia," *Nuevo Amanecer Cultural* (Managua), 24 enero 1987, p. 2.

27. Joaquín Pasos, "Conferencia sobre Vicente Huidobro," in *Joaquín Pasos: 1914-1947* (León, Nicaragua: Cuadernos Universitarios, 1972), p. LXXXIII.

28. Paul Ricoeur, *The Symbolism of Evil*, trans. Emerson Buchanan (Boston: Beacon, 1967), p. 265.

29. Cuadra, "Prólogo a *Breva Suma*," op. cit., p. 33. Also, cf. *Popol Vuh*, trans. Dennis Tedlock (New York: Touchstone/Simon and Schuster, 1985), p. 84. In what might be considered a true mythic antecedent to "Canto de guerra de las cosas," all the abused household utensils in the *Popol Vuh* rebel against the wooden people: "Their faces were crushed by things of wood and stone. Everything spoke: their water jugs, their tortilla griddles, their plates, their cooking pots, their dogs, their grinding stones, each and every thing crushed their faces."

30. For this note on the significance of "the man with three staves," I would like to thank Prof. Don Gifford, who recently retired from teaching English at Williams College.

31. Cleo McNelly Kearns, *T. S. Eliot and Indic Traditions: A Study in Poetry and Belief* (Cambridge: Cambridge University Press, 1987), p. 211.

32. Hoefler, "Algunos temas," p. 33.

33. Urtecho, "La tierra baldía de Joaquin Pasos," p. 3.

Chapter 5. Salomón de la Selva: Testimonial Poetry and World War I

1. See Pedro Henríquez Ureña, "Salomón de la Selva," *El Figaro* (La Habana), 6-IV-1919, pp. 11-12; reprinted in *Homenaje a Salomón de la Selva: 1959-1969* (León, Nicaragua: Cuadernos Universitarios, 1969), p. 13:

> Salomón de la Selva had enlisted in the English Army, toward the middle of 1918, when he had just published his first book of poems in English. From the middle of 1917, he had been planning to enter the ranks and fight in the just war: in the training camp he had won the right to be a lieutenant. But the U. S. Army stubbornly refused to admit him unless he became a U. S. citizen. The poet declared that he would not give up his Nicaraguan citizenship. Finally, sick of useless efforts, he enlisted as a soldier in England, the country of one of his grandmothers.

See also Salomón de la Selva, prólogo, *El soldado desconocido* (Managua: Nueva Nicaragua, 1982), p. 9:

I should explain that I had the good fortune of serving as a volunteer under the flag of King George V, the colors of my father's mother. For this reason, I was able to write this poem.

2. Salomón de la Selva, *El soldado desconocido* (1922; 1971; 1975; Managua: Nueva Nicaragua, 1982).

3. See Stefan Baciu, "Salomón de la Selva precursor," in *Homenaje a Salomón de la Selva 1959-1969* (León, Nicaragua: Cuadernos Universitarios, 1969), p. 103. Baciu makes the point that *El soldado desconocido* "paves the way to humanitarian and social poetry," two important characteristics of Hispanic American poetry written after the Cuban Revolution.

4. José Emilio Pacheco, "Nota sobre la otra vanguardia," *Casa de las Américas* 118 (enero-febrero 1980): 105.

5. Salomón de la Selva, *Tropical Town & Other Poems* (New York: John Lane, 1918).

6. Henríquez Ureña, *Homenaje a Salomón de la Selva*, p. 17.

7. Ibid., p. 18.

8. Alice Meynell, "Decivilised," in *The Rhythm of Life and Other Essays* (London: John Lane, 1896), pp. 7-8.

9. See Salomón de la Selva, "Tropical Town," *The Book of Poetry: Collected from the Whole Field of British and American Poetry. Also Translations of Important Poems from Foreign Languages*, ed. Edwin Markham, 10 vols. (New York: W. H. Wise, 1926), 3:785. The bizarre introduction to the anthologized poem is worth quoting in part:

> His Central American ancestry counts Indian chiefs and Spanish conquistadores, and one of his grandmothers was an English noblewoman. . . . In 1910, on the death of his father, the Nicaraguan Congress decreed his adoption as the ward of the nation, making him virtually their poet laureate.

10. Henríquez Ureña, *Homenaje*, pp. 17-18.

11. Ibid., p. 18.

12. José Coronel Urtecho, "En Nueva York, con el poeta Salomón de la Selva," in *Homenaje a Salomón de la Selva: 1959-1969* (León, Nicaragua: Cuadernos Universitarios, 1969), p. 63.

13. Ibid., p. 64.

14. Ibid., pp. 66-67.

15. Ibid., p. 66.

16. Jon Silkin, introduction, *The Penguin Book of First World War Poetry*, 2nd ed. (New York: Viking Penguin, 1981), p. 29. Hereafter referred to in the text as *PBFWWP*.

17. Henríquez Ureña, *Homenaje*, pp. 15-16.

18. Among Mejía's many projects left unfinished when he died in 1985, was a plan to publish de la Selva's complete works.

19. Siegfried Sassoon, *Siegfried's Journey: 1916-1920* (New York: Viking, 1946), pp. 212-13.

20. Jorge Eduardo Arellano, letter to the author, 25 September 1988.

21. See Pacheco, "Nota sobre," p. 105.

22. See Rubén Darío, *Eleven Poems of Rubén Darío*, trans. Thomas Walsh and Salomón de la Selva (New York: Hispanic Society of America, 1916). As a translator from Spanish into English, de la Selva recreates in strict English rhyme and meter Darío's rhymed modernist poems in Spanish.

23. See Silkin, *Penquin Book of First World War Poetry*, pp. 29-39.

24. Alfred E. Cornebise, introduction, *Doughboy Doggerel: Verse of the American Expeditionary Force 1918-1919* (Athens: Ohio University Press, 1985), pp. xi-xii.

25. See John H. Johnston, *English Poetry of the First World War: A Study in the*

Evolution of Lyric and Narrative Form (Princeton: Princeton University Press, 1964).

26. See *Voices from the Great War*, ed. Peter Vansittart (New York: Avon, 1985), p. 26.

27. Ibid., p. 33.

28. Jon Silkin, *Out of Battle: The Poetry of the Great War* (London: Oxford University Press, 1972), pp. 58-59.

29. Cornebise, *Doughboy Doggerel*, p. ix.

30. Lucía Graves, "Poetas en la guerra, el grito oculto," *El País* (Madrid), 11 noviembre 1988, p. 36.

31. Johnston, *English Poetry of the First World War*, pp. 18-19.

32. Graves, "Poetas en la guerra," p. 36.

33. Oscar Williams, ed., *The War Poets: An Anthology of the War Poetry of the 20th Century* (New York: John Day, 1945), p. 4.

34. See Gwen Kirkpatrick, *The Dissonant Legacy of Modernismo: Lugones, Herrera y Reissig, and the Voices of Modern Spanish American Poetry* (Berkeley and Los Angeles: University of Cailfornia Press, 1989).

35. Jorge Eduardo Arellano, "Salomón de la Selva," diss., Universidad Complutense de Madrid, 1985, p. 113.

36. Silkin, *Penguin Book of First World War Poetry*, p. 31.

37. Johnston, *English Poetry of the First World War*, p. 20.

38. John Beverley and Marc Zimmerman, *Literature and Politics in the Central American Revolutions* (Austin: University of Texas Press, 1990), p. 133.

39. Sergio Ramírez, interview, *Culture & Politics in Nicaragua: Testimonies of Poets and Writers* ed. and trans. Steven White (New York: Lumen, 1986), p. 76.

40. De la Selva, *El soldado desconocido*, pp. 8-9.

41. Silkin, *Out of Battle*, 156-57.

42. Edmund Blunden, *War Poets 1914-1918* (London: Longmans, Green & Co., 1958), p. 30.

43. See note 19 on Futurism in the preceding chapter on Joaquín Pasos.

44. Horacio Peña, "Salomón de la Selva: Soldado Desconocido," *La Prensa* (Managua), 17 marzo 1963, p. 1B+.

45. De la Selva, *El soldado desconocido*, pp. 7-8.

46. Ibid., p. 9.

Chapter 6. Translation and Intertextuality in the Poetry of José Coronel Urtecho

1. Jorge Eduardo Arellano, personal interview, 22 November 1986. From 1910-1928, Nicaragua experienced a strictly-imposed "Pax Americana."

2. See Jorge Eduardo Arellano, *El movimiento de vanguardia de Nicaragua (1927-1932): Gérmenes, desarrollo, significado* (Managua: Ediciones de Librería Cultural Nicaragüense, 1971), p. 55. Arellano quotes an article entitled "Invitación a Reaccionar" (Invitation to react), written by Coronel in late 1929:

> Our system of democratic government is our perdition. The democratic idea, false in itself and therefore impracticable, has been the instrument of deception that ambitious adventurers from everywhere have used to lead the people to slaughter. Democracy is a principle of disorder and chaos, fatal for the Latin peoples, and especially for us.

See also José Coronel Urtecho, *Tres conferencias a la empresa privada* (Managua: Ediciones El Pez y la Serpiente, 1974), p. 97. Coronel states:

After all, the humanities have been and are . . . the substance of culture. Even though, of course, it would be excessive to say that the humanities constitute the entire culture or culture itself, there can be no doubt that in certain epochs and countries of the occidental world, one can discern a kind of culture of the culture.

3. Sergio Ramírez, "El concepto de burguesía en dos noveletas," *Revista del Pensamiento Centroamericano* 150 (1976): 95.

4. See José Coronel Urtecho, trans., *Panorama y antología de la poesía norteamericana* (Madrid: Seminario de Problemas Hispanoamericanos, 1949). See also José Coronel Urtecho and Ernesto Cardenal, trans., *Antología de la poesía norteamericana* (Madrid: Aguilar, 1963). The former anthology includes Coronel's nearly one hundred-page introduction to North American poetry (1745-1945) as well as his translations of 45 poets: Bryant, Longfellow, Emerson, Oliver Wendell Holmes, Whittier, James Russell Lowell, Poe, Whitman, Dickenson, Aldrich, Markham, Reese, Robinson, Frost, Masters, Sandburg, Lindsay, Amy Lowell, Crapsey, Branch, Teasdale, Bynner, Oppenheim, Pound, Jeffers, Kreymborg, Wylie, Millay, H.D., Ridge, Stevens, Ransom, Fletcher, Aiken, Bodenheim, Eliot, cummings, Moore, MacLeish, Williams, Hughes, Crane, Benet, Gregory, and Rukeyser. The latter anthology includes a two-page introduction by Ernesto Cardenal as well as the collaborative translations of Cardenal and Coronel of Native American poems followed by poetry by seventy-six poets: Poe, Whitman, Dickenson, Aldrich, Markham, Crane, Reese, Robinson, Frost, Masters, Sandburg, Lindsay, Bynner, Kreymborg, Oppenheim, Johnson, Jeffers, Stevens, Ransom, Bodenheim, Amy Lowell, Crapsey, Branch, Teasdale, Wylie, Millay, H.D., Ridge, Reading, Stein, Pound, Eliot, Moore, Aiken, Williams, Bartolomeo Vanzetti, MacLeish, cummings, Van Doren, Humphries, Hughes, Crane, Benet, Gregory, Penn Warren, Lorentz, Lattimore, Auden, Rukeyser, Shapiro, Agee, Schwartz, Rexroth, Fearing, Patchen, Roethke, Jarrell, Merton, Lax, Laughlin, Viereck, Robert Lowell, Wilbur, Murray, Miles, Brother Antoninus, Ferlinghetti, Levertov, Whalen, McClure, Ginsberg, O'Hara, Ashbery, Lamantia, Snyder, and Frankl. See also Beltrán Morales, interview, *Culture & Politics in Nicaragua: Testimonies of Poets and Writers*, ed. and trans. Steven White (New York: Lumen Books, 1986), p. 90. When asked if poetry from the United States had a very large influence on Nicaraguan poets in the 1960s, Morales replied: "The anthology of North American poetry published by José Coronel Urtecho and Ernesto Cardenal was the Bible for two generations. But I was never too enthusiastic about it, perhaps because, as a friend once said, 'We're under the poetic dollar, poet!'"

5. José Coronel Urtecho, *Panorama y antología de la poesía norteamericana*, p. 9.

6. Ibid., p. 9.

7. José Coronel Urtecho, "El americanismo en la casa de mi abuelo," *Revista Conservadora* 23 (1962): 31.

8. See Coronel Urtecho, *Panorama*, pp. 73-74.

9. See Coronel Urtecho, *Panorama*, pp. 171-78; Coronel Urtecho and Cardenal, *Antología*, pp. 115-30; and Eastman, Allison, et al., *Norton Anthology of Poetry* (New York: Norton, 1970), pp. 952-53.

10. José Coronel Urtecho, "Rápido tránsito," in *Prosa* (San José, Costa Rica: Educa, 1972), p. 186.

11. See Carlos Chamorrro Coronel, "El humanismo de José Coronel Urtecho," *Revista del Pensamiento Centroamericano* 150 (1976): 85.

12. See N. Christoph de Nagy, *Ezra Pound's Poetics and Literary Tradition: the Critical Decade* (Basel, Switzerland: Francke Verlag Bern, 1966), p. 43.

13. Coronel Urtecho, *Prosa*, p. 273.

14. De Nagy, *Ezra Pound's Poetics*, p. 43.

15. Octavio Paz, interview, *The Poet's Other Voice: Conversations on Literary Translation*, ed. Edwin Honig (Amherst: University of Massachusetts Press, 1985), p. 154.

16. See Horacio Peña, "Dos poemas: una actitud," in *Homenaje a José Coronel Urtecho al cumplir 70 años de edad*, ed. Ernesto Gutiérrez (León, Nicaragua: Cuadernos Universitarios, 1976), pp. 195-204. See also Stephen Tapscott, *American Beauty: William Carlos Williams and the Modernist Whitman* (New York: Columbia University Press, 1984), p. 24. Tapscott characterizes Pound's acceptance of Whitman as "a filial reconciliation, in images of grafting a new fruitful branch to an established rootstock."

17. Homer, *The Iliad*, trans. Richmond Lattimore (Chicago: University of Chicago Press, 1962), p. 453. We would like to thank Professor Perry J. Powers from the University of Oregon for his help in tracing this reference in Greek to its source.

18. José Ortega y Gasset, "Miseria y esplendor de la traducción," in *El libro de las misiones* (Buenos Aires: Espasa Calpe Argentina, 1940), p. 166.

19. Kenneth Rexroth, "The Poet as Translator," in *Assays* (New York: New Directions, 1961), p. 20.

20. Duverrán, "Coronel Urtecho," p. 19.

21. José Coronel Urtecho, interview, *Culture & Politics in Nicaragua: Testimonies of Poets and Writers*, ed. and trans. Steven White (New York: Lumen Books, 1986), p. 11.

22. Coronel Urtecho, "El americanismo en la casa de mi abuelo," p. 30.

23. See the three versions of Marianne Moore's "Poetry" in *Observations* (New York: The Dial Press, 1924), n.p.; *Selected Poems* (New York: MacMillan, 1935), pp. 36-37; and *Complete Poems of Marianne Moore* (New York: MacMillan, 1967), p. 36.

24. Donald Hall, *Marianne Moore: The Cage and the Animal* (New York: Pegasus, 1970), p. 41.

25. Ibid., p. 40.

26. Pamela White Hadas, *Marianne Moore: Poet of Affection* (Syracuse, N.Y.: Syracuse University Press, 1977), p. 62.

27. See Ernesto Gutiérrez, introduction, *Pol-la d'ananta katanta paranta* by José Coronel Urtecho (León, Nicaragua: Editorial Universitaria, 1970), pp. XIII-XIV.

28. See José Coronel Urtecho, "El hombre americano y sus problemas," *Revista Conservadora* 14 (1961): 20.

29. See Coronel Urtecho, *Tres conferencias*, pp. 99-100.

30. Lewis Hyde, *The Gift* (New York: Vintage, 1983), p. 235.

31. See Coronel Urtecho, "Marcha triunfal," in *Pol-la d'ananta*, p. 124.

32. Cf. Ernesto Cardenal, "Con Walker en Nicaragua," in *Antología* (Managua: Editorial Nueva Nicaragua, 1983), p. 21. In this poem, Cardenal, too, makes use of Masters' technique of enumerating individuals and their distinguishing characteristics:

> De Brissot, Dolan, Henry, Bob Gray;
> el bandido, el desilusionado, el vago, el buscador
> de tesoros.

33. Coronel Urtecho, "El hombre americano y sus problemas," 21.

34. See John T. Flanagan, *Edgar Lee Masters: The Spoon River Poet and His Critics* (Metuchen, N.J.: The Scarecrow Press, 1974), p. 41. Flanagan summarizes Herbert Ellsworth Childs, "Agrarianism and Sex, Edgar Lee Masters and the Modern Spirit," *Sewanee Review* 41 (1933): 331-43.

35. Coronel Urtecho, *Panorama*, p. 69.

36. José Miguel Oviedo, "Las voces múltiples de Coronel Urtecho," in *Homenaje a José Coronel Urtecho al cumplir 70 años de edad*, ed. Ernesto Gutiérrez (León, Nicaragua: Editorial Universitaria, 1976), p. 220.

37. See Angel del Río, *Historia de la literatura española*, 2 vols. (New York: Holt, 1963), 1: 76-82.

Chapter 7. Ernesto Cardenal and North American Literature: The Formulation of an Ethical Identity

1. See Paul W. Borgeson, Jr., *Hacia el hombre nuevo: poesía y pensamiento de Ernesto Cardenal* (London: Támesis, 1984), p. 30.

2. See Julio Ycaza Tijerino, *La poesía y los poetas de Nicaragua* (Managua: Ediciones Lengua, 1958), p. 135.

3. Cardenal has distanced himself from poems published in the 1940s, such as "Proclama del conquistador" and "La ciudad deshabitada" (The uninhabited city), by not allowing them to be included in any anthologies of his poetry, including the collection of early work, *With Walker in Nicaragua*, edited by Jonathan Cohen.

4. See Borgeson, *Hacia el hombre nuevo*, p. 31.

5. Ibid., p. 32.

6. William Carlos Williams, *The Autobiography of William Carlos Williams* (New York: New Directions, 1951), p. 178.

7. Ibid., pp. 183-84. Although *In the American Grain* is written in prose, most chapters retain a highly poetic use of language. Seldon Rodman includes "Sir Walter Raleigh" in the anthology *One Hundred Modern Poems*.

8. Horace Gregory, introduction, *In the American Grain* by William Carlos Williams (New York: New Directions, 1956), p. xii.

9. Reed Whittemore, *William Carlos Williams: Poet from Jersey* (Boston: Houghton, 1975), p. 199.

10. Archibald MacLeish, *Collected Poems, 1917-1982* (Boston: Houghton, 1985), p. 261.

11. Jonathan Cohen, "In Bryant's Footsteps: Translating 'Con Walker en Nicaragua'," *The American Voice* 6 (1987): 84-88.

12. See Pablo Antonio Cuadra, "Sobre Ernesto Cardenal," *Papeles de Sons Armadans* 187 (1971): 10-11.

13. Margaret Glynne Lloyd, *William Carlos Williams's Paterson: A Critical Reappraisal* (Cranbury, N.J.: Associated University Presses, 1980), p. 130.

14. It would be interesting to approach "Con Walker en Nicaragua" psychoanalytically, given the poet/victim's latent identification with (admiration of?) the oppressor.

15. Stephen Tapscott, *American Beauty: William Carlos Williams and the Modernist Whitman* (New York: Columbia University Press, 1984), pp. 61-62.

16. Gregory, intro., *In the Americna Grain*, p. xi.

17. Mario Benedetti, "Ernesto Cardenal: evangelio y revolución (entrevista)," *Casa de las Américas* 63 (1970): 175.

18. K. K. Ruthven, *A Guide to Ezra Pound's Personae (1926)* (Berkeley: University of California Press, 1969), p. 8.

19. James F. Knapp, *Ezra Pound* (Boston: G.K. Hall, 1979), p. 28.

20. See N. Christoph de Nagy, "Pound and Browning," in *New Approaches to Ezra Pound*, ed. Eva Hesse (Berkeley: University of California Press, 1969), pp. 96-97.

21. William M. Chace, *The Political Identities of Ezra Pound & T. S. Eliot* (Stanford, Ca.: Stanford University Press, 1973), p. 63.

22. Ibid., p. 64.

23. Ibid., p. 33.

24. José Miguel Oviedo, "Ernesto Cardenal: un místico comprometido," *Casa de las Américas* 53 (1969): 37.

25. See Jorge Eduardo Arellano, *El movimiento de vanguardia de Nicaragua 1927-1932): Gérmenes, desarrollo, significado* (Managua: Librería Cultural Nicaragüense, 1971), pp. 52-57. Also see Steven White, *Culture and Politics in Nicaragua: Testimonies*

of Poets and Writers (New York: Lumen Books, 1986), pp. 8-9.

26. Peter Brooker, "The Lesson of Ezra Pound: An Essay in Poetry, Literary Ideology and Politics," in *Ezra Pound: Tactics for Reading*, ed. Ian F.A. Bell (London: Vision, 1982), pp. 17-18.

27. See Borgeson, *Hacia el hombre nuevo*, p. 33; Alfredo Veiravé, "Ernesto Cardenal: El exteriorismo, poesía del nuevo mundo," in *Ernesto Cardenal: Poeta de la liberación latinoamericana*, ed. Elisa Calabrese (Buenos Aires: Fernando García Cambeiro, 1975), p. 96; and Oviedo, "Ernesto Cardenal," op. cit., p. 36.

28. Ezra Pound, "A Retrospect," in *Literary Essays of Ezra Pound*, ed. T. S. Eliot (London: Faber and Faber, 1954), p. 3.

29. Borgeson, *Hacia el hombre nuevo*, p. 35.

30. Benedetti, "Ernesto Cardenal," p. 176.

31. Ezra Pound, *Selected Prose 1909-1965*, ed. William Cookson (New York: New Directions, 1973), p. 284.

32. Knapp, *Ezra Pound*, p. 122.

33. See Ruthven, *Guide to Ezra Pound's Personae*, p. 16.

34. Robert Pring-Mill, "The Redemption of Reality through Documentary Poetry," introduction, *Zero Hour and Other Documentary Poems* by Ernesto Cardenal (New York: New Directions, 1980), p. ix.

35. Ibid., p. x.

36. Robert Pring-Mill, "Acciones paralelas y montaje acelerado en el segundo episodio de *Hora 0*," *Revista Iberoamericana* 48.118-119 (1982): 240.

37. The next fifteen lines of "Hora 0" closely resemble several passages from a Spanish journalist's physical/ psychological portrait of Sandino based on firsthand experience. His account was originally published in 1934. See Ramón de Belasteguigoitia, *Con Sandino en Nicaragua* (Managua: Nueva Nicaragua, 1985), pp. 76-77, 134-135, & 169-170.

38. See Victor Farías, "La poesía de Ernesto Cardenal: historia y trascendencia," *Araucaria* 15 (1981): 107.

39. Robert Pring-Mill, introduction, *Marilyn Monroe and Other Poems* by Ernesto Cardenal (London: Search, 1975), p. 13.

40. Tapscott, *American Beauty*, p. 126.

41. Ibid., p. 138.

42. Isabel Freire, "Pound and Cardenal," *Review* 18 (1976): 42.

43. The titles may be translated as couplets (or song) on the death of Merton and on the death of Manrique's father.

44. See Ernesto Cardenal, "Por una cultura de la paz," in *Hacia una política cultural* (Managua: Ministerio de Cultura, 1982), pp. 189-90. See also, John Beverley and Marc Zimmerman, *Literature and Politics in the Central American Revolutions* (Austin: University of Texas Press, 1990), p. 87. The notes for this page include the bibliographical references to the debate between Cardenal and Daniel Berrigan on the legitimacy of the armed struggle.

45. See Kenneth L. Woodward, "Father Ernesto Cardenal," *Geo*, March 1984, p. 20+. Also see Margaret Randall, *Cristianos en la revolucion* (Managua: Editorial Nueva Nicaragua, 1983), pp. 19-22. In these two interviews, Cardenal explains Merton's role in the genesis of Solentiname.

46. Thomas Merton, letter to Pablo Antonio Cuadra, 4 December 1958, Cuadra's personal archive in Managua. At that time, Merton was translating Cuadra's *El jaguar y la luna*, a book of poems based primarily on Nahuatl mythology.

47. See Azarías H. Pallais, *Antología*, ed. Ernesto Cardenal (Managua: Nueva Nicaragua, 1986), p. 28; see also Beverley and Zimmerman, *Literature and Politics*, p. 59. Certain critics view the Nicaraguan poet Azarías H. Pallais (1885-1954) as an important antecedent to liberation theology. The issue is problematic, as Cardenal himself

points out, given Pallais' great admiration of Franco and Falangist Spain, especially in the infrequently-cited work *Epístola católica a Rafael Arévalo Martínez* (Lima: Compañía de Impresiones y Publicidad, 1947).

48. Henry Cohen, "Daniel Boone, Moses and the Indians: Ernesto Cardenal's Evolution from Alienation to Social Commitment," *Chasqui* 11 (1981): 23.

49. Boris de Rachewiltz, "Pagan and Magic Elements in Ezra Pound's Poetry," *New Approaches to Ezra Pound*, ed. Eva Hesse (Berkeley: University of California Press, 1969), p. 183.

50. See Lilia Dapaz Strout, "Nuevos cantos de vida y esperanza: los *Salmos* de Cardenal y la nueva ética," in *Ernesto Cardenal: Poeta de la liberación latinoamericana* (Buenos Aires: Fernando García Cambeiro, 1975), pp. 109-31. The critic, in her Jungian approach to the *Salmos*, takes the persona poem into the realm of modern psychology and the process of individuation. In this sense, the poet internalizes the positive and negative definitions of ethical behavior as exemplified in the external world.

51. Oviedo, "Ernesto Cardenal," p. 44.

52. Gordon Brotherston, *Latin American Poetry: Origins and Presence*, (Cambridge: Cambridge University Press, 1975), pp. 11-12.

53. Ibid., p. 12.

54. Ernesto Cardenal, ed. and trans., *Antología de poesía primitiva* (Madrid: Alianza, 1979), p. 15.

55. Jerome Rothenberg, *Technicians of the Sacred* (New York: Doubleday, 1968), p. xxiv.

56. Thomas Merton, "The Sacred City," in *Ishi Means Man: Essays on Native Americans* (Greensboro, N.C.: Unicorn, 1976), p. 65.

57. See Eduardo F. Elias, "*Homenaje a los indios americanos* de Ernesto Cardenal: Lecciones del pasado," *Chasqui* 12 (1982): 49.

58. Paul Ricoeur, *The Symbolism of Evil*, trans. Emerson Buchanan (Boston: Beacon, 1967), p. 67.

59. Pablo Antonio Cuadra, introduction, *Muestra de la poesía hispanoamericana del siglo xx*, 2 vols., ed. J. Escalona-Escalona (Caracas: Editorial Ayacucho, 1985), 2:792.

60. See Fernando Jorge Flores, "Comunismo o reino de Dios: una aproximación a la experiencia religiosa de Ernesto Cardenal," in *Ernesto Cardenal: poeta de la liberación latinoamericana*, ed. Elisa Calabrese (Buenos Aires: Fernando García Cambeiro, 1975), p. 168.

61. David Murray, "Pound-Signs: Money and Representation in Ezra Pound," in *Ezra Pound: Tactics for Reading*, ed. Ian F.A. Bell (London: Vision, 1982), p. 64.

62. Thomas Merton, "War and Vision," in *Ishi Means Man: Essays on Native Americans* (Greensboro, N.C.: Unicorn, 1976), p. 20.

Bibliography

Apter, Ronnie. *Digging for the Treasure: Translation after Pound*. New York: Peter Lang, 1984.

Aggler, William F., ed. *Baudelaire Judged by Spanish Critics*. Athens: University of Georgia Press, 1971.

Arellano, Jorge Eduardo. "Ernesto Cardenal: De Granada a Gethsemany (1927-1957)." *Cuadernos Hispanoamericanos* 289-290 (1974): 163-83.

_____. "Esbozo biográfico de Joaquín Pasos." In *Joaquín Pasos 1914-1947*, pp. 46-52, León, Nicaragua: Cuadernos Universitarios, 1972.

_____. *El movimiento de vanguardia de Nicaragua (1927-1932): Gérmenes, desarrollo, significado*. Managua: Ediciones de Librería Cultural Nicaragüense, 1971.

_____. Introduction. *Muestra de la poesía hispanoamericana del siglo XX*. 2 vols. Edited by J. Escalona-Escalona, pp. 2: 792-96. Caracas: Ayacucho, 1985.

_____. *Panorama de la literatura nicaragüense*. Managua: Ediciones Nacionales, 1977; rpt. Managua: Nueva Nicaragua, 1982.

_____. "Pablo Antonio y el movimiento nicaragüense de vanguardia." *La Prensa Literaria*, 20 abril 1991, pp. 4-5+.

_____. "Los *Poemas nicaragüenses*." *La Prensa Literaria*, 20 July 1985, p. 6.

_____. "Los poetas de la generación del 40." *Ventana* 19 (1985): 2-5.

_____. "Salomón de la Selva y la otra vanguardia." *Anales de Literatura Hispanoamericana* 18 (1989): 99-103.

_____. Introduction. *El tiempo es hambre y el espacio es frío*, by Alfonso Cortés, pp. 1-6. Managua: Ediciones Americanas, 1981.

Arellano, Jorge Eduardo, Margarita López, et. al., eds. *Azul . . . y las literaturas hispánicas*. Managua: Biblioteca Nacional "Rubén Darío"; México: UNAM, Instituto de Investigaciones Bibliográficas, 1990.

Argüello, José. "Dios en la obra de Ernesto Cardenal." *Amanecer* (Managua) 34-35 (1985): 27-29.

Bachelard, Gaston. *The Poetics of Space*. Translated by Maria Jolas. Boston: Beacon, 1969.

Baciu, Stefan. "Salomón de la Selva precursor." In *Homenaje a Salomón de la Selva 1959-1969*, pp. 96-109. León, Nicaragua: Cuadernos Universitarios.

Balladares, José Emilio. *Pablo Antonio Cuadra: La palabra y el tiempo, secuencia y estructura de su creación poética*. San José, Costa Rica: Editorial Libro Libre, 1986.

Barili, Amelia. "Borges on Life and Death." *New York Times Book Review*, 13 July 1986, pp. 1+.

Baudelaire, Charles. *Les Fleurs du Mal*. Edited Jacques Crépet and Georges Blin. Paris: Librairie José Corti, 1942.

_____. *The Mirror of Art: Critical Studies*. Edited and translated by Jonathan Mayne. London: Phaidon, 1955.

_____. "Le Peintre de la Vie Moderne." *Sur le dandysme*. Edited by Roger Kempf, pp. 189-230. Paris: Bibliotèque 10/18, 1971.

Bays, Gwendolyn. *The Orphic Vision: Seer Poets from Novalis to Rimbaud*. Lincoln: University of Nebraska Press, 1964.

Benedetti, Mario. "Ernesto Cardenal: evangelio y revolución (entrevista)." *Casa de la Américas* 63 (1976): 174-183.

_____. "Joaquín Pasos o el poema como crimen perfecto." *Joaquín Pasos 1914-1947*. León, Nicaragua: Cuadernos Universitarios, 1972.

Benjamin, Walter. "The Task of the Translator." In *Illuminations*, edited by Hannah Arendt, translated by Harry Zohn. New York: Schocken, 1969.

_____. "The Work of Art in the Age of Mechanical Reproduction." In *Illuminations*, edited by Hannah Arendt, translated by Harry Zohn. New York: Schocken, 1969.

Beverley, John, and Marc Zimmerman. *Literature and Politics in the Central American Revolutions*. Austin: University of Texas Press, 1990.

Bloom, Harold. *Agon: Towards a Theory of Revisionism*. Oxford: Oxford University Press, 1982.

Blunden, Edmund. *War Poets 1914-1918*. London: Longmans, Green, 1958.

Borgeson, Jr., Paul W. *Hacia el hombre nuevo: Poesía y pensamiento de Ernesto Cardenal*. London: Támesis Books, 1984.

Brooker, Peter. "The Lesson of Ezra Pound: An Essay in Poetry, Literary Ideology and Politics." In *Ezra Pound: Tactics for Reading*, edited by Ian F. A. Bell, pp. 9-49. London: Vision, 1982.

Brotherston, Gordon. *Latin American Poetry: Origins and Presence*. Cambridge: Cambridge University Press, 1975.

Cabrales, Luis Alberto. *Política de Estados Unidos y poesía de Hispanoamérica*. Managua: Publicaciones del Ministerio de Educación Pública, 1958.

Cáceres, Ester de. *Significación de la obra de Jules Supervielle en la cultura uruguaya*. Montevideo: Instituto de Estudios Superiores de Montevideo, 1943.

Campbell, Joseph. *The Inner Reaches of Outer Space: Metaphor as Myth and as Religion*. New York: Alfred Van Der Marck Editions, 1986.

Cardenal, Ernesto. "Alfonso Cortés." *Revista del Pensamiento Centroamericano* 101 (1969): 27-32.

_____. *Antología*. Managua: Editorial Nueva Nicaragua, 1983.

_____. *Antología*. San José, Costa Rica: Educa, 1972.

_____, trans. and ed. *Antología de poesía primitiva*. Madrid: Alianza Editorial, 1979.

_____. *Cántico cósmico*. Managua: Nueva Nicaragua, 1989.

_____. *Canto nacional*. México: Siglo XXI, 1973.

_____. "La democratización de la cultura." In *Hacia una política cultural*, pp. 245-65. Managua: Ministerio de Cultura, 1982.

_____. "La ciudad deshabitada." *Cuadernos Hispanoamericanos* 25.1 (1946): 211-19.

_____. *En Cuba*. Buenos Aires: Carlos Lohlé, 1972.

_____. *Epigramas: poemas*. México: Universidad Nacional Autónoma de México, 1961.

_____. *El estrecho dudoso*. San José, Costa Rica: Educa, 1971.

_____. *El evangelio de Solentiname*. Salamanca: Ediciones Sígueme, 1975.

_____. *Gethsemani, ky*. México: Ediciones Ecuador, 1960.

_____. "El grupo de vanguardia en Nicaragua." *Revista de crítica literaria latinoamericana* 15 (1982): 71-76.

_____. *Homenaje a los indios americanos*. León, Nicaragua: UNAN, 1969.

_____. "Hora 0." *Revista Mexicana de Literatura* (1957-1960).

_____. *La hora cero y otros poemas*. Barcelona: El Bardo, 1971.

_____. "Joaquín Pasos: un joven que no ha viajado nunca." *Cuadernos Americanos* 6.4 (1947): 124-127.

_____. "Joaquín Pasos." In *Joaquín Pasos 1914-1947*, pp. 13-26. León, Nicaragua: Cuadernos Universitarios, 1972.

_____. *Mayapán*. Managua: Ediciones de Librería Cardenal, 1968.

_____. *Oración por Marilyn Monroe y otros poemas*. Medellín: Ediciones La Tertulia, 1965.

_____. *Oráculo sobre Managua*. Managua: Editorial José Martí, 1973.

_____. *Los ovnis de oro: poemas indios*. México: Siglo XXI, 1988.

_____. "La paz mundial y la Revolución de Nicaragua." In *Hacia una política cultural*, pp. 205-16. Managua: Ministerio de Cultura, 1982.

_____. *Poemas reunidos: 1949-1969*. Edited Antidio Cabal, Caracas: Universidad de Carabobo, 1972.

_____. *Poesía escogida*. Barcelona: Barral Editores, 1975.

_____, ed. *Poesía nicaragüense*. Buenos Aires: Editorial Lohle, 1971; rpt. Havana: Casa de las Américas, 1973; rpt. Managua: Nueva Nicaragua, 1981; rpt. Managua: Nueva Nicaragua, 1986.

_____. "Por una cultura de la paz." In *Hacia una política cultural*, pp. 187-97. Managua: Ministerio de Cultura, 1982.

_____. "Proclama del conquistador." In *Nueva poesía nicaragüense*. Madrid: Seminario de Problemas Americanos, 1949.

_____. *Salmos*. Medellín: Universidad de Antioquia, 1964.

_____. *Tocar el cielo*. Managua: Nueva Nicaragua, n.d.

_____. Introduction. *Treinta poemas de Alfonso* by Alfonso Cortés, pp. 11-14. Managua: Editorial Nueva Nicaragua, 1981.

_____. *Vida en el amor*. Salamanca: Ediciones Sígueme, 1980.

_____. *Vuelos de victoria*. León: UNAN, 1985.

_____. *With Walker in Nicaragua*. Translated by Jonathan Cohen. Middletown, Conn.: Wesleyan University Press, 1984.

Cattaui, George. *Orphisme et prophétie chez les poétes français: 1850-1950*. Paris: Librairie Plon, 1965.

Chace, William M. *The Political Identities of Ezra Pound & T. S. Eliot*. Stanford, Ca.: Stanford University Press, 1973.

Chamorro Coronel, Carlos. "El humanismo de José Coronel Urtecho." *Revista del Pensamiento Centroamericano* 150 (1976): 81-89.

Childers, James Saxon. *Sailing South American Skies*. New York: Farrar & Rinehart, 1936.

Cohen, Henry. "Daniel Boone, Moses and the Indians: Ernesto Cardenal's Evolution from Alienation to Social Commitment." *Chasqui* 11 (1981): 21-32.

Cohen, Jonathan. "In Bryant's Footsteps: Translating 'Con Walker en Nicaragua.'" *The American Voice* 6 (1987): 79-81.

Cóleno, Alice. *Les Portes d'ivoire*. Paris: Librairie Plon, 1948.

Concha, Jaime. *Vicente Huidobro*. Madrid: Ediciones Júcar, 1983.

Cornebise, Alfred E., ed. *Doughboy Doggerel: Verse of the American Expeditionary*

Force 1918-1919. Athens: Ohio University Press, 1985.

Coronel Urtecho, José. "El americanismo en la casa de mi abuelo." *Revista Conservadora* 23 (1962): 25-31.

_____. "Anotaciones acerca de la Revolución." *Nicaráuac* 3 (diciembre 1980): 55-75.

_____. "Anotaciones y exageraciones sobre *La montaña es algo más que. . . .*" *Nicaráuac* 7 (junio 1982): 39-42.

_____. "Conversación con Carlos." *Nicaráuac* 13 (diciembre 1986): 69-77.

_____. *Diez cartas al pater*. Managua: Ediciones Nacionales, n.d.

_____. "El hombre americano y sus problemas." *Revista Conservadora* 14 (1961): 16-21.

_____. "En Nueva York, con el poeta Salomón de la Selva." In *Homenaje a Salomón de la Selva 1959-1969*, pp. 59-77. León, Nicaragua: Cuadernos Universitarios, 1969.

_____. *Líneas para un boceto de Claribel Alegría*. Managua: Nueva Nicaragua, 1989.

_____. "No volverá el pasado." *Nicaráuac* 1 (mayo-junio 1980): 131-33.

_____. *Paneles de infierno*. Managua: ENIEC, 1981.

_____, ed. *Panorama y antología de la poesía norteamericana*. Madrid: Seminario de Problemas Hispanoamericanos, 1949.

_____. *Pol-la d'ananta katanta paranta*. León, Nicaragua: Editorial Universitaria, 1970.

_____. *Prosa*. San José, Costa Rica: Educa, 1972.

_____. *Prosa reunida*. Managua: Editorial Nueva Nicaragua, 1985.

_____. *Rápido tránsito (al ritmo de norteamérica)*. Managua: Nueva Nicaragua, 1985.

_____. "Resistencia de la memoria." *Revista del pensamiento centroamericano* 150 (enero-marzo 1976): 98-107.

_____. "Siendo pintado por Dieter Masuhr o, Autorretrato con pintor." *Nicaráuac* 10 (agosto 1984): 93-114.

_____. "Sobre la universalidad nicaragüense." *El nicaragüense* by Pablo Antonio Cuadra, pp. 143-64. Madrid: Ediciones Cultura Hispánica, 1969.

_____. *Tres conferencias a la empresa privada (y epílogo en memoria de Joaquín Zavala Urtecho)*. Managua: Ediciones El Pez y la Serpiente, 1974.

Coronel Urtecho, José, and Ernesto Cardenal, ed. *Antología de la poesía norteamericana*. Madrid: Aguilar, 1963.

Coronel Urtecho, José, Pablo Antonio Cuadra, and Joaquín Pasos, trans. "Traducciones de poesía francesa del movimiento de vanguardia." *El Pez y la Serpiente* 24 (1981): 139-83.

Cortés, Alfonso. "La belleza perfecta." Reproduced in the "Apéndice" of Francisco Fuster's "Alfonso Cortés: vida e ideas." *Revista Conservadora del Pensamiento Centroamericano* 101 (1969): 51-52.

_____. *Las coplas del pueblo*. Managua: Editorial Alemana, 1965.

_____. *La odisea del istmo*. Guatemala: Tipografía Latina, 1922.

_____. *El poema cotidiano*. León, Nicaragua: Editorial Hospicio, 1967.

_____. *Poemas eleusinos*. León: Talleres del Hospicio San Juan de Dios, 1935.

_____. *Poesías*. Managua: Imprenta Nacional, 1931.

_____. *Las puertas del pasatiempo*. Managua: Editorial Alemana, 1967.

_____. *Las siete antorchas del sol*. León: Imprenta Hospicio, 1952.

_____. *Tardes de oro*. León: Tipografía de J. Hernández, 1934.

_____. *El tiempo es hambre y el espacio es frío*. Edited by Jorge Eduardo Arellano. Managua: Ediciones Americanas, 1981.

_____. *Treinta poemas de Alfonso*. Edited by Ernesto Cardenal. Managua: El Hilo Azul, 1952. Reprint; Managua: Ediciones Librería Cardenal; San José, Costa Rica: EDUCA, 1970; and Managua: Editorial Nueva Nicaragua, 1981.

Cuadra, Pablo Antonio. "Alfonso, discípulo del centauro Quirón." *Revista Conservadora del Pensamiento Centroamericano* 101 (1969): 24-26.

_____. *The Birth of the Sun: Selected Poems (1935-1985)* Translated by Steven F. White, Greensboro: Unicorn, 1988.

_____. *Breviario imperial*. Madrid: Cultura Española, 1940.

_____. *Entre la cruz y la espada: mapa de ensayos para el reduscubrimiento de América*. Madrid: Instituto de Estudios Políticos, 1946.

_____. *Hacia la cruz del sur*. Madrid: Acción Española, 1936; Reprint; Buenos Aires: Comisión de Argentina de Publicaciones e Intercambio, 1938.

_____. Introduction. *Muestra de la poesía hispanoamericana del siglo XX*. 2 vols. Edited by J. Escalona-Escalona, pp. 788-92. Caracas: Editorial Ayacucho, 1985.

_____. *El nicaragüense*. Madrid: Ediciones Cultura Hispánica, 1969.

_____. *Obra poética completa*. 8 vols. San José, Costa Rica: Editorial Libro Libre, 1983-1988.

_____. *Poemas nicaragüenses*. Santiago, Chile: Editorial Nascimento, 1934.

_____. "Poetry and the Temptations of Power." In *Lives on the Line*, edited by Doris Meyer, pp. 281-89. Berkeley: University of California Press, 1988.

_____. "La prensa norteamericana y el sandinismo." *Resistencia* (Miami) 2.4 (julio 1988): 3-6.

_____. "Prólogo a *Breve Suma*." In *Joaquín Pasos 1914-1947*, pp. 27-35. León, Nicaragua: Cuadernos Universitarios, 1972.

_____. *Promisión de México y otros ensayos*. México: Editorial Jus, 1945.

_____. "Sobre Ernesto Cardenal." *Papeles de Sons Armadans* 187 (1971): 5-33.

_____. *Torres de Dios*. Managua: Ediciones de la Academia Nicaragüense de la Lengua, 1958. Reprint; Managua: El Pez y la Serpiente, 1985.

Dapaz Strout, Lilia. "Nuevos cantos de vida y esperanza: Los *Salmos* de Ernesto Cardenal y la nueva ética." In *Ernesto Cardenal: Poeta de la liberación latinoamericana*, edited by Elisa Calabrese, pp. 109-31. Buenos Aires: Fernando García Cambeiro, 1975.

Darío, Rubén. *Antología poética*. Buenos Aires: Losada, 1966.

_____. *Eleven Poems of Rubén Darío*. Translated by Thomas Walsh and Salomón de la Selva. New York: Hispanic Society of America, 1916.

_____. *Nuestro Rubén Darío*. Managua: Ministerio de Cultura, 1984.

_____. *Poesía*. Edited by Ernesto Mejía Sánchez. Caracas: Biblioteca Ayacucho, 1977.

_____. *Rubén Darío: poesía*. Introduction by Pere Gimferrer. Barcelona: Planeta, 1987.

De Costa, René. *Vicente Huidobro: The Careers of a Poet*. Oxford: Oxford University Press, 1984.

Del Río, Angel. *Historia de la literatura española (tomo 1)*. New York: Holt, Rinehart and Winston, 1963.

De Nagy, N. Christoph. *Ezra Pound's Poetics and Literary Tradition: The Critical Decade*. Basel, Switzerland: Francke Verlag Bern, 1966.

_____. "Pound and Browning." In *New Approaches to Ezra Pound*, edited by Eva Hesse, pp. 86-124. Berkeley: University of California Press, 1969.

De Rachewiltz, Boris. "Pagan and Magic Elements in Ezra Pound's Poetry." In *New Approaches to Ezra Pound*, edited by Eva Hesse, pp. 174-97. Berkeley: University of

California Press, 1969.

Drost, Wolfgang. "De la critique d'art Baudelairienne." In *Baudelaire: Actes du Colloque de Nice (25-27 mai 1967)*, pp. 79-88. Monaco: Annales de la Faculté des Letres et Sciences Humaines de Nice, 1968.

Duverrán, Carlos Rafael. "Coronel Urtecho o la palabra en libertad." *Revista del Pensamiento Centroamericano* 150 (1976): 18-22.

Eigeldinger, Marc. "Baudelaire et l'alchimie verbale." *Etudes Baudelairiennes II*. Neuchâtel: Editions la Baconnièrre, 1971.

_____. *Le Platonisme de Baudelaire*. Neuchâtel: Editions la Baconnièrre, 1951.

Eliade, Mircea. *The Myth of the Eternal Return, or, Cosmos and History*. Princeton: Princeton University Press, 1954.

Elias, Eduardo F. "Homenaje a los indios americanos de Ernesto Cardenal: Lecciones del Pasado." *Chasqui* 12 (1982): 45-60.

Eliot, T. S. *The Complete Poems and Plays, 1909-1956*. New York: Harcourt, Brace, 1962.

_____. *The Waste Land and Other Poems*. New York: Harcourt, Brace & World, 1962.

Ehrhart, W. D. *Carrying the Darkness: American Indochina—The Poetry of the Vietnam War*. New York: Avon, 1985.

Farías, Victor. "La poesía de Ernesto Cardenal: Historia y trascendencia." *Araucaria* 15 (1981): 101-18.

Favres, Yves-Alain. *Supervielle: la rêverie et le chant dans Gravitations*. Paris: Librairie A. G. Nizet, 1981.

Fernández, Francisco de Asis, ed. *Poesía política nicaragüense*. Managua: Ministerio de Cultura, 1986.

Ferrán, André. *L'Esthétique de Baudelaire*. Paris: Nizet, 1968.

Flanagan, John T. *Edgar Lee Masters: The Spoon River Poet and His Critics*. Metuchen, N.J.: The Scarecrow Press, 1974.

Flores, Fernando Jorge. "Comunismo o reino de Dios: una aproximación a la experiencia religiosa de Ernesto Cardenal." In *Ernesto Cardenal: Poeta de la liberación latinoamericana*, edited by Elisa Calabrese, pp. 159-90. Buenos Aires: Fernando García Cambeiro, 1975.

Frank, Joseph. *The Widening Gyre*. New Brunswick, N.J.: Rutgers University Press, 1963.

Freire, Isabel. "Pound and Cardenal." *Review* 18 (1976): 36-42.

Fuster, Francisco. "Alfonso Cortés: vida e ideas." *Revista Conservadora del Pensamiento Centroamericano* 101 (1969): 1-53.

Genette, Gérard. *Palimpsestes: La littérature au second degré*. Paris: Editions du Seuil, 1982.

Graves, Lucía. "Poetas en la guerra, el grito oculto." *El País* (Madrid) (11 noviembre 1988): 36.

Greene, Tatiana W. *Jules Supervielle*. Genève: Librairie E. Droz, 1958.

Gregory, Horace. Introduction. *In the American Grain* by William Carlos Williams, pp. ix-xx. New York: New Directions, 1956.

Guardia de Alfaro, Gloria. "Visión del mundo o centro espiritual de Pablo Antonio Cuadra a través de su evolución temática." *Revista del Pensamiento Centroamericano* 177 (1982): 38-51.

Gutiérrez, Ernesto. Introduction. *Pol-la d'ananta katanta paranta* by José Coronel Urtecho, pp. IX-XX. León, Nicaragua: Editorial Universitaria, 1970.

Hadas, Pamela White. *Marianne Moore: Poet of Affection*. Syracuse, N.Y.: Syracuse University Press, 1977.

Hall, Donald. *Marianne Moore: The Cage and the Animal*. New York: Pegasus, 1970.

Hamilton, Ian. *Robert Lowell: A Biography*. New York: Vintage, 1983.

Harlow, Barbara. *Resistance Literature*. New York: Methuen, 1987.

Henríquez Ureña, Pedro. "Salomón de la Selva." *El Fígaro* (La Habana) (6 abril 1919): 288-89. Reprint; *Homenaje a Salomón de la Selva: 1959-1969*, pp. 13-19. León, Nicaragua: Cuadernos Universitarios, 1969.

Hiddleston, James. *L'univers de Jules Supervielle*. Paris: Librairie José Corti, 1965.

Hoefler, Walter. "Algunos temas en la poesía de Joaquín Pasos." Diss., Universidad Austral de Chile, 1971.

Honig, Edwin, ed. *The Poet's Other Voice: Conversations on Literary Translation*. Amherst: University of Massachusetts Press, 1985.

Houston, John Porter. *The Design of Rimbaud's Poetry*. New Haven: Yale University Press, 1963.

Huidobro, Vicente. *Obras completas*. 2 tomos. Edited by Hugo Montes. Santiago: Andrés Bello, 1976.

Hyde, Lewis. *The Gift: Imagination and the Erotic Life of Property*. New York: Vintage, 1983.

Hyslop, Lois Boe. *Baudelaire, Man of His Time*. New Haven: Yale University Press, 1980.

Johnston, John H. *English Poetry of the First World War: A Study in the Evolution of Lyric and Narrative Form*. Princeton: Princeton University Press, 1964.

Johnson, Kent, ed. and trans. *A Nation of Poets: Writings from the Poetry Workshops of Nicaragua*. Los Angeles, Ca.: West End Press, 1985.

Jonas, Hans. *The Gnostic Religion*. Boston: Beacon, 1963.

Kearns, Cleo McNelly. *T. S. Eliot and Indic Traditions: A Study in Poetry and Belief*. Cambridge: Cambridge University Press, 1987.

Kermode, Frank. "T. S. Eliot." In *Voices & Visions: The Poet in America*, edited by Helen Vendler. New York: Random House, 1987.

Kirkpatrick, Gwen. *The Dissonant Legacy of Modernismo: Lugones, Herrera y Reissig, and the Voices of Modern Spanish American Poetry*. Berkeley: University of California Press, 1989.

Knapp, James. *Ezra Pound*. Boston: G. K. Hall, 1979.

León-Portilla, Miguel. "The *Chalca Cihuacuicatl* of Aquiauhtzin: Erotic Poetry of the Nahuas." Translated by Daniel Morgan Miller. *New Scholar* 5.2 (1978): 235-62.

———. *Trece poetas del mundo azteca*. México: UNAM, 1972.

LeShan, Lawrence, and Henry Margenau. *Einstein's Space and Van Gogh's Sky*. New York: Macmillan, 1982.

Lloyd, Margaret Glynne. *William Carlos Williams's Paterson: A Critical Reappraisal*. Cranbury, N.J.: Associated University Presses, 1980.

Lowell, Robert. *Imitations*. New York: Farrar, 1961.

MacLeish, Archibald. *Collected Poems, 1917-1982*. Boston: Houghton, 1985.

Mallarmé, Stéphane. *Oeuvres complètes*. Paris: Librairie Gallimard, 1945.

Manuel, Frank E., and Fritzie P. Manuel. *Utopian Thought in the Western World*. Cambridge: Harvard University Press, 1979.

Markham, Edwin, ed. *The Book of Poetry: Collected from the Whole Field of British and American Poetry. Also Translations of Important Poems from Foreign Languages*. 10

vols. New York: W. H. Wise, 1926.

Martínez Estrada, Ezequiel. "El nuevo mundo, la isla de *Utopia* y la isla de Cuba." *Cuadernos Americanos* 127 (1963): 88-122.

Martínez Rivas, Carlos. "Dos murales U. S. A." *Cuadernos Hispanoamericanos* 181 (1965): 20-28.

_____. *La insurrección solitaria*. México: Editorial Guarania, 1953. Reprint; San José, Costa Rica: EDUCA, 1973; Managua: Editorial Nueva Nicaragua, 1982.

_____. "Morales: una observación y cuatro preguntas." *Nicaráuac* 10 (agosto 1984): 175-78.

Masters, Edgar Lee. *The Spoon River Anthology*. New York: Macmillan, 1942.

Mauriac, François. "Charles Baudelaire the Catholic." In *Baudelaire: A Collection of Critical Essays*, edited by Henri Peyre. Englewood Cliffs, N.J.: Prentice-Hall, 1962.

Maxwell, D. E. S. *The Poetry of T. S. Eliot*. London: Routledge & Kegan Paul, 1952.

Melançon, Joseph. *Le spiritualisme de Baudelaire*. Montreal and Paris: Editions Fides, 1967.

Merton, Thomas. *Ishi Means Man*. Greensboro, N.C.: Unicorn, 1976.

_____. Introduction. *Las ramas universales* by Alfonso Cortés, pp. 1-2. Managua: Editorial Alemana, 1964.

_____. "Prólogo." In *Vida en el amor* by Ernesto Cardenal, pp. 9-19. Salamanca: Ediciones Sígueme, 1980.

Messiaen, Pierre. *Sentiment chrétien et poésie française: Baudelaire, Verlaine, Rimbaud*. Paris: Les Editions Marcel Dubin, 1947.

Meynell, Alice. "Decivilised." In *The Rhythm of Life and other Essays*. London: John Lane, 1896.

Moore, Marianne. *Selected Poems*. New York: Macmillan, 1935.

Morales, Beltrán. *Sin páginas amarillas*. Managua: Ediciones Nacionales, 1975. rpt. Managua: Editorial Vanguardia, 1989.

Murray, David. "Pound-Signs: Money and Representation in Ezra Pound." In *Ezra Pound: Tactics for Reading*, edited by Ian F. A. Bell, pp. 50-78. London: Vision Press, 1982.

Nelson, William. Introduction. *Twentieth Century Interpretations of Utopia*, edited by William Nelson, pp. 1-11. Englewood Cliffs, N.J.: Prentice-Hall, 1968.

O'Hara, Edgar. "Ernesto Cardenal: Poeta de la resurrección." *Inti* 18-19 (1983-1984): 107-15.

Ordóñez Argüello, Alberto. "Poemas de un joven que no sabe inglés." *La Nueva Prensa* (Managua), 5 agosto 1937, n.p.

Ortega y Gasset, José. "Miseria y esplendor de la traducción." In *El libro de las misiones*. Buenos Aires: Espasa Calpe Argentina, 1940.

Oviedo, José Miguel. "Ernesto Cardenal: un místico comprometido." *Casa de las Américas* 53 (1969): 29-48.

_____. "Las voces múltiples de Coronel Urtecho." In *Homenaje a José Coronel Urtecho al cumplir 70 años de edad*, pp. 217-26. León, Nicaragua: Editorial Universitaria, 1976.

Pacheco, José Emilio. "Nota sobre la otra vanguardia." *Casa de las Américas* 118 (enero-febrero 1980): 103-7.

Pade, Werner. "El pensamiento de Carlos Marx y su vigencia en la lucha actual por la paz." *Ventana* 30 (marzo 1985): 5-6.

Pagels, Elaine. *The Gnostic Gospels*. New York: Random House, 1979.

Paillar, Claire. *Mitos primordiales y poesía fundadora en América Central.* Paris: Editions de la CNRS, 1989.

Pallais, Azarías H. *Antología.* Edited by Ernesto Cardenal. Managua: Nueva Nicaragua, 1986.

_____. *Epístola católica a Rafael Arévalo Martínez.* Lima: Compañía de Impresiones y Publicidad, 1947.

_____. *Piraterías.* Managua: Talleres de la ECSA, 1951.

Pasos, Joaquín. *Breve suma.* Managua: Nuevos Horizontes, 1945.

_____. "Carta sobre la muerte." *Los Lunes de la Prensa* (Managua), 27 enero 1947, p. 2+.

_____. "Conferencia sobre Vicente Huidobro." *Joaquín Pasos 1914-1947.* León, Nicaragua: Cuadernos Universitarios, 1972.

_____. "Fragmento inédito de 'Canto de guerra de las cosas.'" *La Prensa Literaria*, 19 enero 1991, p. 1.

_____. "Un libro con ojos, nariz y boca," *El Diario Nicaragüense* 10 Jan. 1935, pp. 1+.

_____. *Poemas de un joven.* México: Fondo de Cultura Económica, 1962. Reprint; Managua: Editorial Nueva Nicaragua, 1983; México: Fondo de Cultura Económica, 1984.

_____. "Señoras y Señores, ¡mucho cuidado con esta poesía!" *Ya!* 12 (1941): 13+.

_____. "La vida es muerte: juguete trágico." *La Prensa Literaria* (Managua), 5 mayo 1984, p. 8.

Paz, Octavio. *El arco y la lira.* México: Fondo de Cultura Económica, 1956.

_____. "Baudelaire as Art Critic: Presence and Present." In *On Poets and Others*, translated by Michael Schmidt, pp. 50-65. New York: Seaver, 1986.

_____. *Cuadrivio.* México: Joaquín Mortiz, 1965.

_____. "Presencia y presente: Baudelaire crítico de arte." In *El signo y el garabato*, pp. 31-45. México: Joaquín Mortiz, 1973.

_____. *Sor Juana Inés de la Cruz o Las trampas de la fe.* México: Fondo de Cultura Económica, 1982.

Peña, Horacio. "Dos poemas: una actitud." In *Homenaje a José Coronel Urtecho al cumplir 70 años de edad*, pp. 195-204. León, Nicaragua: Cuadernos Universitarios, 1976.

_____. "Salomón de la Selva: Soldado Desconocido." *La Prensa* (Managua), 17 marzo 1963, pp. 1B+.

Picon, Gaeton. "La qualité du présent." *Preuves* 207 (mai 1968): 24-26.

Pound, Ezra. *A B C of Economics.* Tunbridge Wells, England: The Pound Press, 1953.

_____. *A B C of Reading.* New Haven: Yale University Press, 1934.

_____. *The Cantos.* New York: New Directions, 1970.

_____. *Literary Essays of Ezra Pound.* Edited by T. S. Eliot. London: Faber, 1954.

_____. *Selected Poems.* New York: New Directions, 1957.

_____. *Selected Prose 1909-1965.* Edited by William Cookson. New York: New Directions, 1973.

Pring-Mill, Robert. "Acciones paralelas y montaje acelerado en el segundo episodio de *Hora 0.*" *Revista Iberoamericana* 118-119 (1982): 217-40.

_____. Introduction. *Marilyn Monroe and Other Poems* by Ernesto Cardenal, pp. 7-32. London: Search, 1975.

_____. "The Redemption of Reality through Documentary Poetry." Introduction. *Zero Hour and Other Documentary Poems* by Ernesto Cardenal, pp. ix-xxi. New York:

New Directions, 1980.

Pulver, Max. "Jesus' Round Dance and Crucifixion According to the Acts of St. John." In *The Mysteries: Papers from the Eranos Yearbooks*, edited by Joseph Campbell, pp. 169-93. Princeton: Princeton University Press, 1955.

Ramírez, Sergio. "El concepto de burguesía en dos noveletas." *Revista del Pensamiento Centroamericano* 150 (enero-marzo 1976): 95-97.

_____, ed. *Ventana (edición facsimilar)*. Managua: Nueva Nicaragua, 1990.

Randall, Margaret. *Cristianos en la revolución*. Managua: Editorial Nueva Nicaragua, 1983.

Rawlence, Christopher, ed. *About Time*. London: Jonathan Cape, 1985.

Rexroth, Kenneth. "Gnosticism." In *Assays*, pp. 131-42. New York: New Directions, 1961.

_____. "The Poet as Translator." In *Assays*, pp. 19-40. New York: New Directions, 1961.

Ricoeur, Paul. *The Symbolism of Evil*. Translated by Emerson Buchanan. Boston: Beacon, 1967.

Riffaterre, Michael. *Text Production*. Translated by Terese Lyons. New York: Columbia University Press, 1983.

Rimbaud, Arthur. *Oeuvres*. Edited by Suzanne Bernard. Paris: Editions Garnier Frères, 1960.

Ritter, Gerhard. "*Utopia* and Power Politics." In *Twentieth Century Interpretations of Utopia*, edited by William Nelson. Englewood Cliffs, N.J.: Prentice-Hall, 1968.

Robichez, Jacques. *Gravitations de Supervielle*. Paris: Societé D'Edition D'Enseignement Supérieur, 1981.

Robinson, James S., ed. *The Nag Hammadi Library*. New York: Harper & Row, 1977.

Rodríguez, Ileana. "Poetas y poesía." *Nuevo Amanecer Cultural* (Managua), 24 enero 1987, pp. 3+.

Román, José. *Maldito país*. Managua: Ediciones El Pez y la Serpiente, 1983.

Rothenberg, Jerome. *Technicians of the Sacred*. New York: Doubleday, 1968.

Ruff, Marcel A. *L'esprit du Mal et l'esthétique baudelairienne*. Paris: Librairie Armand Colin, 1955.

Rumi, Jalal al-Din. *Mystical Poems of Rumi*. Translated by A. J. Arberry. Chicago: University of Chicago Press, 1969.

Ruthven, K. K. *A Guide to Ezra Pound's Personae (1926)*. Berkeley: University of California Press, 1969.

Sacks, Oliver. *Awakenings*. New York: Dutton, 1983.

Sassoon, Siegfried. *Siegfried's Journey: 1916-1920*. New York: Viking, 1946.

Sassoon, Siegfried. *Collected Poems*. New York: Viking, 1949.

Schaefer, Claudia. "A Search for Utopia on Earth: Toward an Understanding of the Literary Production of Ernesto Cardenal." *Crítica Hispánica* 4.2 (1982): 171-79.

Schneider, Pierre. "Le découverte du présent." *Preuves* 207 (mai 1968): 4-6.

Selva, Salomón de la. *Acolmixtli Netzahualcóyotl*. México: Talleres Gráficos de la Editorial Cornaval, 1958.

_____. *Antología Poética*. Edited by Jorge Eduardo Arellano. Managua: UNAN, n.d.

_____. *Canto a la independencia ncaional de México*. México: Imprenta Arana Hermanos, 1955.

_____. *Elogio del pudor*. México: Turanzas, 1943.

_____. *Evocación de Horacio*. México: 1949.

_____. *Evocación de Píndaro*. San Salvador: Ministerio de Cultura, 1957.

_____. *La guerra de Sandino o pueblo desnudo*. Managua: Nueva Nicaragua, 1985.

_____. *Las hijas de Erectheo*. Panamá: Andreve, 1933.

_____. *Ilustre familia*. México: Talleres Gráficos de La Nación, 1954.

_____. *Oda a la tristeza y otros poemas*. México: Antorcha, 1924.

_____. *Sandino: Free Country or Death*. Edited by Jorge Eduardo Arellano. Managua: Biblioteca Nacional de Nicaragua, 1984.

_____. *El soldado desconocido*. México: Cultura, 1922. Reprint; San José, Costa Rica: EDUCA, 1971; México: Juan de la Selva, 1975; Managua: Editorial Nueva Nicaragua, 1982.

_____. *Tropical Town and Other Poems*. New York: John Lane, 1918.

_____. *Versos y versiones nobles y sentimentales*. Managua: Banco de América, 1974.

Sénéchal, Christian. *Jules Supervielle: Poète de l'univers intérieur*. Paris: Librairie Les Lettres, 1939.

Silkin, Jon. *Out of Battle: The Poetry of the Great War*. London: Oxford University Press, 1972.

_____, ed. *The Penguin Book of First World War Poetry*. 2nd ed. New York: Viking Penguin, 1981.

Smith, Janet Lynne. *An Annotated Bibliography of and about Ernesto Cardenal*. Tempe, Ariz.: Center for Latin American Studies, 1979.

Stabb, Martin S. "Utopia and Anti-Utopia: the Theme in Selected Essayistic Writings of Spanish America." *Revista de Estudios Hispánicos* 15.3 (1981): 377-93.

Starobinski, Jean. "De la critique à la poésie." *Preuves* 207 (mai 1968): 16-23.

Steiner, George. *After Babel: Aspects of Language and Translation*. New York: Oxford University Press, 1975.

Supervielle, Jules. *Choix de Poèmes*. Paris: Gallimard, 1947.

_____. *Gravitations*. Paris: Gallimard, 1925.

Tapscott, Stephen. *American Beauty: William Carlos Williams and the Modernist Whitman*. New York: Columbia University Press, 1984.

Tedlock, Dennis, ed. and trans. *Popol Vuh*. New York: Touchstone/Simon & Schuster, 1985.

Tirado, Manlio. *Conversando con José Coronel Urtecho*. Managua: Editorial Nueva Nicaragua, 1983.

Torres, Edelberto. *Sandino y sus pares*. Managua: Editorial Nueva Nicaragua, 1983.

Tunnerman Bernheim, Carlos. "La poesía nicaragüense y universal de Pablo Antonio Cuadra." *Revista del Pensamiento Centroamericano* 177 (1982): 70-79.

Urtecho, Alvaro. "Pablo Antonio Cuadra o la vuelta de los tiempos." *La Crónica Literaria* 29, 31 mayo 1989, pp. 1+.

_____. "La tierra baldía de Joaquín Pasos." *Nuevo Amanecer Cultural* (Managua), 24 enero 1987, pp. 1+.

Valdés, Jorge H. "The Evolution of Cardenal's Prophetic Poetry." *Latin American Literary Review* 23 (1983): 25-40.

Valle-Castillo, Julio. "Carlos Martínez Rivas o la soberbia verbal." *Nuevo Amanecer Cultural* 517, 16 junio 1990, pp. 2+.

_____. "Joaquín Pasos: el poeta de la vanguardia," *Nuevo Amanecer Cultural* (Managua), 24 enero 1987, pp.1+.

_____. Introduction. *Poesías escogidas* by Joaquín Pasos, pp. 7-41. México: Comunidad Latinoamericana de Escritores, 1974.

_____. Introduction. *Poetas modernistas de Nicaragua (1880-1927)*, pp. xiv-xv. Managua: Colección Cultural Banco de América, 1978.

Vansittart, Peter, ed. *Voices from the Great War*. 2nd ed. New York: Avon, 1985.

Varela-Ibarra, José. *La poesía de Alfonso Cortés*. León, Nicaragua: Editorial Universitaria, 1976.

Veiravé, Alfredo. "Ernesto Cardenal: El exteriorismo, poesía del nuevo mundo." In *Ernesto Cardenal: Poeta de la liberación latinoamericana*, edited by Elisa Calabrese, pp. 61-106. Buenos Aires: Fernando García Cambeiro, 1975.

Vivier, Robert. *Lire Supervielle*. Paris: Librairie José Corti, 1971.

Wellinga, Klaas S. *Nueva cultura nicaragüense (debate sobre el realsimo)*. Buenos Aires: Utopías del Sur, 1989.

Whisnant, David E., "Rubén Darío as a Focal Cultural Figure in Nicaragua: The Ideological Uses of Cultural Capital," *Latin American Research Review* 27.3 (1992): 7-49.

White, Steven F. "Amor, soledad y paraiso en tres poetas nicaragüenses contemporáneos." *La Prensa Literaria*. (22 febrero 1992): 4-5.

_____. "Breve retrato de Joaquín Pasos," *Inti* 21 (1985): pp. 67-73.

_____, ed. and trans. *Culture & Politics in Nicaragua: Testimonies of Poets and Writers*. New York: Lumen Books, 1986.

_____. "Entrevista con Carlos Martínez Rivas." *Cuadernos Hispanoamericanos* 469-70 (julio-agosto 1989): 93-104.

_____. "Ernesto Cardenal and North American Literature: Intertextuality and the Formulation of an Ethical Identity." *Inti* 31 (primavera 1990): 106-18.

_____. "The Eschatological Voyaage in the Poetry of Joaquín Pasos and T. S. Eliot." *The Literary Half-Yearly* 29.2 (July 1988): 192-202.

_____. "Martínez Rivas y Baudelaire: dos pintores de la vida moderna." *Cuadernos Hispanoamericanos* 469-70 (julio-agosto 1989): 81-92.

_____, ed. and trans. *Poets of Nicaragua: 1918-1979*. Greensboro, N.C.: Unicorn Press, 1982.

_____. "Salomón de la Selva: Poeta comprometido de la 'otra' vanguardia." *Revista Iberoamericana* 157 (oct.-dic. 1991): 915-21.

_____. "Traducción e intertextualidad: el diálogo de José Coronel Urtecho con la literatura norteamericana." *Estudios Filológicos* 24 (1989): 103-10.

_____. "Translation in Nicaraguan Poetry as a Literary Weapon against Imperialism." *Translation Perspectives* 6 (1991): pp. 165-71.

Whitman, Walt. *Complete Poetry and Selected Prose*. Boston: Houghton, 1959.

Whittemore, Reed. *William Carlos Williams: Poet from Jersey*. Boston: Houghton, 1975.

Williams, Oscar, ed. *The War Poets: An Anthology of the War Poetry of the 20th Century*. New York: John Day, 1945.

Williams, Thomas A. *Mallarmé and the Language of Mysticism*. Athens: University of Georgia Press, 1970.

Williams, William Carlos. *The Autobiography of William Carlos Williams*. New York: New Directions, 1951.

_____. *In the American Grain*. New York: New Directions, 1956.

Woodward, Kenneth L. "Father Ernesto Cardenal," *Geo* (March 1984): 20+.

Ycaza Tijerino, Julio. *La poesía y los poetas de Nicaragua*. Managua: Ediciones Lengua,

1958.

Yepes Boscán, Guillermo. "Hacer el poema con el aliento del mito y el lodo de la historia" (introduction). *Siete árboles contra el atardecer* by Pablo Antonio Cuadra. Caracas: Ediciones de la Presidencia de la República, 1980.

Yúdice, George. "Poemas de un joven que quiso ser otro." *Inti* 18-19 (otoño 1983-primavera 1984): 1-10.

Zepeda-Henríquez, Eduardo. *Alfonso Cortés, al vivo*. Managua: Imprenta Nacional, 1966.

_____. "Joaquín Pasos: sabiduría y temporalidad." *Joaquín Pasos 1914-1947*. León, Nicaragua: Cuadernos Universitarios, 1972.

_____. *Mitología nicaragüense*. Managua: Editorial Manolo Morales, 1986.

Zimmerman, Marc, ed. *Nicaragua in Reconstruction and at War: The People Speak*. Minneapolis: Marxist Educational Press, 1985.

Zimmerman, Marc, with Bridget Aldaraca, Edward Baker, and Ileana Rodríguez, eds. *Nicaragua in Revolution: The Poets Speak*. Minneapolis: Marxist Educational Press, 1980.

Index

221